Leadership
Communication
as Citizenship

Leadership Communication *as* Citizenship

Give Direction to Your Team, Organization, or Community
as a Doer, Follower, Guide, Manager, or Leader

John O. Burtis
University of Northern Iowa

Paul D. Turman
South Dakota Board of Regents

Los Angeles | London | New Delhi
Singapore | Washington DC

For information:

SAGE Publications, Inc.
2455 Teller Road
Thousand Oaks,
   California 91320
E-mail: order@sagepub.com

SAGE Publications India Pvt. Ltd.
B 1/I 1 Mohan Cooperative
   Industrial Area
Mathura Road, New Delhi 110 044
India

SAGE Publications Ltd.
1 Oliver's Yard
55 City Road
London EC1Y 1SP
United Kingdom

SAGE Publications Asia-Pacific
   Pte. Ltd.
33 Pekin Street #02-01
Far East Square
Singapore 048763

Printed in the United States of America

Library of Congress Cataloging-in-Publication Data

Burtis, John Orville.
Leadership communication as citizenship/John O. Burtis, Paul D. Turman.
   p. cm.
Includes bibliographical references and index.
ISBN 978-1-4129-5499-0 (cloth)
ISBN 978-1-4129-5500-3 (pbk.)

   1. Leadership—Social aspects. 2. Communication. 3. Interpersonal communication. I. Turman, Paul D. II. Title.

HM1261.B88 2010
158'.4—dc22   2009028256

This book is printed on acid-free paper.

09   10   11   12   13   10   9   8   7   6   5   4   3   2   1

Acquisitions Editor:	Todd R. Armstrong
Editorial Assistant:	Aja Baker
Production Editor:	Astrid Virding
Copy Editor:	Gillian Dickens
Typesetter:	C&M Digitals (P) Ltd.
Proofreader:	Dennis W. Webb
Cover Designer:	Glenn Vogel
Marketing Manager:	Jennifer Reed Banando

Brief Contents

UNIT IV: USE STORIES TO UNITE YOUR GROUP'S EFFORTS

Detailed Contents

UNIT III: DEVELOP YOUR COMMUNICATION SKILLS TO ENHANCE YOUR DIRECTION-GIVING

Chapter 6: Figure Out How to Communicate Effectively   119

List of Tables

Preface

The purpose for this book is to help you shape the choices made by a team, organization, or community that is important to you. All such groups need a sense of purpose and direction. You can help shape that sense of purpose by affecting your group's direction.

What is group direction? Consider the following examples. A frustrated someone might say, "This team is going nowhere, fast!" When optimistic, someone might exclaim, "We are finally on the right track again as an organization." When depressed about the group, "Our business seems to be falling apart." If excited, "Our town is really cooking now, all sorts of new possibilities are opening up" or "I look at this move as an adventure for our worship community." Each statement shows part of what different individuals think about their group's direction.

Each example is a brief account of one group member's perceptions about where his or her group is headed—and about how well the group is doing in its efforts to get there. Where we end up as a group is not something that "just happens to us." Group direction is something we help to create, shape, and sustain through our communications with other group members.

If you want to help give direction to a group that is important in your life, you need to know that all organizations, communities, and teams are shaped by a relatively limited set of direction-giving communications: communication processes and skills that you can learn.

❖ WHY SHOULD GROUP DIRECTION CONCERN YOU?

If you are a manager or leader, it is obvious that you need to be concerned with the effectiveness of your group as a whole. But what if you are just one of many people in a group? You may feel that what you have to offer is unimportant. If you think so, we hope to change your mind.

Groups can face a range of issues that require direction-giving acts by various members. A recession requires each of our businesses, school districts, and families to reexamine our priorities and procedures. The sudden death of a coach forces an assistant to assume head coaching responsibilities midseason and everyone on the team to take on more responsibility. A hostile takeover bid, an especially effective opponent, or a series of terrorist attacks necessitates efforts to redraw alliances and identify new sources for needed resources. Rarely is a group made stronger under such circumstances by simply relying on its leader to shape its reply.

No team, organization, or community can succeed without direction-giving efforts on the part of most, if not all, of its members. Does that mean everyone needs to be a leader? Well, that depends on what you mean by leadership. In this book, we show how everyone can help give direction to a group: as a leader, manager, guide, follower, or doer. All of these are types of direction-givers. All five types can be important, but the most common forms are necessary in every group (the doer, follower, and guide).

❖ EVERYONE ON A TEAM, WORKING IN AN ORGANIZATION, OR LIVING IN A COMMUNITY SHOULD HELP THAT GROUP TO THRIVE

Leadership Communication as Citizenship is about how people give direction to their various groups. We discuss effective leadership in the context of citizenship, emphasizing the opportunities and responsibilities each of us has for helping our own groups to thrive.

The thesis we develop is: Each of us has an obligation to try to find ways of assisting our group's efforts to thrive. This requires using direction-giving skills to help frame the story of our group's experience. There is a social contract, called citizenship, which comes from blending our own efforts and energies with those of any group of other people. Membership always involves responsibility as well as privileges. You should expect to participate when you become part of a group, and you have the right to expect that others will contribute as well.

It is the nature of all groups that they must be maintained and given direction. This is always the work of the citizen. The social contract applies regardless of the type of group you are in (whether family or team, complex bureaucracy, or streamlined committee; from public to private organizations, governmental to business enterprises, educational to religious to community institutions, civic to social movements—every size and type of group in which people work or play together). The work of the citizen must be done regardless of the role you play in a group (whether leader or follower, CEO or line worker, team star or bench warmer, teacher or student, parent or child, board member or stakeholder). The citizen helps shape the group.

We each help give direction to our groups: intentionally or not; for good or for ill. The only question is whether we give direction well. To do so, we must act in a manner that others judge to be both effective and appropriate. To do that, each of us needs to know what it takes to be effective as a doer, follower, guide, manager, and leader. We also need to develop the skills that help us to frame our group's experience: the group's story. This involves figuring out how to help create effective experiences for our group.

The five direction-giving types outlined in this book provide a framework that helps us understand what is needed by groups of all sizes and purposes. This framework and our citizenship argument provide a perspective from which to address timely issues of executive compensation, ethical responsibility within a chain of command, how civic institutions are perpetuated, how identity politics and constructions drive group direction, and how individuals relate to their group. *Leadership Communication as Citizenship* will help you imagine and frame your contributions to the team, organization, or community that is important to you.

❖ UNIQUE FEATURES OF THE BOOK

A readable story is told, the basics of which are found in unit and chapter titles (see the following bullets from the Brief Contents). They frame our story of leadership.

- *Understand your power as a direction-giver.* So, you want other people to work well together? Distinguish between three direction-giving options: doing, following, and guiding well. Understand that other direction-giving options may be needed: managing or leading well.

- *Develop your own strategies for giving direction well.* Use leadership theory and research to prepare yourself to give direction. Develop a framework and position yourself for giving direction.

- *Develop your communication skills to enhance your direction-giving.* Figure out how to communicate effectively. Help shape effective experiences and expectations for citizenship in your group.

- *Use stories to unite your group's efforts.* Help shape the story of your organization, team, or community. Develop the framing skills needed by every direction-giver. Leadership vision is a crisis-based direction-giving story.

The chapters can be read out of sequence. Each unit and chapter can be stand-alone reading. The objective is that you be able to go directly to materials that are most important to you. While you are there, you will find suggestions that help you figure out where else in the book you might want to go. The story of the book is a well-integrated argument, but it is accessible without having to read all the chapters in order.

A diversity of sources and leadership contexts inform the book. Pertinent research, theory, and best practices are synthesized from a variety of successful practitioners taken from a range of leadership contexts. Ideas are included from scholars in organizational and group communication, management, I/O psychology, sociology, political science, persuasion and influence, public and interpersonal communication skills, and argumentation.

❖ ACKNOWLEDGMENTS

From John O. Burtis: This book is a 30-year experience story. Along the way, some highlights (and my thanks to): Michael E. Hadley gives me a definition of demagogue that (6 years later I find) helps me to understand when George Shapiro directs my attentions and energies away from the evocations of advertising and toward competing conceptions of leadership, Robert L. Scott gets me to consider the epistemic nature of various chats, and Ernie Bormann alerts me to the benefits of teasing out symbolic convergences. To Henry Tkachuk, who likes and becomes the first to use the "trichotomy" of direction-giving types (guide, manager, leader) in a college classroom, and to M. Scott Poole, who tells an NCA audience that the guide concept is intriguing. To Phil Clampitt and Kelby Halone, whose insights and support save and significantly alter the first book (*Group Communication Pitfalls:* without a first there would be no second). To John Fritch, who says the first book is written beautifully, and to Paul H. Ephross, whose book review says our approach to grouping and direction-giving provides a "rich, provocative, and creative conceptual vocabulary that will resonate for readers" and leaves him "with a feeling of joy and some mild existential sadness."

To the reviewers for the current book, who added momentum to the project in part by giving SAGE the courage to carry on with authors whose first book is a not oft-purchased read: Sue Currey (St. Edward's University), G. L. Forward (Point Loma Nazarene University), Brian L. Heuett (Southern Utah University), Robert S. Littlefield (North Dakota State University), Dan Peterson (Missouri State University), Kathleen M. Propp (Western Michigan University), and Denise Vrchota (Iowa State University). Their general enthusiasms and insightful criticisms wring useful adjustments from tired minds.

All of these folks provide actionable nuggets of useful criticism or encouragement that create energy for crafting this text. Were it not for the direction they provide, you would be holding something else in your hands right now. Finally, I have experience coauthoring with 35 people over the past three decades, and Paul Turman is one of only three who really keeps up with (and seems somehow able to handle) the sporadic spewings I tend to toss about. When things need getting done, there is nobody I know who is better at the doing.

From Paul D. Turman: My thanks to Bill Seiler, who helped guide my efforts during my time at Nebraska; to Ann Barnett, who developed an interest in the value, qualities, and irregularities that constitute group interaction; to my wife Shelly and my three sons Lincoln, William, and Gabe, who continue to foster my love for communication scholarship. I also thank the reviewers for their thoughtful comments, which were valuable in bringing the text to its current state. In the end, I would like to thank John, whose vision has come throughout beautifully in the pages of this text. It is wonderful that our initial conversation about direction-giving has produced two transformational books.

Reviewer List

Sue Currey, St. Edward's University

G. L. Forward, Point Loma Nazarene University

Brian L. Heuett, Southern Utah University

Robert S. Littlefield, North Dakota State University

Dan Peterson, Missouri State University

Kathleen M. Propp, Western Michigan University

Denise Vrchota, Iowa State University

UNIT I

Understand Your Power as a Direction-Giver

1

So, You Want Other People to Work Well Together?

❖ ❖ ❖

Getting people to work well together is a challenge. No matter the role you play on a team, in an organization, or for a community, getting others to do what you want can feel like working with a bunch of chickens or cats. Try to get chickens to move calmly in a particular direction and they will scatter frantically before you (and behind), going every which way including up. Try to focus a cat on something uninteresting to it and you will be treated as beneath contempt. You may as well try to converse with a cabbage! Fortunately, getting people to work well together is a little easier than herding birds or focusing felines. It is the purpose of this book to help you figure out how to become more effective when you try to give direction to groups of people.

It can be difficult to believe that your own actions matter much when it seems that the whole world is run by feuding and impervious governments, giant and impersonal corporations, and various religions that seem determined to contradict and condemn each other. Explanations for what is happening in the world are dominated by talk about enormous economic exchanges and the activities of a few key people who seem to wield the hammer of change all by themselves.

In this book, we try to change that predominant framing, arguing that it is really interacting people who shape the groups that shape the world.

The title of the first unit in this book incorporates our assumption that: *You have power as a direction-giver in your team, organization, or community.* In this first chapter, we explain that your power to get things done usually comes from getting other people to work well together. We identify five ways you can shape your group as you help to give it direction. These five ways can be useful to you in any group: from a team to a complex organization, from disjointed social movements to formal campaigns to legally incorporated communities. Understanding the ways to give direction to a group helps give you more power as a direction-giver in your group.

Being able to give direction well is important to you and to others in your group: to anyone who wants the group to succeed. To give direction to others, it helps to know the processes people use to give direction to each other as members of a group. It also helps to know why they think they need to be in the group. Why are they on this team, working in this business, or a member of this community? When you find out what motivates the people in a group, you can figure out the kind of direction they are willing to receive from you for their group. As motivation changes, so can the kind of direction you attempt to provide. Our thesis is that *each of us is responsible for helping our own groups to thrive, which requires our best direction-giving efforts to help frame effective experiences for our groups.*

❖ GROUPS CAN CREATE A COMMUNITY, CALM A COMPLEX ORGANIZATION, OR MOVE MILLIONS

> "Never underestimate the power of a small group of dedicated people attempting to change the world. In fact, that is the only thing that ever has."
>
> Margaret Mead

When something significant changes in our world, it is human nature to try to explain what is happening. Explanations tend to attribute simple causes for change. Leadership, as a concept, treats causality as emanating from the acts of a key person (e.g., the star member of a team, the founder of the organization, the governor, the CEO).

Some people tend to treat causes and consequences as the work of the gods or God or joss or fate or karma or magic: Some spirit or force or the universe is blamed in their accounts about what happens that is bad or good. Other people tend to explain the failure or success of a team, organization, or community as the consequence of efforts made by a prominent group member, usually labeled the leader. During the past two centuries, more and more people use leadership as part of their accounts.[1]

Leadership is a concept that helps us answer questions about why things happen. It helps us to organize our stories of significant change. Why is it so useful? Well, first, because there are times when a single person's efforts do make the difference. Regardless, second, it is easier to frame a compelling story about what is happening in a business or country around a central person than it is to accurately detail the myriad interactions among many people that are the more likely causes (Meindl, Ehrlich, & Dukerich, 1985). If people are not buying accounts that seem too complex, when they are unwilling to use fate or the gods to explain what is happening, then making a story about acts of leadership can be compelling.

Something to Think About and Discuss With Others

We like heroes and villains: to adore or to hate. But real people and how they behave are rarely so purely good or bad or alone in their doings. In 2006, the University of Miami's (Florida) football season was marred by a brawl before the start of a game early in the season. Thirteen Hurricane players were suspended, and head coach Larry Cocker was fired at the end of the season just 4 years after he was lauded for coaching Miami to a national championship. Getting another coaching job was difficult for Cocker, who said that the 2006 brawl was a topic raised in the first 30 seconds of subsequent employment interviews. Ask yourself what a simple causal story omits. A team brawls/wins. Who is the coach? That is who is responsible. That is who must be blamed: either praised or denigrated.

---

[1]"The word leadership is a sophisticated, modern concept. In earlier times, words meaning 'head of state,' 'military commander,' . . . 'chief,' or 'king' were common . . . [to differentiate] the ruler from other members of society. A preoccupation with leadership, as opposed to headship based on inheritance, usurpation, or appointment, occurred predominantly in countries with an Anglo-Saxon heritage. Although the *Oxford English Dictionary* (1933) noted the appearance of the word 'leader' in the English language as early as the year 1300, the word 'leadership' did not appear until the first half of the nineteenth century . . . [and] did not appear in most other modern languages until recent times" (Bass & Stogdill, 1990, p. 11).

The enormity of what happens in the world can overwhelm someone who wants to make a difference. That is especially true when explanations assign causality for what is going on to an impersonal bureaucracy, or to a concentration of power in the hands of one or a few highly-placed individuals, or to the whims of the gods. Any bureaucracy, any concentration of power, any institutionalized process of control ultimately serves more as a mechanism for change than as its source. Instead, important intentional changes almost always can be traced back to interactions among people. As people talk, they can help to instigate and to breathe life into and to shape something that becomes meaningful over time.

The acts of a single person are always necessary but rarely sufficient for successful change. Without attention and thrust provided by others along the way, most acts fade into obscurity. For example, Thomas Jefferson is recognized for drafting the Declaration of Independence. However, that document carries little weight without the signatures of the other delegates. It is made more powerful because the colonial representatives agreed to work at their task until they reached sufficient consensus that they were able to join together in a "unanimous declaration" of independence. It is made more powerful still because more than 200 years later, people continue to group together in ways that make it so. *Interactions among, contributions from, and thrust provided by several people are part of almost every idea animated into meaningful life.*

Here is how the process works. A person or two (probably as a result of interacting with others) becomes interested in making a change. That person or two will try to recruit others to support their cause. As like-minded individuals begin to group together, the interactions they share and the work they do become the basis for starting and animating the change. The change that they work toward becomes clearer to them as they talk about it. Each story they tell, each interaction they share, and every minor little decision they make can help to shape the change.

This process is in play whether you are in a family or find yourself in the most complex of bureaucracies. Each person can make a difference to the group. Each group has the potential to influence other groups. *When a few people start grouping together, they can co-construct acts that set great waves of change into motion: acts that can change their world.* Interacting groups of interacting people create, shape, and sustain the mightiest to much meeker social institutions: everything from the United States of America to a small worship community outside Tehran.

Every social institution is a human collaboration. We must collaborate in order to interact, and we must collaborate in order to work together. Grouping is the name we give to all the many ways people collaborate. *Grouping* is people bending and blending their ideas and energies so that they can accomplish something together (Burtis & Turman, 2006). People group together in collaborative service to a shared task, ideal, or social institution.

Grouping includes any collaboration, even across time and place. Grouping can be found on any team or in any boardroom where those involved can communicate directly. However, grouping is also accomplished outside small, shared-moment entities. Whenever and however people interact to try to blend their ideas and efforts, they are grouping. It is also something we do over time and in service to less organized tasks or distinct organizations. Tom Jefferson and others in that group collaborated around their attempt to declare independence. What they accomplished was not just a product—they instigated an ongoing grouping process. By continued grouping efforts over time, in service to the evolving group called the United States, a form of the entity they began continues to this day.

Groups of interacting people play an important role in most significant human endeavors. After the shootings at Virginia Tech in 2007, a few individuals perceived the need to develop a campus alert system to notify students of impending danger. Their perception that they need to respond to the shootings in a positive manner creates an exigency for them to group together and develop a plan. As they group together, they perceive an unfolding flow of new exigencies about how their interaction is playing out and what, in turn, they should do. Over time, their initial interactions spawn actions by other groups of people and the development of campus alert systems across the country. Grouping is how we collaborate. *It is while we are grouping together that giving direction to each other becomes important.* That is where you and this book come into the picture: You can decide to improve your ability to give direction to whichever collaborations matter most to you in your life.

Whatever it is that you want to accomplish in life, other people are probably needed to provide some thrust in support of your efforts. If you want to be successful, you need to group effectively with others who help you accomplish your ends. No small team or large bureaucracy operates with a single mind: Some involve tens, hundreds, even thousands of small groups of interdependent, interacting people whose efforts become the lifeblood of effective action. *So, you need other people to work well together.*

❖ GROUPING, GROUP DIRECTION, AND DIRECTION-GIVING ARE HUMAN RESPONSES TO EXIGENCIES

You cannot work well with others unless at least a few of those others are willing to do so too. And people are only willing to help breathe life into an idea or enterprise if they perceive an exigency to do so. To give direction well, you must figure out what motivates others, over time, to be in the group and to try to help the group. People perceive exigencies that guide their choices regarding various possible activities in a group. The exigencies they perceive help them decide what they are willing to do and what they are not.

An *exigency* is a particular, compelling impulse that you simply must try to communicate with others to address (see Table 1.1). An exigency is an imperfection or opportunity marked by a sufficient amount of urgency that it stimulates your strategic attempt to communicate with someone in order to address the exigency (Bitzer, 1968). If the urgency you feel is not sufficient to stimulate a specific communication

Table 1.1	Examples of Exigencies for Grouping

- "Oh no," thinks Paige, "our quarterly report shows expenses spinning out of control so much that I've got to talk to my division managers and to corporate so that we can begin to develop a plan for cutting equipment costs somehow."

- "Glory be," says Cornelia to her friends, "this park is a mess. It would be fun to talk to the auxiliary: Find who else is interested in getting together and making this place presentable."

- "Would you like to get some coffee with me?" asks Rune, who wants to cultivate a social relationship with someone special at his workplace.

- Hiram claims that we need to take top-soil erosion seriously, which is why I think we ought to organize a seminar on the subject.

- "I wonder," muses Pagan, a senior adviser to the president of the United States, "which of you will step forward to be the person in charge of our task force to study cyber-terrorism."

- "Doggone it," ruminates Clee, "I'm certain that the health services market is going to strengthen significantly over the next decade as the boomers retire and I'm in no position alone to take advantage of it unless maybe I can get a group of you guys, my old college peeps, to join me in setting up an investment circle."

attempt designed to address the exigency, it is not an exigency because it fails to motivate an aspect of your interaction (or some other closely related action). The reasons people have for being in a group and for acting in different ways over time in that group can be boiled down into the various, changing exigencies they perceive, which they use to help them make their grouping choices (Burtis & Turman, 2006).

The exigencies people perceive provide windows into their motives and help shape their choices. In particular, grouping exigencies help explain direction-giving and direction-receiving choices. If you understand the exigencies in play, they can help you refine your efforts to give direction to a group. It is the grouping exigencies that people perceive that they use to help guide their choices. You need to keep that in mind, regardless of what your reasoning tells you ought to matter to them more. Understanding the exigencies in play can help you understand seemingly irrational actions and seemingly intractable individual choices.

When you need other people to work well together, what do you do? You might begin by talking to a few people about your idea or concern. That talk may result in some of those others joining you in an effort to act effectively together. Others may spend their energies attacking what you suggest. In either case, you provide direction to a group as you attract their attention to your idea. In short, once you attempt grouping or direction-giving in response to a perceived exigency, that attempt can become an exigency for the actions of others. It was, in part, parental outrage about the lack of warning for students at Virginia Tech that drew the attention of other parents, university officials, and lawmakers around the country.

When you must rely on others, it creates a double burden for you. Not only must you find a way to communicate effectively with those people about the exigencies that concern you, but you must also find a way to communicate effectively about the exigencies that concern them. At Virginia Tech, for example, some of the grouping efforts after the shooting did not focus on an early alert system but rather on expanding access to weapons for all students across campus so they could directly respond to such attacks. There are always choices to be made about which direction the group should take: Offering direction to a group helps people make their choices.

The exigencies we perceive become evident in how we engage a group, including how we frame and respond to our situation. Framing a compelling story can help to orient others to your point of view. To get people to work well together, you must frame a story that creates an exigency for action in their minds. Do not just assume that they will do what you say. You need to find a way to fuel a sense of exigency in them. If you fail, they may not pay attention to you at all or they may begin to actively oppose your efforts. Framing a compelling story can include telling about the experience your group could be having if others will behave as you suggest. Framing a compelling story about a potential group experience is at the heart of many successful attempts to provide direction to a group.

For grouping to be effective over time, people must begin to converge upon a shared sense of *group direction*. This convergence manifests as a shared set of words, meanings, and stories that grouping people think represent their group: their common concerns, their shared experiences, and the outcomes they desire from being in the group. The people in any team, organization, or community co-construct direction for their group using such shared terms and ideas. Their converged-upon sense of *direction* will probably include the following:

1. "who" and "what" grouping people think that they are as a system,

2. "where" and "why " grouping people think that they want to go to be successful in their enterprise,

3. "how" they think that they want to go about getting to their desired vision/outcome, and

4. "how well" they think that they are doing in their efforts.

The sense of a group's direction may vary among its members, with some believing that the group is going in the right direction, others who do not like where the group is going, and still others who do not much care. For example, some may sense that group direction is healthy and dynamic ("we are really doing some good work here!") or that their group is struggling ("we are going nowhere; we are lost and confused"). The direction may even be destructive ("we are tearing ourselves apart bickering," "I'm sick of this group: You can all go to hell!"). Whether the group is succeeding, flailing about, or failing, individual members probably have a sense of the group's direction. However, effective groups have a shared and productive sense of direction. For that to happen, it must be co-constructed: Effective groups require effective direction-giving.

Direction-giving happens whenever a grouping individual commits an act or makes a statement that commands the attention of others in the group. The action may be good or bad for the group, may help to move it in a negative or positive direction, or may function to reinforce what is already under way. Direction-giving can involve many tens, hundreds, even thousands of communicative interactions.

Messages are created and exchanged in attempts to co-construct some shared sense of what the group is and should be doing. Members may take turns suggesting or providing direction to their group, or one member may predominate as a direction-giver in a given case or set of circumstances.

Direction-givers are people who help to co-construct a sense of direction for the group. *Anyone who helps a group to thrive (or to fail) is a direction-giver.* Direction-giving happens whenever a group member helps to orient or to move the group: focusing or employing the attentions and energies of those who are grouping. Whenever someone is providing direction to a group, it means that others are focusing on what the direction-giver has to offer. Usually grouping involves people taking turns offering or providing direction to the group. Members tend to alternate giving direction and receiving direction from others in the group. Sometimes direction is offered, but nobody takes the bait. Sometimes the direction offered is attacked by others. Through such give-and-take, interacting people begin to co-create and share a sense of their grouping experience: the story of their group. Every group needs effective direction-givers in order to thrive.

Giving direction well requires rhetorical sophistication. Knowing how the exigencies that are perceived may affect choices regarding what direction someone will accept is at the heart of that sophistication. Effective direction-giving is always a rhetorical process. *Rhetorical* acts are tactical or strategic attempts to use communication or other symbolic behavior to accomplish your desired ends. You are being rhetorical when you try to influence someone. *Rhetoric* manifests in the persuasive aspects of your message: the words and deeds you use to try to influence someone's choices. If you forget the rhetorical nature of your attempts to give direction, you are much less likely to frame compelling stories for the group's consideration and much less likely to be effective.

Something to Think About and Discuss With Others

In 2005, Cindy Sheehan held a silent vigil outside President Bush's Crawford, Texas, ranch in part because her son was killed in action in 2004. Her rhetorical choice encouraged others to join her grouping effort and was one of the acts that inspired debate about U.S. action in Iraq. Others around the country used a variety of other rhetorical strategies to support or oppose the war (rallies, marches, parades, Web sites, speeches, town hall meetings, and support for candidates with particular war positions). What other rhetorical efforts are in play as people attempt to initiate, perpetuate, change, or stop war choices?

Becoming aware of grouping exigencies is a valuable rhetorical resource because being in touch with those exigencies can help you to make more informed interaction choices. You need to figure out which of your possible words and deeds might best help to get other people to work well together. To do so, you must consider the exigencies they perceive as most compelling in a particular situation and/or over time.

Because exigencies change as people interact, so will a group's needs. Each group needs different types of direction-giving efforts over time. Each type is a different approach to giving direction. Each type may be needed by a group at different points in time. Each person may act as each of the different types over time. What distinguishes among types of direction-givers is a combination of the exigency perceived for needing direction and the direction-giving behavior that should be offered to the group in response.

What groups of people are willing to hear in the moment affects what direction they are willing to receive. All such choices filter through the exigencies they perceive as most important to their group at a given point in time. They also consider how well the direction that is offered seems to address those exigencies and they consider the communication credentials and direction-giving skills of the person who is offering direction. Each person who tries to provide direction to the group will find that their efforts are usually accepted by others only to the extent that those others think that the offered direction fits the situation as they perceive it to be.

Consider the following descriptions about various types of groups. Even from the snippet provided, you can tell whether the group is heading in the right direction or requires change.

- "Our company is really making progress now."
- "Our town is falling apart. Everyone seems to be leaving and if they close the school, they might just as well shut us down."
- "Our team's preparations are on track, but we are still kind of just sputtering along."
- "Our potential merger is like a love affair; it feels like an adventure, but it is a trip with an unknown destination, and we just cannot risk getting seduced into this scheme."
- "If we want real change in this country, we have got to reject the old ways and form a new covenant, which we can use to transform ourselves."

Each statement frames the group's experience from the perspective of the person making the account. Each frame suggests a longer story attached to that person's opinion regarding the presence or absence of effective direction-giving in his or her group. The first group appears to our storyteller to be well managed. The second apparently needs drastic change in order to survive a crisis. The third may need some form of additional guidance to improve performance. The fourth should avoid making a drastic change in direction. The fifth group may not even exist yet, except as an exigency for action in the mind of the person trying to call others to arms against what is happening in their country. The exigencies being framed are different in each of the scenarios, and so each group requires efforts from a different type of direction-giver.

The exigencies people perceive for grouping should help determine the type of direction-giving you offer or provide. The more closely you can tie your direction-giving attempts to the exigencies people perceive for grouping, the more potential you have to be effective.

❖ DIRECTION-GIVING TYPES INCLUDE THE WORK OF A DOER, FOLLOWER, GUIDE, MANAGER, AND LEADER

All grouping members play a part in giving direction to and in receiving direction from others in the group regardless of whether they are the supervisor, chairperson, president, head honcho, or prince of particularly pertinent personnel. What matters more than any particular title or position is what the individual does that provides direction to a group. Across the almost infinite number of possible direction-giving acts, five general forms of direction-giving behavior tend to recur (doing, following, guiding, managing, and leading), which we translate into the five types of direction-givers: a doer, follower, guide, manager, and leader. As a set, *the five types show how any member can help give direction to a group:* to help a group to thrive.

The differences between types of direction-givers matter. When you attempt to act as each type of direction-giver, you must demonstrate to the group that you have the specific communication credentials and skills required of that type. It is those varying credentials and skills that allow you to give a particular type of direction well (see Chapters 2 and 3). A group may be willing to accept direction from you as a doer but not as a guide. Or, it may be willing to use you as a guide one day and not the next.

Cindy Sheehan acts as a guide while her silent protest attracts the attention and support of others. However, she failed in her 2008 bid to get elected to Congress, which means that voters decide not to make her into one of the managers entrusted to help make decisions about funding the war. Different groups, perceiving different exigencies and different direction-giving skills on her part, are differently willing over different times to accept the different types of direction-giving she offers.

Sometimes the same group receives different types of direction from the same individual over time. Former Army Chief of Staff General Shenseki was a manager until his retirement during the second Bush administration. Then, he could no longer influence the Iraq war as a manager, but he could offer guideship through his insights into the long-term implications of a current war plan. When he was asked to give direction by the Obama administration, it is again as a manager, this time over the Department of Veterans Affairs.

There are five types of direction-givers (Burtis, 1995; Burtis & Turman, 2006). Brief definitions show why each type tends to recur (see Table 1.2). A *doer* offers direction to a group by taking the initiative to act on behalf of the group. A doer's work begins alone but is on behalf of the group and must, over time, draw attention from others in the group for the doer's work to provide any direction to the group. Acting as a doer is a type of direction-giving that initiates something that does not require interaction until the point at which the group decides whether to accept the fruits of the doer's work. A *follower* offers direction to a group by providing support for the direction-giving attempt of another person. A follower gives direction by enhancing or limiting the group's momentum as it responds to the direction initiated by other people. A *guide* offers direction to a group by providing something on which the group can focus its attentions for the moment.

Doers, followers, and guides can play key direction-giving roles and are always necessary for effective groups. Managers and leaders are additional, specialized types. A *manager* has the formal responsibility and authority to offer direction by attempting to marshal the resources of the group. For example, a manager may oversee group processes, personnel, or other resources (e.g., time, money, equipment). A *leader* offers a transformative vision for the future of a group facing its end. As a set, the five types name the kinds of direction groups may need, given the shifting exigencies they face. Further elaboration on each of the types is useful at this point, and we provide detailed discussions of the communication credentials and skills involved in acting as each type of direction-giver in Chapters 2 and 3.

A *doer* takes the initiative to act on behalf of a group. This individual takes responsibility upon himself or herself. He or she undertakes a task, makes some contribution to a task, and/or completes a task that

Table 1.2	Direction-Giving Acts by Type of Direction-Giver
A doer takes initiative to act.	You must take the initiative to do something that is needed or wanted by the group. Then the fruits of your act must be considered and accepted by the group as its own. You provide direction as a doer when the group accepts your fruits as its own or is otherwise affected by the process of having considered your work.
A follower provides support.	You must put your own efforts behind the direction given by another person. Or, you must clearly withhold that support, essentially saying "no" or "not yet" or "not you" to the direction-giving attempt. Your acts must provide direction by enhancing or reducing group momentum initiated by others.
A guide focuses the group's attention.	You must interact with the group in a manner that focuses their attention on what you are doing or saying. You do that by providing them with something they want or need to see, hear, question, or try. While the group's attention is on any other type of direction-giver, she or he is also, in that moment, acting as a guide.
A manager marshals a resource.	To be a manager, you must have a formal position with the authority to marshal a system resource: e.g., budget; personnel; priorities. Making decisions about how to marshal those resources is how you act as a manager.
A leader offers a vision.	You must articulate and/or personify a group-transformative vision made salient by system-threatening crisis.

can somehow help the group. It is a form of direction-giving that can be initiated without interaction, at least up to the point at which the group decides whether to accept the fruits of the doer's work. In the end, of course, the group has to decide whether to receive the fruits of the doer's work as its own. If so, the doer's act may enhance the group's efforts to complete its work (serving a task function for the group) or to maintain viability (serving a relationship function for the group). To be effective as a doer, your work should enhance, change, or perpetuate group direction, perhaps simply by freeing up group resources for other action. For example, some NFL players offer to take a reduction in salary to free up space under the team's salary cap so that other key personnel can stay with the team.

The doer's act may be solicited by the group or done without interaction, in hopes that the group will someday accept the doer's work as its own. For example, a school board member who is a manager in her or his own right decides alone to develop a new approach to presenting data to the public about the school district's performance. Acting alone, undertaking a task that no other board member or mandate makes necessary, means this manager is attempting to provide direction as a doer. When she or he finishes the work and presents it to the board, if other board members embrace the new approach, or if the group is otherwise affected by the process of having to consider the merits of the new approach, the initiating member has provided direction as a doer.

A *follower* offers direction to a group by providing (or withholding) support for the direction-giving attempt of another person. A follower's acts give direction by enhancing or limiting the group's momentum. To be effective as a follower, you must decide whether to put your own efforts behind the direction offered by someone else. If so, you should try to do so effectively. If not, you should clearly withhold your support, in which case you essentially say "no" or "not yet" or "not you" to the direction-giving attempt (Frye, Kisselburgh, & Butts, 2007; Perreault, 1997). For example, the new reporting structure presented to school board members must gain followership from at least one other member to develop any momentum as a change. Without such followership, a doer's or guide's efforts are likely to be rejected or ignored.

Only when needed direction from followers and/or doers is not forthcoming does the remarkable importance and potency of these two direction-giving types become fully evident. Some doers and followers actually become key direction-givers in a group (see Table 1.3). When denied the ongoing contributions of people willing to do and to follow, most groups will quite literally seize up and stop functioning almost immediately. Any group member can be a doer, and most members in every group move frequently in and out of the follower role, even the president or CEO. In fact, groups tend to suffer when a key direction giver is unable to ever follow effectively when useful direction is offered by other group members. Further, most effective group members, regardless of their role, will take on the doer role at times to instigate initiative, create change, or otherwise create an impression that they are making a sufficient contribution to the group.

A *guide* offers direction to a group by providing something on which the group can focus its attentions in the moment. A guide is the person who, in the instant, has the attention of the group. A guide

Table 1.3	Key Direction-Givers May Emerge Over Time

A *key direction-giver* is someone to whom others look for guidance on a given subject, in using a particular process, or in hopes of a particular type of direction. People become key direction-givers after their contributions prove to be crucial or consistent over time.

Crucial contributions are made during *critical incidents* (see Chapter 8), which are when a direction-giver's contributions substantially change the group's experience from then on.

Consistent contributions are made as the group learns to look again and again to the same person because they want that person's direction-giving contributions again and again over time.

Anyone given a management position and anyone who emerges as a leader is a key direction-giver for a group. There may be others as well (i.e., people whose doing, following, or guideship activities teach the group to trust their contributions and to request them regularly over time).

probably offers direction by "answering" whatever "question" (e.g., concern, discomfort, interest, or uncertainty) other grouping members are experiencing regarding what they should do now/next. For example, hesitant board members might raise important questions about the impact of a new reporting structure on student performance. What purposes can it serve? Will this reflect favorably on our district? What administrative costs are involved? Both raising pertinent questions and offering up possible answers to them help to shape group decision-making. Both focus attention on the person asking or answering the question. In those moments, that person is playing the important direction-giving role of a guide. Even the devil's advocate or a follower who says no serves as a guide as his or her objections are considered by others. Raising important issues helps guide the group and provide it with direction.

To be an effective guide, you must interact with the group in a manner that focuses the attention of other people in the system on what you are doing or saying. When you guide, you are helping to orient the group in this moment of the life of the system. You can do that by providing them something they want or need to question, hear, observe, or try out themselves.

The range of possible guideship acts is quite broad—for example, the jokester breaks the ice for a new group, the oldest member shows the way because she or he best knows the territory the group must cover, the expert demonstrates a new process for, or explains a difficult idea to, the group, the hired consultant helps the group attempt to manage conflict, or the CEO briefs the group on a proposed merger. Further, when a doer, follower, manager, or leader explains her or his work or ideas to the group, in that moment, as the group's attention is on her or him, that person is serving as a guide. Consequently, any direction-giver will be effective in part because of her or his guideship skills and not solely because he or she is an effective leader, manager, or doer. Regardless of the other roles you may play, your guideship skills will probably be exercised at times in every group that matters much to you.

Multiple people should be able to play a guideship role, often in quick succession. Each should be able to offer direction when they have expertise, information, perspective, or pertinent questions or concern that can help orient the group or improve its efforts or deliberations. In an egalitarian group that shares responsibility and power, all grouping members should tend to move in and out of guideship roles. Even heavily hierarchical bureaucracies are more likely to be healthy and effective to the extent that guideship behavior is allowed and encouraged among its members.

The health of most groups correlates to how well its members are able to contribute while acting as these first three direction-giving types. Not everyone, however, needs to act as a leader or manager and not every group requires the efforts of someone at managing or at leading.

A *manager* offers direction to a group from a position of formal authority over others in the group. The manager uses that authority to marshal some of the resources of the group (e.g., group process, personnel, budget, or supplies; the record of the group's decision-making; the group's agenda and/or long-term plans; and/or other resource). It is not the title that makes you a manager; it is doing the work expected of the person in your position. You act as a manager when you make decisions about how to marshal group resources that are under your purview.

Managers (if a group needs one) tend to hold a relatively long-lived and stable position. Some groups employ the efforts of many managers, each with a specified set of resources to marshal on behalf of the group (e.g., a board, a CEO, a CFO, multiple vice presidents, and a myriad of mid-level directors, heads, supervisors, and chairpersons). The fraternity president, head coach of a soccer team, regional division head in a *Fortune* 500 company, and Senate majority leader are individuals vested with a job of acting as a manager for their respective groups. Each is responsible for overseeing group resources and is faced with related decisions. For example, who might be in the next pledge class, what players will start in the first game of the season, which of several possible mergers under consideration by corporate will get the full-throated support of the division, or what might comprise the agenda for the Senate?

A *leader* offers a transformative vision for the future of a group facing its own end. A leader (if a group has one) articulates the hopes and dreams of a group in crisis. Leadership is vision made salient by crisis (Burtis, 1995). A leader offers direction by articulating a group-transformative vision and may personify that vision when it is made salient by crisis.

During the world's economic upheaval at the end of the first decade in the 21st century, fears are given voice that what might be happening is the start of a great depression. In the United States, first a Republican and then a Democratic administration issue statements framing the situation as a crisis. "We must do something" and "the greatest risk is in doing too little" are frames used by both Bush and Obama people. Showing a shared sense of urgency that there is a crisis results in some level of agreement that drastic action is necessary. Translating agreement into sweeping programmatic changes of transformative leadership vision for how to escape the crisis is much more difficult.

Some claim that the lessons of the Great Depression of the 1930s should guide any vision for today. Others disagree about what lessons are learned from the Great Depression. Countries disagree about how to approach the crisis: Some favor more drastic solutions as others advise caution. People in positions of power within each country disagree. Leadership options to transform the status quo are advocated, but those visions get locked in struggle against more managerial plans: options that advocate incremental, careful changes. Over time, many people try to cobble together something approximating a vision that gains sufficient traction to work.

Crisis can help make a vision salient, but a vision does not provide leadership until it gets sufficient support from needed constituencies to support group-transformative action. Perhaps some of the countries and industries around the world can manage their way through the crisis without suffering the pain of a transformation wrought of leadership vision. When vision is in play, and regardless of the particulars of the vision, you can expect harshly competing claims: both about what is happening and about what ought to be done next. Even then, some will say that a vision is in play, and others will deny that fact. Violently coalescing and competing framings of the crisis and of the appropriate vision for response are at the center of leadership, which makes us grateful that most groups never require such leadership.

Effective direction-givers help shape the grouping experience. All five types of direction-givers are necessary to understand how groups become successful even though not every group requires all five types. (We discuss the skills necessary for each of the five in Chapters 2 and 3.) We hope that you can tell from the brief descriptions that there are ways for you to become a more active and effective direction-giver for your group. You have contributions you can make that will help your groups to thrive.

❖ EVERYONE HAS THE OBLIGATION TO HELP HIS OR HER GROUP TO THRIVE: THE SOCIAL CONTRACT OF CITIZENSHIP

Part of the thesis for this book is that each of us has an obligation to try to find ways of assisting our group's efforts to thrive. In fact, the subtitle for the book was supposed to be *Leadership Communication as Citizenship: Give Direction to Your Team, Organization, or Community as a Doer, Follower, Guide, Manager, or Leader.* Our argument assumes that a *social contract* manifests as we blend our efforts and energies with those of other people. We name this social contract *citizenship*. It requires us all to help our groups thrive by using our direction-giving skills to help frame and shape our group's experience. This direction-giving responsibility is a duty of participation: a membership obligation we ought to feel as we become part of a group.

Group membership always involves responsibility as well as privileges (Gastil, 1992[2]). Why? Because *we each always help give direction to every group we are in*: intentionally or not, well or poorly. It is the nature of groups that they must be co-constructed, given direction, and sustained. Doing so is always the work of the citizen. This responsibility applies regardless of the role we play (leader or follower, CEO or line worker, team star or bench warmer, teacher or student, parent or child, board member or stakeholder). The social contract applies regardless of the type or size of the group we are in. The only question is whether we do so with good or bad effects: whether we help our group to thrive, or let it be less than at its best, or to falter (see Table 1.4).

---

[2]Those who are denied volition, or freedom of choice, or who are otherwise without the means of exercising volition are excepted by some theorists (see Gastil, 1992) from the burdens and privileges of the social contract (e.g., slaves, infants, criminals, and individuals deemed to be of less than full mental capacity).

Table 1.4	Violators of the Social Contract: Those Who Do Not Help Their Group Thrive

The *social contract* obligates people to each other in two ways. The obligation is on each individual to try to help his or her group to thrive. The obligation is on the group, as a collective, to each individual. As a consequence, we judge poorly those who violate the contract. Several terms name behaviors that do not help a group to thrive. Each of these, though direction-givers, violate the social contract, reduce their group's ability to thrive, and deprive their group of its due. What terms would you add to the following list?

- *Social loafers* let others carry their part of the load (Latane, Williams, & Harkins, 1979).
- *Passive members* acquiesce to others rather than taking a stand (Burtis & Turman, 2006[a]).
- *Saboteurs* try to undermine the group's efforts to reach its goals.
- *Tyrants* force outcomes without taking direction from others—eviscerating the concepts of direction-giving, leader, and follower (Burns, 1978[b]).

a. See Burtis and Turman (2006) for an elaboration of additional pitfall possibilities and remedies for every grouping enterprise.

b. Burns (1978) distinguishes leaders from tyrants by pointing to when members can no longer provide direction as followers. He raises nagging questions: Can an evil genius, acting badly, be a great leader? He says no. Are people, forced into passivity by a tyrant's brutality, really followers? We say no; not unless they find a way to rise up or to enjoy.

A person or group *thrives* if it is healthy, has prospects, and can anticipate and adapt to change as a regular and ongoing response to its circumstances. A complex organization does not thrive as a group unless smaller groups within it thrive and spread their health to the larger organization. A country does not thrive as a group unless various groups engaging its citizens also thrive. A family does not thrive as a group unless the various supra-groups in which it is nested and that help to sustain it are also thriving (e.g., employment, educational, civic, leisure, food production, and governmental groups). Human action and interaction make some groups thrive and others falter or wither away. The obligation of citizenship is to help co-create the direction a group takes. That means helping those in the group figure out what they need to do for their group to thrive (see Chapter 7).

The remainder of the thesis for this book is that, to be effective as we help give direction to our groups, each of us should develop the skills involved in helping to frame and shape our group's experiences and the accounts we make and share about those experiences. This also means learning what it takes to be effective as a doer, follower, guide, manager, and leader. This allows each of us to find ways to make a contribution to our group. *If we do not recognize the potential value of our own contribution, we will almost certainly diminish or distort it.*

Each of us needs to help shape the story of our group's experience. Our contributions are especially important in helping negotiate the values and actions that we use to co-construct the future of our group. This is the work of every grouping member, not just a job for the manager or leader (Kouzes & Posner, 1993). For example, a new congregation needs to converge upon a joint framing for its mission to ensure that members are moving toward similar goals. Should we focus on growing our congregation? Should we focus on our role in the larger community or on the spiritual lives of our individual members? How does our decision-making structure affect our outreach? Such pragmatic questions are value-based choices about the direction the new congregation wants to take.

In every group, people frame the grouping situation, including which exigencies we ought to use to orient our group. People frame the processes they think we might employ. People frame the outcome options they want us to choose. Framing is "a quality of communication that causes others to accept one meaning over another" (Fairhurst & Sarr, 1996). We help shape a group's experience and give it direction as we affect how it converges around key framings.

❖ IN CONCLUSION

Understanding the process of grouping, direction-giving, and communicating is fundamental to your effectiveness. In Chapters 2 and 3, we elaborate on the skills needed to employ your five direction-giving options to help shape the direction and story of your group's experiences. In Chapters 4 and 5, we review contemporary leadership theory and research and then walk you through a process for developing your own framework for giving direction well. Understanding basic communication processes and skills can enhance your efforts to help your group (Chapters 6 and 7). We also discuss the communication skills specific to direction-giving (framing and shaping stories of grouping experiences) in Chapters 8 through 10. All of these can help you shape the story of your group regardless of the type of direction-giving you provide.

This material will be useful as you make connections between it and your grouping experiences. To make that connection, be intentional, proactive, and alert. Look for ways to boil down useful ideas into nuggets you can easily remember. Then use those to try to change what you do in your own groups. (We explain in Chapter 8 why nuggets are a useful direction-giving tool, but for now, we encourage you to practice looking for "small treasures you can put to use later.") You have to translate the material into your own specific circumstances. Then, if you decide to become more effective, you might actually begin to change your part of the world.

2

Distinguish Between Three Direction-Giver Options

Doing, Following, and Guiding Well

In the first unit of this book, we focus on the power you can have as a direction-giver. The second and third chapters in that unit elaborate on the different skills needed by each of five direction-giving types. In this chapter, we focus on the first three types (doer, follower, and guide) because of how closely intertwined they are in most group interactions. They tend to be the most frequently ignored types of direction-givers in other books, which focus more on the last two types of direction-givers (manager and leader). To give direction well as a doer, follower, or guide means doing so in a manner that is effective and that others will judge to be appropriate.

Doers, followers, and guides are often more integral to group effectiveness than are managers and leaders. That is because they are so deeply involved in co-constructing the vitally important convergences of meaning that the group uses to represent itself. These convergences in meanings are found in shared, member-accepted accounts: about the group's past experiences, the nature of the group's current situation, how group members should behave, and where the group is trying to go in the future. Followers help do all this by selecting which direction-giving attempts they will accept and which they will oppose or ignore. Doers help by working to complete something that they personally can accomplish for the benefit of the group. Guides help orient the group to each moment and choice faced by the group throughout its lifetime. Combined, the activities of these three direction-giving types help to frame and shape the experience story of every group.

We treat each type of direction-giver in turn. We begin by discussing the exigencies you look for to decide when your group needs the efforts of a doer, follower, or guide. Then we discuss the differing credentials you must demonstrate when you attempt to act as each type of direction-giver. Finally, we outline the communication skills you need to be effective during each type of direction-giving attempt.

❖ SPECIFIC EXIGENCIES, CREDENTIALS, AND COMPETENCIES FRAME EACH TYPE OF DIRECTION-GIVER

Let's begin by remembering why and how it is that we work with others. We first perceive an exigency that we think should result in us interacting with someone else. Then, as we attempt to interact with them, we perceive additional exigencies that make us think that we need to begin to move in the same direction as a group. The exigencies we perceive help us to decide when and how to offer direction to others and when and from whom to accept direction. We test the direction other people offer to our group against the exigencies we perceive. Then we decide how we think that we and our group ought to behave in response (see Chapter 1).

Our concern with exigencies is explained in three steps. First, the exigencies that we perceive for grouping tend to change as group efforts and interactions unfold. Change comes from an evolution of the circumstances under which we are grouping, including any adjustments we make in our task, personnel, process, or desired outcomes. Second, changing exigencies change perceptions of the kind of direction-giving a group needs. Group situations are dynamic and continually change. As a result, each group needs different types of direction-giving over time. Third, knowing the exigencies and communication competencies specific to each direction-giving type helps you become more personally effective over time in your own groups.

Effective direction-givers (1) respond appropriately to the grouping exigencies perceived by others in a group. Each direction-giving attempt is accepted only to the extent group members perceive that a group's needs and interests are matched by the direction offered (see Table 2.1).

Effective direction-givers also (2) behave in ways that attract attention and trust from others. Getting the group to accept your contributions depends on whether they are willing to pay attention to you as a potentially useful source of direction.

Sometimes, what you offer might match their perceived exigencies but still fail to stir their support. For example, new members in a group may have their ideas disregarded because of institutional memory: "We tried that already" or "We don't do things like that" may be the group's response. Some members have so little credibility that the idea they try to get a group to pay attention to is ignored until someone else raises that same idea and the group says "all right!" If a group does not trust you as a direction-giver, they will probably accept direction from others.

Table 2.1	Exigencies and Definitions by Direction-Giving Type: Doer, Follower, Guide	
The Exigency for This Type Direction-Giver Is:	*Direction-Giver*	*Definition of Type*
"We need xyz." The group wants or needs (or could benefit from) something, which doesn't require grouping or interaction to accomplish.	**Doer**	Person(s) who takes the initiative to act on behalf of the group
"Help me!" Someone's attempt to act requires someone else's grouping attempt in response in order to be successful, improved, or fail: e.g., a follower may offer a supportive or cooperative reply; an alteration; rejection.	**Follower**	Person(s) who provide(s) or withhold(s) support or momentum for a direction-giving attempt offered by another person
"What now?" The group needs or wants something on which to focus as a group: e.g., the group needs or wants instruction, an orientation, explanation, or entertainment.	**Guide**	Person(s) who provide(s) something on which the group can focus its attentions for the moment

The group's attention and trust manifests mostly from what you do and say, in part in response to the credentials you offer and in part to the communication skills you demonstrate. Credentials suggest your capacity to give direction and are inherently tied to any competency you demonstrate as you attempt to give direction. The group's assessment of your credentials and communication competencies will vary according to the type of direction-giving you attempt to provide and by the type they think is needed for their group (see Table 2.2). The credentials you provide and the skills you exhibit both help frame the group's perceptions of what you have to offer as a direction-giver.

Table 2.2	Credentials and Competencies by Direction-Giver: Doer, Follower, Guide	
Direction-Giver	Credential	Communicator Competency
Doer	Actions to accomplish something competently	(1) Sense of self-efficacy that supports (2) taking initiative to (3) act competently. Competent action requires (a) the ability and willingness to perceive an impulse to act, (b) completing an act in a manner that bears fruit, and (c) getting the fruits of the act considered by the group. The group's decision to accept fruits from a doer's act as the group's own requires effective guideship either from the doer or from someone else.
Follower	Actions that create the impression of a willing, able, and desirable affiliation	Affiliative receptivity requires (1) ability to "listen" for need; (2) willingness to blend one's efforts with another's direction; (3) ability to adapt behaviorally to support or oppose that direction; all based in (4) a sense of self-efficacy; and ability to (5) co-create a communicative and relational climate conducive to receiving direction (e.g., the ability to ask questions, to interact effectively while following, to raise concerns).
Guide	Actions that create the impression of credibility	(1) Credibility and (2) ability to engage the group's attention (e.g., to be able to articulate a thought, question, frame, process, proposed option, or idea that focuses the group's attention) or to facilitate others so that they can engage the group.

Credentials are required for licensure in some jobs, but for us, credentialing is a natural, informal grouping phenomenon (Olson, 1987). We define a *credential* as an experience, skill, or attitude of yours that might be useful to the group. *Credentialing* is any act by which you tell or show the group your experience or skill. Demonstrating an elegant speaking style might help credential you as a minister or presidential candidate just as Adrian Peterson's record-setting acts as a running back for Oklahoma stoked the desire of NFL teams to draft him. When you credential yourself in a group, you suggest a reputation for yourself as a potential direction-giver.

Especially as grouping members get to know one another, we tend to swap accounts of our past, present, and future activities. Doing so is part of our credentialing. Sharing accounts and stories is how we build a narrative about ourselves that tells about, among other things, our experiences, interests, character, and competencies. As we credential, people get a feel for what it is like to work with us and to take direction from us.

Credentialing is something that you can insert intentionally into your interactions with others, but your credentials are also enhanced (or diminished) unintentionally as you interact and offer direction. Every direction-giving act is a potential credential. Others judge us by what we say about ourselves but also by our actions and attitudes. Once you say or do something others find worthy of attention, they are more likely to look your way again. *Think of direction-giving as a dance in which group members decide when and from whom they accept direction.*

❖ GIVING DIRECTION AS A DOER REQUIRES COMPETENCE

The opening scene from Steven Spielberg's movie *Amistad* shows Joseph Cinqué, a real, historical figure, chained in the hold of a slaver sailing from Cuba to the United States in 1839. Working in the dark, Cinqué tries to separate an iron spike from a wet board in the hull of the ship. Bloody fingers finally foist the nail from its clenched wooden clutch. He uses the freed metal to set loose other chained men and women and together they kill or subdue their captors.

Cinqué's acts are those of a doer. The group needs something done, and he is strong enough to do that work. Once released from their chains, everyone starts to attack their captors. There is no leader, no manager. The freed people merely do or blend their followership with others who are doing: adding their force to the struggle, turning the momentum of their grouping attempt (which is strongly opposed, with superior weapons, by those running the ship) into a successful insurrection. *La Amistad* was theirs. Their story, told eventually to the U.S. Supreme Court, echoes down to us through 170 years of history. As Spielberg tells it, theirs is a powerful example of how doers and followers can animate a group.

A doer is any individual who initiates action that can then be used to affect the task or relational aspects of grouping (Burtis & Turman, 2006). To act as an effective doer, you must initiate something alone that is needed or wanted by, or somehow beneficial[1] to, your group. The doer does not have to be the only one who can do the act; she or he is just someone who does an act on behalf of the group. If a group needs its meeting room unlocked and a group member gets the key to unlock the room before anyone else arrives, that individual serves the group as a doer. If a group member looks up key information related to the group's charge and brings a synopsis to the next meeting, that member serves as a doer. If a CEO spends time between board meetings thinking of a new initiative for the board to consider, he or she acts as a doer in hopes of making the board or broader organization more effective in the future. If you limit your direction-giving to just the interactive types of efforts, then you forego useful activity options and the rhetorical resources and credentials that tend to go along with showing initiative as a doer.

The root for the word *doer* is tied historically to the concept of "the act," which remains the basic unit of doing. A doer's act is comprised of (1) *impulse,* which is the perception of a need to do something; (2) *self-guided effort,* which is an individual's response to the impulse; and (3) *consummation* or completion of the act. However, for an act to provide direction, it must affect grouping, which requires (4) the fruits of the act to be *brought to the group* and (5) *considered* by the group in a way that affects the group's experience.

Something to Consider

Be on the lookout for things that might need doing. Keep track of ideas and/or jobs the group discusses that require finishing. Piggyback, with permission, on the best ideas for action that you pick up from others. Doing so allows you to do work that is likely to be appreciated by others when you do it on behalf of your group and it helps position you as part of the "institutional memory" for your group.

---

[1]Those who act alone to hurt or disable a group are saboteurs.

When a doer's act is completed, consideration by the group of its fruits can result in a variety of effects. For instance, the group can choose (1) to accept the fruits or (2) may find that "failed fruits" help them to shape norms for future behavior (e.g., to set criteria for work they would be willing to accept). Whether accepted or not, the doer's work can continue to provide direction for the group well after the act itself is completed, as is the case with Jefferson's successfully accepted efforts as the doer who wrote the Declaration of Independence.

Everyone in the group may have the ability to help out as a doer, and several or all grouping members may engage in such efforts. The duration of the doer's role can be quite short, but it lasts as long as is needed to complete enough of a task to justify bringing work to the group for consideration. For example, a co-worker who purchases a birthday card that others can sign helps serve the relational needs of the group. Sometimes doing can involve a substantial commitment in time (e.g., a research team member who "likes" to enter data may help every research project team he or she is on to successfully complete their task). The most effective groups often have members who figure out when it is appropriate to do something for the group and who make it their business to be sure that the stuff that needs doing gets done.

A Group's Need Creates an Exigency for a Doer

The exigency for an act of "doing" is that a person perceives that something should be accomplished on behalf of the group. This requires imagining such an action or task (the impulse part of an act) and perceiving the need to act alone in service to the group. Such exigencies can originate in the individual doer or from the group. For example, if Bill Gates perceives an exigency but only makes a brief comment about it,[2] he might still stimulate someone else to act as a doer in response to his comment. Perhaps the group makes a list of tasks that someone needs to do.

The dynamics of doing and how your act will be perceived by others both change with the source of initiative and how it is acted upon.

---

[2]The rhetorical force of any exigency created in response to such comments may differ according to who utters them. For example, there is no particular sense of urgency attached if it is nobody in particular who makes the comment, but if a manager or leader or particularly well-respected guide makes the suggestion, it carries at least a whisper of potential promise for reward to the one who acts in response. Perhaps the promise from heeding such a germinal comment is that that idea deserves attention so one's work will not be wasted; perhaps it is that those who heed the manager will be remembered at bonus time.

Regardless of origin, a doer's act has powerful potential force in a group. When the act is competent, a doer can exert considerable influence over the direction of a group.

Something to Consider

The more volition or free choice you use when taking on a task and the greater the autonomy and judgment you exercise while doing the task, the more the act approximates doing and the less it approximates following. The greater the time commitment required by an act that a group may not accept, the greater the risk involved in spending your resources that way. Acting without a request or some other sign of support from the group can change how willing other grouping members are to receive the fruits of your work: It affects their attributions and expectations. Effective doers usually earn more *idiosyncrasy credits* than effective followers. Such credits are a group's willingness to allow the doer to break group norms because of the doer's contributions to the group. Doers can become heroes (as Cinqué did). A key follower's fruits, unfortunately, are more likely attributed to the person who gave them direction.

❖ CREDENTIALING AS A DOER REQUIRES YOU TO ACCOMPLISH SOMETHING COMPETENTLY

A doer credentials by *accomplishing something competently. Competence* requires completing a job effectively. As Kouzes and Posner (1993) explain, "To commit to doing something that you have no capacity to perform is either disingenuous or stupid. There is nothing courageous about boldly saying you will successfully . . . [do something you] know you have neither the skills nor the resources to do it" (p. 69).

"Effectiveness," however, is a subjective judgment. It involves preferences about the process used and about the outcome that results. Figuring out what other people value in these regards will help you figure out what standards of performance they will apply to your work as a doer. In short, for a doer, it is rarely "the thought that counts."

Showing competence begins with finding and seizing opportunities to show initiative. *Initiative* is a combination of the impulse to try something and the willingness to expend the energy needed to get that something started. Taking initiative shows your willingness to spend your energy and to take some risk on behalf of your group. Of course, every type of direction-giver must show some level of initiative.

What makes some doers unique is that they do not have any formal authority to take the initiative. That increases the risk and also the potential benefits. Consequently, acts of doing sometimes reverberate more than other direction-giving acts. In addition, over time an effective doer gets to be relied upon by others who decide that he or she is to be trusted to do a particular kind of work. That creates status and idiosyncrasy credits that can turn into influence. That influence often extends beyond the subject matter of the doer's act into other group needs.

To show your competence, you need a sense of self-efficacy. *Self-efficacy* is your belief in your own ability to act in ways that will make you effective.[3] It supports your willingness to take the initiative to act on behalf of the group. Fortunately, being effective as a doer can begin with small acts. *Small successes strengthen and broaden your sense of self-efficacy over time*, allowing you to work your way up to more significant direction-giving acts on behalf of your group. They also help you to credential with others in your group. For example, a new team member can demonstrate willingness to take on jobs that experienced members no longer like to do. Over time, appreciation for that orientation can broaden into their support for you doing other activities.

❖ COMMUNICATING COMPETENTLY BLENDS YOUR ACT AS A DOER INTO THE GROUP'S NEED

The one prerequisite to acting well as a doer (for doing well) is to act with competence. But the process for effective doing is complicated because it also requires blending your act and its fruits with the perceptions others have regarding group needs. Although the first three steps of an act do not require interaction, the blending of the act into the story of the group may.

You *may* need to communicate with others at several times along your way toward completing an act (e.g., prior to taking the initiative to act on behalf of your group, during the process of completing the act, and/or after your act is completed and its fruits taken to the group for their consideration). If you cannot anticipate the level of need for staying in touch with your group and/or if you lack the skill to interact well at those key times, you will require help from someone else who

---

[3]See, for example, Zorn (1993), Bandura (1997), and Koesten, Miller, and Hummert (2002).

can ease the way for you. To get a feel for the level of communication your group might require during your attempts as a doer, start small and then grow your acts.

Once you make your choice to act, and while doing, be graceful. Take care in how you undertake, complete, and share the fruits of your work. Be aware of the toes or turf of others in your group: Be aware of their own activities and priorities. After your act is consummated, plan its presentation—don't just plop your fruits down on your group. You, or someone, must guide the group's attention into considering the fruits of your act in a way that helps the group feel inclined to accept those fruits as its own. To do that, you must learn when and how to take initiative in a way that is appreciated by your group.

We counsel practicing humility about your work. That is difficult when you are probably ego-engaged with your efforts and feel proud of your fruits. However, others must see the merit of your work as well. They will struggle to do so if they perceive either you or your fruits as a threat. They may not know how to orient to your unexpected "gift." Is it a Trojan horse? Does your effort mean that they are not carrying their own fair share of the work? Such confusions sometimes manifest as criticism. In some cases, doing can be like throwing a surprise party. The negative reactions of others can be difficult and frustrating if you are someone who likes to do.

It can take time for a group to learn that it is safe to accept work from a doer. Developing a climate that allows your group to well and gently receive a doer's contributions and a history of successful experiences are useful but ongoing co-constructions in most effective groups.

❖ GIVING DIRECTION AS A FOLLOWER REQUIRES AFFILIATIVE RECEPTIVITY

Ginger Rogers, a dancer and actress, is described by various sources as becoming famous by spending her life following. She did, they say, everything that her more famous dance partner, Fred Astaire, did. However, she "did it backwards and in high heels." She was receptive to his direction. When he chose to work with her, it was because she provided a desirable affiliation. A dancer who follows helps co-create the dance with a dancer who leads. Both are responsible for the nature and quality of the dance. In effective dancing (and grouping), the one who follows exerts a positive influence. She or he works to create a vital, physical tension with the one who leads. Both are necessary. Without a follower, there would be no dance.

To act as an effective follower, you must bend and blend your own efforts, ideas, and support into direction provided by others. The question of followership is the question of whom to support: Which direction should be taken, and what action best helps the group to thrive? Perhaps X suggests "this way" and L acts as a follower when replying "OK" or "sounds good but let me think about it a bit" or "yes, this way is good but I need to go slowly." Perhaps Y says, "Well this is an unexpected problem," and M acts as a follower by saying, "I think so too; how can I help?" Perhaps Z says, "Here, give me a hand will you?" and N acts as a follower by nodding and shouldering half the load. A person who follows adds momentum to the direction he or she agrees to receive (Burtis & Turman, 2006).

When one group member follows the direction given or offered by another person, that direction "becomes more real." Other members must now pay more attention to it than when it is the input of a single individual. When a follower throws her or his support behind the direction suggested by someone else, she or he helps get the group going in that direction. A follower adds momentum even to direction given by a boss.

Deciding who or what to support also results, directly or indirectly, in turning down other followership options. When nobody follows a direction-giver's attempt, potential followers are essentially saying "no" or "not yet" or "not you." For example, perhaps Q says, "We should try it this way instead," and nobody responds directly; then, after a pause O looks at J and says, "Tell me more about your weekend." Saying yes to any one direction is essentially saying no to others. As group members begin to follow, other options lose momentum or go unsaid.

Something to Think About and Discuss With Others

A lieutenant is a potent, specialized form of followership. A lieutenant, once her or his decision to follow is made, becomes proactive. She or he becomes vocal and active in support of another member's ideas or of that person's candidacy to become a key direction-giver in the group (see Table 1.3 in Chapter 1). A lieutenant

(Continued)

(Continued)

is a follower who begins advocating on behalf of the person whose direction-giving he or she supports (advocating = articulating, elaborating upon, recruiting others to the cause, supporting). Their followership becomes guideship, not as a means for advancing their own ideas but rather as a means for advancing the direction-giving of another member. Are there people in your group who should receive such support from you? Are there any who support you in this way? Bormann (1996) says that until you attain the support of a lieutenant in your group, your potential contributions as a key direction-giver for the group may not be realized.

The followership role can be short in duration, taking only the time to accomplish a coordinated action. For example, following occurs whenever grouping members listen to and take direction from their fellows as they exchange guideship duty. People who give direction by following probably also play the roles of doer, guide, manager, or leader. So, no person is inherently "a follower"; rather, he or she may act as a follower when his or her support is needed.

Followership is often found in transitions from one grouping experience to another (i.e., when instructions or orders are passed down through an organization). For example, a division head may be effective only to the extent that he or she can follow the dictates of the president. And almost any superviser needs, at times, to listen to and take direction from feedback provided by underlings. Consequently, everyone in every successful group probably moves in and out of a followership role.

Effective followers provide direction. Someone who acts as an effective follower can become as important to a group as anyone else. Followership is making choices that dedicate you to action. It is fundamental to any effective group and, like guideship, is necessary for the success of all other direction-giving types.

In sum, the dance metaphor is a more useful framing for followers than are widespread pejorative and derogatory framings that a follower is "less than" other members. Beware connotations that a person who follows is someone of low caliber who is weak, lacks initiative, or is otherwise not useful or important. When you need to make such negative attributions about someone, we suggest you replace the word *follower* with terms from Table 1.4 in Chapter 1. Such labels fit better on people who do not help their group to thrive: passive member and social loafer. They are more accurate frames for the poor grouping behaviors that are so often wrongly attributed to followers.

Followers select which direction-giving options they will accept, attempt to adjust, ignore, or reject. These are fundamental direction-giving choices for a citizen. All such choices about whom, whether, how, and when to follow help shape the group experience and determine whether a group will thrive.

❖ A DIRECTION-GIVER'S INITIATIVE CREATES AN EXIGENCY FOR A FOLLOWER

The exigency for followership manifests as a perceived need for someone's support. Such support is required to build the momentum needed to put (or keep) the group on a desired path. Potential followers decide if desired support will be provided. Usually a need for support is created by someone whose efforts can only be completed after someone else engages with them. Politicians say, "I need your vote." Coaches say, "We can only win together." A new employee says, "Someone better show me how to do this." Should the potential follower stand with, ignore, or oppose the ideas or efforts being proposed? Followership is useful whenever grouping acts require, or could benefit from, someone's support.

Brainstorming sessions demonstrate how natural and influential are the processes of responding to exigencies to follow. As people are taught to brainstorm, they are told to engage in the uncritical, uninterrupted, free exchange of ideas—no matter how crazy some of the ideas may be. During the process, however, an idea may be tossed out that resonates with the group. Members begin to focus all of their attention and energy pursuing that idea. The rules of brainstorming say that they are not supposed to focus on one idea, but the exigency to follow changes the rules. When people act on an impulse to follow, the future direction of their project is shaped as they throw in their support.

❖ CREDENTIALING AS A FOLLOWER REQUIRES SHOWING YOU OFFER AN ABLE AND DESIRABLE AFFILIATION

In some cases, credentialing well may be as necessary for a follower as it is for other types of direction-givers. All followers are not created equal. Consequently, some people will be sought out for their followership, and others may find that their help or support is grudgingly accepted if at all. To credential as a follower, you must create the impression that you offer a willing, able, and desirable affiliation: a combination we call *affiliative receptivity*. The combination manifests from actions that put you into consideration when someone in your group needs support.

To *affiliate* is to enter into a useful relationship with another person. When you create such a relationship, it is an *affiliation*. To be *affiliative* is to try to behave in ways that help that relationship prosper. Being affiliative can involve trying to work, play, or do other interactions well on behalf of the relationship. To be *receptive* is to show a readiness, willingness, and ability to accept something—in this case, an affiliation offered[4] by someone else.

In grouping, being affiliative requires sending messages, through words or deeds, that show your support for or alignment with the ideas expressed by others (or with the actions they advocate or undertake). In grouping, receptivity means showing yourself to be ready and willing to affiliate and, while doing so, to bend and blend your own efforts into support for the ideas or actions of others. Taken together, showing your affiliative receptivity means demonstrating through your words and deeds that you are a willing, able, and desirable person with whom to associate. If you do, others will be more open to your offers of support, will be more likely to think of you when they need support, and may even seek out your support in advance when they think about beginning a new enterprise.

Something to Consider

Some people act as a particular type of follower so long or so well that they become so identified with those they follow that their affiliation becomes almost formal (a right-hand man, go-to gal, confidant, devotee, or disciple). Such people can wield tremendous influence, but their position can also be counterproductive if they are judged by others in the group to be part of "a couple" whose loyalties are more strongly tied to their relational affiliation than to their group affiliation.

---

[4]If you do not like people or social interactions, it may be difficult to show affiliative receptivity, but it is not impossible. Followership is a partially guided interaction and is constrained by the grouping context. Indeed, some people who like to be social might not like to follow because they are unwilling to do the work. Others, however, who are not socially inclined may thrive on the social contact they can get from an opportunity to interact as a follower under the auspices of a work-related context: The context helps guide the social interaction involved, easing the person's way through what might otherwise be a difficult relationship to help co-construct.

❖ COMMUNICATING COMPETENTLY BLENDS YOUR FOLLOWERSHIP WITH A DIRECTION-GIVER'S EFFORTS

To be successful as a follower, you must communicate with sufficient competence to identify need in others, to establish the parameters of that need and of how you might provide support, and to adapt your efforts during the followership efforts that ensue. Your ability to identify the needs of others requires listening carefully for opportunities to provide support (see Chapter 6). You should also be alert to behavioral and nonverbal cues signaling someone is accomplishing less than they might if they had help (or, perhaps, that someone is struggling). Once you identify what you think may be a need, interaction negotiating how to follow can begin.

> ### Something to Consider
>
> A follower's offer of affiliation may get rejected. He or she may be perceived as lacking the ability to follow well because of some personal limitation or personality problem. A person viewed as unavailable or too busy might not be asked to follow or may be turned down when he or she offers. A person viewed as lacking initiative, as undependable when asked to complete a task, or as having unsavory associations or political leanings will also be viewed as a poor candidate for affiliation.

Your efforts to interact well with others as you explore the nature of their need and of how you might act in support require sensitivity and tact. Keep in mind that, though it costs you to provide support, it can also cost others to accept your support. Also challenging is adapting behaviorally over time to better support their work. Both require discourse about subjects that can be touchy. The latter, for example, involves interacting about how well what you are trying to do together is being done by the two of you. That is difficult material to broach, much less to engage well. Doing so can easily result in one or both of you becoming ego-defensive.

Discussing and modifying the processes we are using as we interact is the most likely topic of communications that improve the quality of outcomes in small groups (Hirokawa, 1990). That lesson can be applied to other grouping contexts as well. However, effectively addressing what we are doing well and poorly requires interactions that are challenging at best. To follow well means being willing to raise uncomfortable subjects such as our performance together, and to be flexible and emotionally resilient in response to the discussions that ensue.

You will become more adept at such interactions and at adapting your efforts in response the more you orient yourself toward believing in the value of followership in general. Doing so can help you to embrace the particular contributions you might make as you follow. Over time, blending your efforts effectively into the work of others will enhance your reputation (both in general and as a desirable affiliation) and also your self-efficacy: your sense that you can accomplish what you intend to accomplish.

The activities involved in following well become especially challenging when the person in need of a follower is not aware of that need (or does not want help despite their need). Others know how to ask for help but are not adept at using it (e.g., struggling to organize helpers or to delegate). Such difficulties can distort your efforts to follow well. Your best response to such difficulties is to continue your own efforts to co-construct a communication climate that is conducive to helping others receive your help (see Table 2.3).

Table 2.3	Creating a Conducive Communication Climate: Communication Imagination

To get others to see you as an affiliative partner can depend on whether you create a relationally supportive communicative climate between yourself and a direction-giver. This requires a combination of four factors that Engen (2002) calls *communicative imagination.*

(1) *Symbolic awareness* is your tendency to pay attention to and understand the meanings that people make out of the words and deeds they use and see others using.

(2) *Narrative imagination* is your tendency to "read," to their satisfaction, the experience stories others have had or hope for, even when their stories are quite different from your own.

(3) *Moral intelligence* is your appreciation of the effects your words and deeds have on others as well as your ability to sense how the words and deeds of others may be affecting you.

(4) *Feedforward impulse* is thinking through possible effects of your words and deeds before using them on someone else so that you can modify them in advance and enhance your interactions.

One final point on affiliative receptivity: Time matters. Though you can choose to follow only after careful consideration, momentum may be lost or provided by someone else while you deliberate. That may diminish the potency of the followership you offer. In some cases, a constrained, subdued, and slow-to-warm affiliation is reasonable, given the circumstances and individuals involved. However, affiliative receptivity is usually demonstrated by openness, quickness of under-standing, and interest in new actions, ideas, and people.

You should be on the lookout for opportunities to follow. Many direction-giving attempts can be understood as invitations to follow. You can show your interest or support in how you respond, breathing life into choices that shape the group in ways that you value.

❖ GIVING DIRECTION AS A GUIDE REQUIRES CREDIBILITY

Guiding involves getting others to focus their attention: perhaps on you, perhaps on an item or process that you need them to understand. To guide well, you must provide something on which the group *ought* to focus: something that might somehow help the group in its ongoing efforts to thrive. For example, a guide can be a jokester, breaking the ice in a tense meeting or for a new group; a guide can be the individual facilitating group attempts to manage conflict; a guide can be the one who emcees a celebratory gala at the spring board meeting or the CEO who delivers the year-end report. To guide well, you must interact in a manner that gains, focuses, and keeps the attention of others until you have finished what it is you are doing or saying.

As you command the group's attention, you cannot count on your words having the desired effects unless you play the guideship role well. For instance, an effective guide may be the person who frames the issues in a way that helps the group orient to its task or decide how to change its direction (see Chapter 9). For example, making an argument for increased spending for education in your state may not accomplish what you desire unless you include relevant student performance data, evidence of decreasing graduation rates, and statistics about the effects of teacher shortages. Whatever it takes, the effective guide focuses the group's attention in a manner that helps the group decide what to do in the moment (Burtis, 1995).

The term *guide* originated hundreds of years ago in the idea that a person may "know something" so is best suited to "show the way" for others who do not. This locates guideship in specialized knowledge or expertise. We significantly broaden the construct. In grouping, an effective guide is any individual who can read the group's needs and focus the group's attention on the question, issue, topic, concern, discomfort, interest, or uncertainty members are (or should be) experiencing in the moment. A guide "answers" the group's "question" of what they will be doing next, so guideship should come in the form of a system-orienting, rhetorically appropriate response to grouping exigencies rather than to the individual whims of the guide.

Each and every one of us is likely to have opportunities to try to guide, even the most seemingly inconsequential group member. For example, while a state senator is speaking in support of a bill, she or he is serving as a guide and will be effective because of her or his guideship skills (and not just because she or he has acted as an effective doer by writing a worthy piece of legislation and not just because this person is an effective manager who has marshaled strong support from others for the bill).

Doers must act briefly as guides if they present the fruits of their labors for the group's consideration. Even followers act as a guide when announcing their decision to follow (e.g., to support someone, to interact with the person they are following in order to improve the process they are using) or when they express concerns about a direction they are contemplating, indicate confusions they have about what the group is doing, or report on how well their efforts are coming along. During the time while your talk or action commands the attention of the group, you are guiding the group.

Guideship can vary in duration, subject matter, and rhetorical intensity. All grouping members can and probably should move in and out of a guideship role, and multiple members can play the role of guide, nearly simultaneously and in quick exchange. Most groups cannot succeed unless members have relatively seamless opportunities to start and stop trying to guide.

❖ EVERY GROUP NEEDS DIRECTION AT MANY POINTS IN TIME, CREATING THE GUIDESHIP EXIGENCY

Every group needs something on which to focus as a group or else individuals will begin to go their own way and the group will begin to come undone. The need to focus manifests as various perceived exigencies for guideship. For example, the group may need someone to show them a process for proceeding, a technique to address their confusions, a description of the proper role each member should play, an idea that addresses a difficult choice, or a plan to attain a desirable outcome. An attempt at guideship provides a direction-giving option: creating an exigency to consider changing or sustaining group direction. This happens whenever someone trots out an idea or activity that attracts group attention from whatever else they might be doing or thinking.

❖ CREDENTIALING AS A GUIDE REQUIRES YOU TO CREATE AN IMPRESSION OF CREDIBILITY

Credibility is the key credential required of someone who tries to guide. Your attempts to guide will be effective only to the extent that others judge you to be credible as their guide. You can credential credibility by talking about past experiences that you think indicate your ability to address specific issues or processes currently facing the group. And/or, you can credential by attempting to provide the direction that is needed by the group and, over time, show that your contributions are competent (Burtis, 1996, 1997).

You might even be asked to guide. For example, groups often hire consultants to help guide them, and some groups create formal positions to encourage experienced members to serve as guides. For instance, the "past president" position doesn't hold formal authority in a nonprofit organization, but that position allows a former manager to continue to help guide the group by bringing institutional memory and experience into the group's attempts to set its future direction.

Credibility is not something you have; it not yours to assume. Regardless of who you are, what you know, or what experiences or skills you offer, your credibility is a judgment made by others. Their judgment modulates their willingness to receive direction from you. Their judgment translates into the foundation of your ability to catch and hold their attention.

Credibility is a dynamic judgment. It changes with the evolving situation and with the unfolding relationship the group shares with you. To credential credibility, focus on situation-germane experiences, mention your attitude and orientation to the particular task or process in play, and be willing to walk the walk required to work well with others in your group. Each reflects on the credibility others perceive in you as you try to guide.

❖ COMMUNICATING COMPETENTLY, YOUR GUIDESHIP OUGHT TO TAKE CARE WITH A GROUP'S ATTENTIONS

Effective guideship is impossible unless you are paid attention to: given consideration by the group. The person with a reputation of having silly or irrelevant things to say and the person with a reputation for not performing as promised will have difficulty guiding regardless of the quality of their particular attempt. To get serious consideration, you must be able to engage the group's attention and then be perceived as sufficiently credible to justify their continued focus on your words or deeds. To be credible, you must be viewed by other grouping members as having something worthwhile to say or for them to do. To be credible, you must build your ethos.

Aristotle defines *ethos* as the ability you have to be persuasive because of who you are (and not because of the reasoning and evidence behind what you have to say and not because of the emotions you get people to feel). Research shows that ethos matters: a recording of the same speech is more persuasive when people are told it is given by someone who is respected by them than when it is attributed to someone who is not respected: the *same* speech (cf. Haiman, 1949)!

As people judge your credibility, they consider three aspects of who you are. First, your intentions or what Aristotle calls your *good will*. Do others think you are looking out for their best interests and the group's, or are you just looking out for number one? They ask, "Are you safe?" as they wonder about your character, integrity, honesty, trustworthiness, fairness, ethics, and authenticity.

Second, you are judged by your facility with grouping processes or with the subject matter of the group's work. Such knowledge or skill is what Aristotle calls *good sense*. People wonder, are you really the most intelligent, informed, trained, expert, competent, or experienced member to guide the group given what we face in this moment?

Third, you are judged by how similar your values and ideas are perceived to be relative to their own. This is an assessment Aristotle calls *good moral character*. They wonder, are you one of us; can we trust you as having the same values and basic beliefs we have, or are you somehow different from us, motivated by values we do not share? Just knowing these three aspects of their judgments about you allows you to focus on actions that help build your ethos in one or more of those three general ways.

Think of the plethora of opinion polls each election cycle. Pollsters ask us which candidate we would prefer to invite into our own home or to share a beer with. We are asked to assess which has our interests at heart, cares about me, will help me, or feels my pain. Such questions are trying to get at your perceptions of the candidate's credibility, and it seems that many candidates will do almost anything to build their ethos for the voters. Apparently, the judgments we make about a potential direction-giver's ethos matter quite a bit when we choose among those we want elected to manage our city, state, or country.

❖ IN CONCLUSION

Potent forms of change can be wrought from small direction-giving acts. The "butterfly effect" (sometimes depicted in movies, especially about time travel) is an idea from chaos theory. It says the flapping wings of a butterfly can begin a chain of events that create an ever-increasing rumble of change that echoes around the world or down through the ages. Applied to direction-giving, the idea is that small direction-giving choices and activities can result in major changes over time. Let this idea encourage your imaginings about how you might contribute. What can you offer as a doer, follower, or guide? You can help to shape the story of the group experiences that matter most to you.

3

Understand That Other Direction-Giving Options May Be Needed

Managing or Leading Well

This chapter focuses on communicating well as a leader or manager, which means doing so effectively and in a manner that others will judge to be appropriate. It is the third and final chapter in our first unit, which details the options you have for exerting your power as a direction-giver in your own team, organization, or community (as a doer, follower, guide, manager, or leader).

In this chapter, we focus the bulk of our attentions on the exigencies people perceive for needing leadership or management and on how the differences in those exigencies affect their expectations. Managing and leading are two different direction-giving types, and each provides you with different options. The differences between management and leadership exigencies can signal the differing credentials others will expect you to have if you try to act as a manager or as a leader. Each type of direction-giving also requires specific communication competencies that people in a group will expect of anyone trying to act either as a leader or as a manager.

❖ THERE ARE MANY NAMES FOR LEADERSHIP: DEFINITIONS TOO

Conceptions vary tremendously about what leadership is and about what activities it involves. In fact, Bernard Bass, a scholar whose work we rely heavily upon in this section, says that so many scholars and practitioners have weighed in on the definition of leadership that it seems there are as many definitions as there are people writing about leadership (Bass & Stogdill, 1990[1]).

> "The search for the one and only proper and true definition of leadership seems to be fruitless, since the appropriate choices of definition should depend on the . . . substantive aspects of leadership in which one is interested."
>
> (Bass & Stogdill, 1990, p. 18)

To make use of the plethora of expert conceptions regarding what is important about leaders and leadership, we translate a lengthy list of the ideas that are in play (Bass & Stogdill, 1990). Three clusters organize the conceptions (see Table 3.1). *Direction-giver-oriented views* are based on ideas about leadership that focus explanations for effective direction-giving on whom the direction-giver is or on a particular style or type of activity that he or she does. *Direction-receiver-oriented views* focus on what is supposed to be happening to the folks who receive direction. *Grouping-activity-oriented views* focus explanations on grouping and direction-giving processes rather than on the people who co-construct them. Each and all of these conceptions are useful to us as we try to understand direction-giving processes, dynamics, and skills.

---

[1] In our opinion, the best, single encyclopedic resource on the subject of leadership is a reference work that began as the *Handbook of Leadership* but has added the names of its authors to its title through ongoing revisions. Written first by Ralph Stogdill, the handbook is an exhaustive literature review (the 1974 edition was based on a review of 3,000 publications) that was updated in 1990 by Bernard Bass and in 2008 by Bernard and Ruth Bass (Bass & Bass, 2008).

	Bass and Stogdill's Review of Competing Conceptions About Leadership
Table 3.1	

Our Clusters	Our Paraphrases for Bass and Stogdill's Synthesized Conceptualizations
Direction-giver-oriented-views	Leadership is determined by personality traits: people with "the right stuff."
	Leadership manifests as particular prescribed behaviors or styles.
	Leadership is a particular, differentiated role played by one person.
Grouping-activity-oriented views	Leadership is at the focal point of group processes.
	Leadership is originating and maintaining structure.
	Leadership is the instrument by which the group achieves goals.
	Leadership is an effect of interaction among grouping members.
	Leadership is the interpersonal interactions among grouping members that create positive/negative influence.
	Leadership is some combination of all these various conceptions.
Direction-receiver-oriented views	Leadership is a power relationship: the force of the leader versus the resistance of the follower.
	Leadership is inducing compliance by putting psychological pressure on followers.
	Leadership is persuasion that moves the minds and emotions of followers.

Much of what others study or describe as leadership is different from the definition we use for the term, but most of their work nestles nicely under our broader term: direction-giving. In fact, Bass and Stogdill's (1990) own definition is a good example. From an exhaustive review of competing definitions and conceptions, they conclude that

leadership is an interaction between two or more members of a group that often involves a structuring or restructuring of the situation and the perceptions and expectations of the members. Leaders are agents of change.... Leadership occurs when one group member modifies the motivation or competencies of others in the group . . . directing . . . attention of other members to goals and the paths to achieve them. It should be clear that . . . any member of the group can exhibit some amount of leadership, and the members will vary in the extent to which they do. (pp. 19–20)

Of course, we will stick with our more specialized definition of leadership in this book, but we like how Bass and Stogdill's definition encompasses the territory of interest to us. In fact, we think that their definition fits nicely when we attach it instead to our terms, *direction-givers* and *direction-giving* (see Chapter 1). For example, note how they mention a potential direction-giving role that can be played by every group member. We also agree with their use, throughout their book, of the umbrella terms *group* and *direction*, to discuss a very wide range of systems (e.g., complex bureaucracies and communities; historical, social, and political movements; small teams) and every conceivable direction-giving activity.

In sum, we find the work of many leadership and management scholars and skilled practitioners to be useful. We hope to translate the most useful parts for you by fitting them into, in one way or another, the conceptual framework for direction-giving and direction-givers that we explain in this book. In this chapter, we focus on the exigencies, credentials, and communication competencies specific to managers and leaders (see Table 3.2). We also provide a much more extensive review of contemporary leadership theory and research in Chapter 4.

If you are not currently in a managerial position and hope forever to avoid the sort of group-transformative crisis that requires leadership, you may wonder if this chapter is relevant to you. We think so. You are certainly in groups where others act as managers. The material here can help you understand their experiences and to find ideas useful in your efforts to work well with them. Also, because you engage in the first three types of direction-giving (doing, following, and guiding), understanding how these last two types differ can help you be more effective at the first three. Finally, be aware of the possibility that you might someday find yourself managing or leading. Whether intended or not, being successful in life tends to result in such things happening. When it does, the obligations of leadership or of management may quite literally be thrust upon you.

Table 3.2	Definitions, Exigencies, and Credentials for Managers and Leaders

	Manager	*Leader*
Definition	Person(s) in a position vested with formal authority over some grouping resource(s) (e.g., personnel, time, money, equipment, facilities, or grouping procedures). The manager marshals the entrusted resource for use in service to the group.	Person(s) who articulate(s) and/or personify a group-transformative vision made salient by crisis or opportunity. Leadership is vision made salient by system-threatening crisis or transformative opportunity.
Exigency	"Someone needs to organize us" or "That's not my job!" or "We need a record in case we get sued." The odious, complex, or everlasting requires formal processes, enforcement, and differentiated role authority.	"And then, everything changed!" System-threatening crisis or opportunity provides sufficient energy to make transformative vision salient.
Credential	Actions that tell the story of past *experience*(s) of success and/or of (a) key *relationship*(s) that help bend the group's will to this person as manager.	Actions that *articulate* (or otherwise show appreciation for and understanding of) the *salient, group-transforming vision*.

❖ GIVING DIRECTION AS A MANAGER REQUIRES THE ABILITY TO MARSHAL RESOURCES

A manager is any group member in a position vested with formal authority over some group resource(s) (Burtis, 1995). *Marshaling* a resource may mean a manager will oversee the finding, gathering, organizing, allocating, and/or use of the resource. For example, as the head coach of Penn State's football team, Joe Paterno is a manager entrusted with marshaling a variety of team resources on behalf of the university (e.g., its physical facilities, equipment, meetings, budget, practice and travel schedule, and personnel—staff and players). He also is in charge of less discrete resources such as the procedures the team has developed over the years (e.g., for planning, disciplining and recruiting players, creating the schedule, and hiring others to help manage and guide the team).

Paterno's job gives him formal authority or what is called *legitimate power*. This means that he officially is allowed and expected to act on issues mentioned above even when he affects other people doing so (French & Raven, 1959). Were one of his players to attempt the same action, he would not have legitimate power to do so. It is the head coaching position that gives Paterno his authority. Legitimate power is created by the group, in this case the university. First a group creates a manager's authority to marshal some of its resources, often including the efforts and energies of other group members. Then the group selects a manager to act on its behalf.

Something to Consider

A manager always has enumerated power and responsibility. *Enumerated powers* are formalized indications for how the authority and responsibility in a manager's job are differentiated from other group work. Formal duties and responsibilities manifest from the group. This means the group agrees they are binding within the group and for its members. Members acknowledge (1) the particular duties and authority of the manager, (2) their own responsibility to accede to or comply with the direction provided by the person who occupies the manager's job, and (3) that the specified individual is the legitimate occupant of that job. If any of those acknowledgments is not made, the manager will struggle.

Marshaling resources can be unpopular and/or difficult work. Resources may be in short supply, creating demand by more than one individual in the group, so there may be politics to sort through. Some processes and decisions are inherently fraught with tensions and difficulties (e.g., hiring, assessing, assigning, promoting, and firing group members). As a consequence, group members are often more comfortable with a formal process for assigning such tasks to a manager than they are doing those tasks themselves (or worse, allowing someone else with chutzpah or clitspah simply to take charge).

For example, most states have a secretary of budget and finance who works on behalf of the governor to coordinate the budget. In difficult economic times, this individual is responsible for making decisions about cutting programs. A manager may, consequently, become unpopular. It is ironic that, because a manager's work is often difficult or unpleasant, we tend to pay our managers more than we pay those who do the work the group actually exists to get done.

Formalizing a management position gives the person in that job some protection from the cyclical bouts of disdain that irate group members feel for the choices a manager has to make. Consequently, a manager is usually in a relatively long-lived, somewhat protected position from which she or he marshals group resources.

Something to Think About and Discuss With Others

Dirty work is often required of a manager, and we differentiate the position with enumerated powers as a consequence. We should never forget, however, that we as group members "willingly" give up some of our own autonomy to a manager because we want them to address particular group exigencies. We might not like to do what others tell us to, but we like even less the chaos or politics that can accompany grouping without management.

A manager should work in service to a group, helping a group fulfill its purposes. A managerial position should emerge from needs a group has, not from the desire a person has to be in charge. Needs that arise during attempts to accomplish group ends provide the only legitimate reasons for the privileges and powers of a managerial position. Managers should be on guard against letting power corrupt their efforts. Managers who forget that should receive a reminder from the group.

A group can have one or more managers (or none). For instance, several people can occupy different managerial positions in a single group (e.g., a treasurer, president, CEO, CFO, vice president, secretary, and any "directors" or "heads" or "managers" or "supervisors"). And many people working together can act as a manager (e.g., a board of directors, trustees, regents). If a position is managerial, it has formal, enumerated authority over a group resource (see Table 3.3).

❖ THE ODIOUS, THE COMPLEX, AND THE EVERLASTING PROVIDE EXIGENCIES FOR A MANAGER

The exigency for a manager manifests out of some peculiarity of grouping activity or task. People work together because they perceive exigencies for doing so (see Chapter 1). As people interact, they perceive additional exigencies that they think suggest how they should interact. In some cases (the peculiarities), people perceive exigencies that should

Table 3.3	Examples of Direction-Givers We Call Managers	
Distinctive, but Still Managerial Roles	*Aspects That Somewhat Distinguish Among These Managerial Role Types*	*Aspects That Unify These Role Types*
Executives (e.g., presidents, CEOs, governors, general officers, admirals, kings, queens, and other sovereigns)	Bottom-line decision-maker: "the buck stops here"; has direct, formal authority to shape the life and activity of the other grouping members; responsibilities and obligations (e.g., to "meet a payroll")	All provide direction to a group from a position of formal authority and all marshal and manage people, processes, or other resources for the benefit of a particular entity or collaboration of entities such as a program, team, organization, bureaucracy, movement, or community
Entrepreneurs, sole proprietors, founder	Creator and nurturer: original visionary	
Senators, board members, oversight committees	Assess others or their systems; seek consensus building; joint decision-makers	
Upper to lower level managers, colonels, directors, captains	Manage resources or groups of people with autonomy though still clearly under the direct authority of others	
Supervisors, sergeant majors	Direct, daily supervision of subgroups of people in an organization; key guides for implementing others' directives	

support certain behaviors, but they ignore the exigency. For example, when Fred stops coming to work on time, or when Omra spends several hours at work each day texting her friends, it can be difficult to know when and how to make an issue of their behavior. Such behavior certainly cannot be allowed to continue, that would be unfair to everyone else. But who should say something? When and how should the behavior be addressed?

When the response to an exigency like these is to ignore or distort your response to them, it is a sign that a grouping peculiarity may be in play and managerial direction-giving needed. People are adept at grouping. When faced by such peculiarities, they seek solutions. Over time, people have learned that they can develop a tool to deal with certain, recurring peculiarities. The tool is a manager. And what a wonderful tool!

Managers are tools? Yep. Having a manager in position to deal with odious, complex, or everlasting peculiarities is a tool for allowing others to get on with their own work (see Table 3.4). Getting on with their own work means that a group can achieve its purpose. Managers are a great tool for helping some groups of people to get their good work done.

The recurrence of some problematic peculiarities is common among long-lived and large groups. For example: "Making our own decisions on promotions and who should get fired is destroying our working relationships" (or we do not feel qualified to make such choices) or "Someone needs to organize and keep track of our budget requests and allocations each year" or "Why isn't there anyone to schedule facilities so that we can keep out of each others' way and get our work done?" or "None of us ever want to document our progress and write year-end reports but it has got to get done again this year" or "We need a formal planning process" or "We need a record of our

Table 3.4	Odious, Complex, and Everlasting Exigencies That Call Forth a Manager

Odious issues provide an exigency for a manager by being extremely unpleasant or by requiring undesirable interactions. Odious issues include *onerous* or difficult or unpopular work that will not likely get done unless someone is assigned to do it or given authority to make others do it.
Complex issues provide an exigency for a manager when grouping complexity increases to the extent that the full attentions of someone are needed just to get grouping processes to continue to flow. Complexity is relative, from the simple work that one individual can keep track of to intensely integrated activities of larger and larger clusters of group efforts.
Everlasting issues provide an exigency for a manager when a chronic problem requires someone to be assigned the chore of dealing with it. A chronic problem does not go away but is manageable. Everlasting issues recur or (just seem to) go on forever. Some are so *contentious* (quarrelsome; likely to cause argument) or *divisive* that group members cannot let them go. Others are so *procedurally encumbered* that the group has to keep reinventing the wheel unless someone is charged with remembering "how we do this." Others are so *litigious* (legally encumbered) that someone must steer the group through its legal obligations and be responsible if the group is sued or audited.

decisions and expenditures in case we get sued or audited: Who will keep records/books for us?" or "Someone really should xyz then lmnop," but nobody wants to take the risk or has the time. In such cases, work that the group feels needs doing is unlikely to be done or done well. That is, unless a particular person, given a differentiated job specifically charged with the work, is assigned by the group to the task and given the authority and resources to succeed.

Something to Think About and Discuss With Others

Beware! Managerial positions are created to respond to the distortions in grouping created by certain peculiarities. However, a managerial position can itself distort how people respond to the exigencies they perceive. As a rule, people should seek and receive direction from others only to the extent that the direction they are offered addresses the grouping exigencies they perceive. Having a manager can create exceptions to that rule. The legitimate power a manager wields creates its own exigencies for obedience. That can be a good thing, or not. "Do it because I said so and I am your mother" is a manager's attempt to use her position to trump other exigencies. So is "do it because I am your boss," which implies that you ought to act as I say or you may get fired (as opposed to "do what I say because it is best for the group that you do"). So, creating a managerial position entails risks. Anything that distorts what grouping members need to do to accomplish group ends is a diminution of what they might accomplish. Such a diminution reduces group effectiveness (Burtis & Turman, 2006).

❖ CREDENTIALING AS A MANAGER IS BASED IN THE STORIES YOU AND OTHERS TELL OF YOUR EXPERIENCE

The credentials of greatest interest to others, as they help select a person to manage their group, are your past *experiences* and any key *relationships* you have. If you know the right people (e.g., your mother owns the company or several members of the board want you for the job), you may have all the credentials you require. (Consequently, you may not need to do any credentialing to get the job, but credentialing as you manage is even more important in such cases.) Usually, however, when a hiring decision is to be made, past experiences are treated as the credential that provides the best predictor of potential managerial effectiveness.

A formal selection process during which you get the chance to describe your experiences and to get others to speak (or write letters of recommendation) on your behalf will almost always be involved in the decision to select a manager. For example, during the 2008 U.S. presidential election, some questioned Barack Obama's experience. His limited time in the U.S. Senate after a short term in the Illinois legislature was one issue. They also questioned the skills a candidate develops from legislative rather than executive work. Senators may have limited experience putting together a cabinet, balancing a budget, or assuming other executive-level responsibilities.

To credential as a manager, you need to tell stories about pertinent experiences. Common ways to tell such stories are a résumé, interview, and references. Prepare to provide clues about your qualifications during any interactions you get to have with group members. Expect them to wonder: How well did your past group perform? Did you help them? How do you treat others, respond to pressure, sort out difficult situations, create options, handle conflict, and make decisions? They are hungry for whatever clues you can provide.

Treat interaction as an opportunity to listen to them and also to provide informative credentialing stories. Treat credentialing as an opportunity to frame your candidacy and to test out ideas that help others and you predict whether you likely will be effective helping them get their work done well. Your focus should be on goodness of fit (whether you are well-suited for helping them get their work done) and not on "winning" the position.

❖ DOING AND INTERPRETING YOUR MANAGEMENT WORK FOR THE GROUP REQUIRES A VARIETY OF SKILLS

Skillful managerial communication is the subject of literally thousands of essays, training sessions, research articles, college and MBA classes, and (hand) books. We cannot address all the relevant subject matter, and our purposes do not include accomplishing that task. Rather, we recommend that you partake widely and deeply from other sources on the subject (see Clampitt, 2005) and suggest the following three keys for you to consider.

First, *position your contributions so that they are* (perceived as) *high-quality work*. The perceptions others develop regarding the quality of your work is important to your effectiveness. Though a manager's job has authority, your direction-giving should still match exigencies that people perceive as important while grouping. Otherwise, over the long haul, people in your group will become disgruntled, and you will be seen, over time, as ineffectual or misguided.

To be an effective manager requires an ongoing credentialing process by which you demonstrate that your work serves the group well (in addition to actually managing well; see "common managerial tasks" below). You should begin by making certain that your contributions help your group to thrive. Then, the stories you tell, your authenticity, and your initiative can help you position those contributions.

Group success is the best credential a manager can have, so keep track of the story of the experiences of your group, especially its trials and accomplishments. Keep track of your story too, especially the parts that help to demonstrate what you have to contribute, the experiences that shape you and the group, and what you and the group value. Weave who you are and what you are doing with the group into the stories you tell of your group's experiences. We are not talking about "padding" your résumé or collecting a list of your own virtues. Rather, we suggest an orienting logic that keeps you *authentic* (honest with yourself, genuine in treatment of others), focused on group success, and that helps those who receive your direction to understand you.

Stay alert for opportunities to show initiative. Seek ways to contribute beyond the minimum obligations of your job. Continue to build your skills as a doer, guide, and follower (see Chapter 2). Such actions provide a good model to others, and, sometimes, the germinal impetus for useful new initiatives to bud and bloom. As a manager, you may have more leeway to exercise initiative than others in your group. However, you must be intentional about using that advantage of your position or it will likely come to naught, drummed out by the day-to-day and cyclical stuff that sucks dry so much of the typical manager's energies.

Common Managerial Tasks

Plan, organize, control, coordinate, provide the means for grouping, provide and maintain group structure, facilitate action and interaction, supervise, motivate, define objectives, maintain goal development, cohesion, and satisfaction (Bass & Stogdill, 1990). Each task suggests a skill set and has a literature you can consult if your position requires that skill (cf. goal-setting[2]). Communication-related managerial

---

[2]See, for example, Locke and Latham (1990); Lee, Locke, and Latham (1989); and DeSouza and Klein (1995).

skills may be required that are tied to such managerial tasks. Additional management communication processes may include negotiating the boundaries of your own group (who is in, who is not, and what it means to be "in" your group), boundary-spanning to other groups while representing your own (e.g., to stakeholders, news sources, regulators, or competitors), and potentially the need to communicate across cultures—social or institutional. Managers may be called on to teach, persuade, inform, or assess others; develop or oversee any problem-solving and decision-making processes used in the group; and record, preserve, and use institutional memory.

Second, make certain to *focus first on work a manager is best positioned to do.* Do not flee odious, complex, and everlasting tasks. Just because you have the authority to delegate some of these does not mean that you always should. The more such tasks you can offer to relieve other group members from having to do, the more appreciative the group will be of your use of your position and the more likely group members will be to help you address thorny issues.

As a manager you may also be best situated to juggle the ongoing need to maintain group protocols while simultaneously engaging processes that adjust protocols in anticipation of changes in the situation facing the group. It helps if you can accept that uncertainties, ambiguities, and equivocations are inherent aspects of managing a group. Groups are always in some degree of flux. Juggling requires personal resources to handle the distress and discomfort involved in such struggles. Taking flight from such work, though it can be appealing to do so, is not a reasonable option for a manager whose job emanates from such peculiarities.

Third, *develop a system-wide perspective.* As a manager, you may be the only one who has the time and latitude to focus significant attention and energy on the whole system. There are a variety of ways to broaden your perspective. For example, orient yourself as someone charged with helping others do their good work. You can be alert for ways identify, encourage, and support people who show the interest or willingness to try to be effective doers, followers, and/or guides for the group. Seek ways to make resources out of difficult people: This includes noticing and helping address the struggles others face.

Think of ways to more effectively frame the stories you tell about group enterprises so that your stories help guide people in the group and those on the outside whose support or acquiescence is needed by the group. Your stories should help create and perpetuate group values, and you need to be intentional about trying to integrate those values into planning processes, the reward system, and any other grouping activities and processes you oversee.

Be on the lookout for change. Managerial thinking involves anticipation, planning, and sequencing. The captain of a ship, like any manager, is more likely to succeed if he or she sees the shoals and squalls that are coming and adjusts course before the ship sails into them. Being able to identify and articulate how change must be dealt with to attain a better future for the group is at the top of the list of admired capacities in effective direction-givers (Kouzes & Posner, 1993). The manager's role tends to be relatively long-lived in part because having a long view and "institutional memory" helps you to be effective at such system-wide concerns.

Something to Consider

It is possible to be good at making decisions about how to marshal group resources and still not be effective as a manager because of poor communication skills. It is also possible to be an effective communicator but poor manager, explaining well what the group needs to do but failing to help the group to thrive because of poor choices made while marshaling group resources.

Marshaling resources is not always communicative work, but it usually ought to be enmeshed in communication processes. Examples include when grouping members ought to be asked for input or when they need to be engaged by a manager in problem-solving, decision-making, or other interdependent processes. Further, translating a manager's work to the group involves the need for guideship (see Chapter 2). For example, managers use communication when announcing and interpreting managerial decisions or when making management-related ideas and activities clear to grouping members. What makes a manager unique as a guide are the formal obligations that make such guideship efforts part of the manager's job description. Also, a manager should anticipate a relatively high frequency of need to act as a guide. If you cannot stand people focusing attention on you, a manager's job may not suit you despite your skills.

Something to Think About and Discuss With Others

Because the charge given a manager is to marshal group resources, there should be an expectation of stewardship for every manager. The bottom-line duty for any direction-giver is to *help the group to thrive*. We pay special attention to the stewardship of a manager because we give that person the formal position that "protects" him or her from "normal" group and direction-giving processes. Our scrutiny is also warranted because distorted reward systems sometimes come with serving as a manager. Such *protections and distortions* are not a source of moral outrage for us, but they can diminish group effectiveness. For example, if too many group resources are tied up in management, it is a *mistake*. If a manager abuses the authority of her or his position, it is an *outrage*. If a manager receives rewards out of sync with grouping quality, such as may be happening when she or he gets million-dollar bonuses as other stakeholders lose their shirts or the group goes bankrupt, it is *poor stewardship*. Every management position needs careful scrutiny so that group efforts do not become too distorted or diluted by the protections and privileges necessary to a management position. Scrutiny can help the group (or its regulators and stakeholders) decide which acts are mistakes, which are poor stewardship, and which are an outrage.

Stewardship means "serving the group" well by making the best use possible of group resources. For a manager, stewardship means marshaling resources with constraint, demonstrating the *group-enhancing values* of carefulness, discretion, efficiency, maximization, and prudence. Shepherding resources requires *due diligence:* attentive, capable, conscientious, organized, resourceful, and thorough efforts over time. Stewardship is an aspect of the social contract (see Chapter 1). All group members should make good use of group resources in attempts to help the group thrive. The manager is particularly accountable.

❖ GIVING DIRECTION AS A LEADER REQUIRES ARTICULATING A GROUP-TRANSFORMATIVE VISION

Some folks think that leadership manifests in almost every form of social influence. A generally accepted alternative view is that leadership is a more limited phenomenon. One way to limit the construct is to separate leaders from other distinct types of direction-givers such as managers: the approach we take.

Many scholars[3] distinguish between direction-giving types. Burns (1978) does so when he discusses *transformational leaders*, who elevate the efforts and motivations of others, and *transactional leaders* who engage in direction-giving that maintains a system (also see Bass and Bass, 2008[4]). The distinctions he and others make are fairly consistent with those we draw between leaders and managers (though our distinction focuses more on a vision of shared group transformation than does his, which focuses more on transformative change in the individual).

Leadership is vision made salient by crisis (Burtis, 1995). For example, Churchill offered a leadership vision to England in the 1930s that fell on deaf ears: It was not yet sufficiently salient. As World War II began, while Great Britain was on the verge of falling, his vision became sufficiently salient to provide leadership and he was able to lead England through the war. As the United States faced economic turmoil during the Great Depression, Roosevelt's leadership vision for transforming the government's relationship with the nation's economy was developed over time while the crisis fueled its salience.

Vision is a metaphor representing a group's sense of the fundamental, transformative change required of it to survive a crisis. Leadership vision transforms a group by providing "a new phenomenological world with which the followers can continue to identify" (Hunt, Boal, & Dodge, 1999, p. 425).

Salience is the perceived importance of something, in this case of transforming a group by following a particular vision to escape a crisis (or to seek transformative opportunity). Crisis, as it stimulates fear, helps transformative vision become salient. A system-threatening crisis provides energy: It stimulates group members to pay the high costs demanded to follow a transformative vision. "There is nothing to fear but fear itself" (FDR) and "If you are going through hell, keep going" (Churchill) are phrases used to help frame and inspire the mind-numbingly difficult effort involved in a transformative struggle to survive.

---

[3]See, for example, Gardner, who notes that "although owners, managers, and officials are in the position to do so, they do not necessarily act as leaders" (Bass & Stogdill, 1990, p. 6). Also see Zaleznik (1977); Muczyk and Adler (2002); Hunt et al. (1999); Bass and Bass (2008); Burtis (1995).

[4]A greatly increased focus on transformational leadership is listed in promotional materials as one of the biggest changes from the 1990 to the 2008 version of the *Handbook of Leadership*, no doubt in part because of contributions Bass made operationalizing the construct over the past 20 years and, we argue, because of how important transformative leadership is to understanding the importance of vision to leadership.

Our definition of a leader involves someone offering a transformative vision for the future of a group facing its own end (Burtis & Turman, 2006). In both the case of Churchill and FDR, during crisis, when they articulated and personified the vision, they acted as a leader, though both also had managerial roles to play.

A *leader* articulates or personifies a vision of group transformation that speaks the hopes and dreams of a group responding to crisis (Burtis, 1995). She or he is usually the person who best articulates or most personifies the vision, but sometimes there are several people acting as a leader. A leader (when there is one) can be anyone who is perceived by the group as closely bound up with creating the direction provided by a vision. However, no specified person or leader is actually needed for a group to take direction from a vision. In other words, a group can experience leadership vision without a leader. The vision, not the leader, exerts leadership.

The leadership vision process can unfold several ways. For example, the civil rights movement in the United States is an ongoing, unfolding grouping effort that had and has many direction-givers, including many leaders. An unfolding vision expressing the importance of equal rights was articulated and promulgated over many years. A variety of people lent their voice, attention, energy, treasure, and body.

During one period in the life of the movement, it gained momentum after a Black seamstress named Rosa Parks refused to give up her seat to a White man on a public bus in Montgomery, Alabama. She and her act were chosen to be lifted up by others in the movement as personifying the movement in the moment. A bus boycott was constructed around her act, making it (and the boycott) critical incidents in the life of the movement (see Chapter 8).

During the same time in the movement, while following the same vision, others became prominent, such as the Reverend Doctor Martin Luther King Jr. Both Parks and King helped personify the vision, but it was he who was more involved in articulating the hopes and dreams of the group. Speaking up for an alternative vision, Malcolm X led those for whom a different process of transformation became salient. In sum, over time, someone or several people may begin to be key direction-givers (see Chapter 1) because of how well they articulate a vision for the group (King). Some may even begin to *personify* or embody the vision for the group (Parks). Others may articulate or personify an alternative vision for the group (X). The transformative vision, not the leader, exerts leadership and it does so only when salient, which requires crisis or transformative opportunity.

Something to Think About and Discuss With Others

A case is often made that it takes charisma to be a leader (see Jermier, 1993; Hunt, Boal, & Dodge, 1999; Mumford & Strange, 2004). The idea is that the person, and not the vision, asserts leadership. We relegate charisma to a different role. *Charisma* is personal magnetism and dynamism: It can inspire interest, enthusiasm, and affection. Charisma manifests in how people respond to an especially potent, compelling, even intoxicating or alluring individual. A charismatic person can marshal attention and energy from others. Doing so, though it does involve influence, does not necessarily involve leading. For example, a charismatic is likely an able guide when he or she chooses to be because this person can get others to focus their attentions and energies (see Chapter 2). However, whether he or she does so to the benefit of the group determines whether this individual guides well. A charismatic is likely to attract support as a manager, but the skills involved in managing well do not require charisma. If a charismatic provides a group-transformative vision made salient by crisis, then he or she is likely to be judged a leader by the group. However, absent group-transformative vision and crisis, the charismatic is not a leader because the group is not experiencing leadership. And, even absent charisma, someone who personifies such a vision under such circumstances acts as a leader. Charisma is not a type of direction-giver; it is a charged relationship between people that may or may not affect direction-giving and direction-receiving (true also about sexual tension and fame).

In Chapter 10, we elaborate on both crisis and vision. We describe how crises range in origin and intensity and how conceptions of vision range from those who see vision as a planning tool, required in every group, to those who use the term to represent group-transformative change. In sum, for now, a leader frames the story of a group's experience through a system-transformative vision made salient by a crisis or opportunity that threatens the group.

❖ A SYSTEM-THREATENING CRISIS OR OPPORTUNITY PROVIDES THE EXIGENCY FOR LEADERSHIP

It is an interaction between crisis and those who perceive it as such that allows leadership to be co-constructed into grouping activities. A *crisis* is a turning point for the group: Afterwards, the group will either be over or fundamentally changed. We operationalize crisis as the point at which the need for a transformation becomes salient to those who must co-construct it. A group that believes it is facing its own end faces a crisis. For example, in 1970, a tragic plane crash killed 75 players and coaches on the Marshal University football team, leading the board of trustees to consider killing the program as well. Instead they decided to hire Jack Lengyel, an inexperienced coach, to see if he could resurrect a team, which later became a top program. The single antecedent condition for leadership is the perception of a crisis (Burtis, 1995).

Perceiving that there is a crisis is antecedent to perceiving exigencies for doing the difficult grouping that is required in response. Someone must frame group circumstances as a survival-threatening crisis, or there will be insufficient rhetorical force animating the call for group transformation. Crisis stirs the pot and changes the equation. When group members perceive a crisis, they can be tempted to try to transform their group. Without the perception of crisis, leadership will likely not be accepted because following such a vision is too exhausting a venture. *Transformation involves substantial time, struggle, risk, and uncertainty: We do not take it on readily and we do not accomplish it easily.*

A salient vision addressing crisis exigencies creates more grouping energy than can be expected or sustained during times of normalcy. In crisis conditions, we can be motivated to "give 110%" to our grouping efforts. We are more likely to climb out of our ruts and become innovative and imaginative. We may become desperate, demanding, and even destructive. We are willing to consider previously "nonnegotiable" subjects and suggestions. During World War II, U.S. citizens on the home front went through considerable hardships over rationed food and materials. Even the difficult choice of sending a son, daughter, father, or mother to serve in the armed forces becomes a price people are willing to endure to preserve a way of life. Crisis makes us willing to take on major risk because our group is in danger. We pay the price, hoping to help our group survive. Simply put, a group cannot thrive if it does not survive.

Grouping members have another choice during times of crisis. Even at the height of an evident crisis, there always seems to be someone who is trying to maintain current protocols: to continue receiving the direction offered by a manager or guide and to reject a leadership vision. Indeed, "the antagonism [between the basic aims of leaders and managers] surfaces during periods of stress and change" (Zaleznik, 1977, p. 68). Some try to "ride it out," hoping the difficult situation they face is not really threatening group survival (smart, if true; denial if not—but hard to tell which when it really matters). For example, prior to Japanese attacks on Pearl Harbor, many Americans felt that entry into World War II was unnecessary. Perception is the key to crisis. How crisis should be framed and acted upon are the essence of the direction-giving options available.

People don't actually become leaders; they act as leaders during times of crisis. The life of leadership approximates the life of the crisis (Burtis, 1995). That is, leadership will be accepted for about as long as the life of the crisis that spawns it. Afterwards, a leader either stops offering that type of direction-giving (as others stop accepting it), focusing on other direction-giving activities, or she or he will get removed from their position of influence in the group. Leadership and leaders are tied to a transformative vision, and such vision is tied to crisis.

❖ CREDENTIALING TO BE SEEN BY OTHERS AS A LEADER REQUIRES YOU TO ARTICULATE A SALIENT VISION

How do you become a leader? You act as one during a time of crisis. A leader is not something you become so much as it is a set of activities in which you engage during a crisis. Activities that articulate or show appreciation for a salient, group-transformative vision are the acts of a leader. These actions can create the perception among others that you best understand, articulate, or personify the group's struggles, hopes, dreams, and transformation.

Something to Consider

You act as a leader when you tell a salient story integrating and framing:

1. the uniqueness of the group—especially of its past, its purpose, and/or its process;

2. the nature of the crisis and of the group's present struggles;

3. the nature of the group's aspirational future, including how to co-construct it; and

4. the uniqueness of the future, transformed group—especially its purpose, its process, and/or how it retains value because of how it maintains ties to its past.

Such framings and stories are the heartbeat of transformative vision (see Chapters 8 and 9).

People act as leaders through an ongoing interaction between crisis and the activities and orientations of those who perceive it as such. Unlike a manager, who is selected by credentialing with past experiences or relationships, a leader credentials in action: articulating a salient vision of change, forged under the pressure of a crisis-fueled fire. A leader is not necessarily someone with a formal position in the group. Being a manager certainly provides a bully pulpit for leadership acts. However, when a manager also acts as a leader, he or she is not effective because of the position she or he holds or because of the management acts he or she provides (though they may be excellent). Rather, anyone's effectiveness as a leader is tied to how effectively they articulate or personify a transformative vision that the group decides is their response to crisis.

Though you might read stories about what leaders have done in the past, such stories are not recipes (interesting, thought-provoking, and even heuristic: but not a recipe). There is sufficient science to the art of management to prescribe what to do to be an effective manager. There is insufficient science in the art of leadership to write that prescription. So, we suggest you not worry about becoming a leader but rather focus on providing the kinds of direction that are more often necessary to help a group to thrive. Let leadership sort itself out for you and your group. If you are fortunate, nobody will ever have to serve your group as its leader. If someone does, and you are fully engaged in your group, you must play your part in helping get the vision co-constructed.

❖ YOUR EFFECTIVE LEADERSHIP IS NOT NECESSARILY TIED TO SPECIFIC COMMUNICATION SKILLS

A leader may be someone who can effectively articulate, elucidate, clarify, or exemplify a transformative vision. A leader may be helpful in creating the vision or in helping set up a process for co-constructing it. A leader may even evoke the vision from other grouping individuals after hearing them share their own stories about the group. A leader may be someone who selects, synthesizes, or resurrects aspects of the vision from the group's own experiences. Whatever the point of engagement, a leader aligns with the vision well enough that its followers are activated, dedicated, and solidified in their hopes and grouping actions. Communication of some sort is almost certainly involved, but leading well does not necessarily require a specific set of communication skills.

Quite excellent and differently skilled individuals become associated by their group with a leadership vision. A few leaders, in fact, have been almost completely silent, working in ways that somehow serve as the exemplar for what others in their group believe the group's vision is all about. Buddha contemplated suffering. Moses mumbled. Joan of Arc raised a sword. Lincoln spoke with unpleasant voice. Gandhi stood in silent protest. Mother Teresa fed poor people. If a group perceives someone as its leader, why quibble over how that person communicates?

❖ BEWARE EASY MISCONCEPTIONS ABOUT THESE FIVE TYPES OF DIRECTION-GIVERS

We have two final issues to mention. First, all types of direction-givers can benefit from skills we attribute to particular direction-giving types: e.g., competence, adaptability, credibility, self-efficacy, and initiative. Further, all group members need to be concerned with how resources are marshaled and how their group responds to crisis. The reason we identify each subject as important to a particular type of direction-giver is because of how people, perceiving particular exigencies, are willing to receive direction.

For example, guides are in special need of credibility to get paid attention to for they have little else on which to hang their hat. Unlike the doer, who when attempting to guide has the fruits of his or her work for the grouping members to consider, and the manager, who has the authority of his or her position to support the guideship attempt, and the follower, who has the fact that someone else gave him or her direction, the guide's need for credibility is uniquely acute. Each direction-giving type has particular need for the skills we attribute most directly to it.

Second, several misconceptions tend to recur as people think about direction-giving and direction-givers (see Table 3.5). For instance, some folks think every group has a doer, follower, guide, manager, and leader. Others think everyone plays just one of those roles. Others think that playing the role of a follower makes you a follower, playing a leader makes you a leader, and so forth. (Does playing the role of Hamlet make you Hamlet?) We suggest you orient toward direction-giving not as though it will tell you who you are but rather as something you strive to do well so that you and your group can thrive.

Table 3.5	Correcting Misconceptions About Direction-Giving and Direction-Givers

- You are not born a doer, follower, or leader; a direction-giving type is not inherent in your personality. Instead, you can *act* as a doer, follower, guide, manager, and/or leader.
- You can fill different direction-giving roles at different times. We move in and out of these roles (except the role of manager and, perhaps, of leader).
- Different people can fill the same direction-giving roles for our group. We can have multiple guides, followers, doers, and even managers over time in our group.
- Effective direction-givers are usually also effective direction-receivers.
- Some groups do not need a manager, and even fewer need a leader.

The distinctions we draw between the direction-giving types are so we can understand them and identify the rhetorical resources they provide. Distinct in theory, the types are almost seamlessly integrated throughout group activities. Do not worry too much about whether an individual is acting as a specific direction-giving type at a particular point in time. Orient instead on which type of direction-giving the group requires in the moment.

❖ IN CONCLUSION

Despite a general cultural bias lauding leadership, no direction-giving type is "better" than the others. Each is necessary, depending on exigencies perceived by grouping people. What is important is that you know you can help give direction to your group and that you orient on what the group needs in order to thrive as you think through your direction-giving options.

People often think, "I am not a leader," thus granting themselves permission to ignore responsibility for what happens in their group. Often what a group most needs is someone able and willing to work well as follower, doer, or guide. We like the metaphor George Shapiro suggests (c.f., Shapiro, 1987). A professor emeritus of leadership communication at the University of Minnesota, he talks about ethical direction-giving as *a complex improvisational dance over ever-changing terrain*. Everyone in a group can play a few notes of the tune and dance a few of the steps.

UNIT II

Develop Your Own Strategies for Giving Direction Well

4

Use Leadership Theory and Research to Prepare Yourself to Give Direction

You have five options for exercising influence as a direction-giver in your team, organization, or community—any group that matters to you: to do, follow, guide, manage, or lead (see Unit I). This second unit contains two chapters that focus on *developing your own strategies for giving direction well*. In this chapter, we review how experts in leadership and management can help us. In Chapter 5, we show you how to develop your own framework for giving direction well.

We use the term *well*, as in "I want to be able to give direction well," to represent judgments other people will make about your efforts. They will decide (1) whether the direction-giving you offer is *effective* in accomplishing what it needs to for the group, and they will decide (2) whether your direction-giver effort is *appropriate* given who you are and given what they think that the group needs. What can you do that will be both effective and appropriate? If someone is bothering you, killing that person is an effective but inappropriate way to get him or her to stop. Giving that person a pickle probably fails to meet both criteria. When people judge a direction-giving attempt as both effective and appropriate, they will think you have given direction well.[1]

Most experts tend to employ one of five basic perspectives to explain giving direction well. Some say that (1) direction-giving effectiveness stems from the *traits* of the individual giving the direction: His or her personal characteristics determine their effectiveness. Others claim that (2) it is the nature of the *situation* that determines a direction-giver's success. Others focus on (3) the *styles* of interaction direction-givers use (e.g., how they involve other group members when working through problems and when making decisions), and still others say the key to understanding effectiveness is to figure out (4) the *contingencies* that should be considered when deciding how to behave as a direction-giver. What matters most to us is (5): Which grouping and direction-giving activities are *functional*? In other words, which acts actually work to address the exigencies people perceive for grouping together in the first place and which acts actually work in a manner that helps a group to thrive (see Chapter 1)?

But we also think that each of the five perspectives has something useful to tell us about direction-giving and about those who give and receive direction. Each perspective has a research tradition that demonstrates some merit. In addition, each has an *intuitive appeal*, which means that it might be more than just a research perspective. Because of their intuitive appeal, each of these five basic ideas might actually be incorporated into the calculations some people make as they work with others, whether or not research indicates that their choice is well founded. Consequently, we explore each perspective by focusing on the intuitive logic that undergirds it.

❖ THE TRAITS PERSPECTIVE FOCUSES ON WHO YOU ARE TO EXPLAIN YOUR EFFECTIVENESS

The first perspective has a research history of interesting and sometimes useful results. The basis for the traits perspective is the idea that your personal characteristics (those you are born with) determine if you will be successful in life generally and effective as a direction-giver in particular. We see a *trait* as a relatively enduring characteristic, something you are born with or that has been developed

---

[1]Communication competence is also measured by these two tests: "a functional test (*is it effective?*) and a social test (*is it appropriate?*)" (Powers & Witt, 2008, p. 250).

in you over enough time that the behavior becomes characteristic of you. Traits include things such as height, sex, gender, intelligence, and introversion/extroversion.

Something to Think About and Discuss With Others

Traits, Nay: The traits perspective says that some people are born leaders: that the potential to give direction well is inherent in the person. This idea evolves from the notion that people who lead are chosen by the gods (*charisma* originates as a term to explain someone who is "touched by God"). Others are born to lead because they inherit their position as king/queen or in the ruling class. As philosophy and political science evolve, groups are constructed that are run by people who earn their position by their individual merits. A traits perspective, consistent with earlier ideas that people are born to lead, evolves to measure the characteristics that people need to be effective. Social scientists measured many variables (see* below), but Stogdill's (1948) synthesis of all available research to that point concluded that no reliable pattern of personality traits adequately explains all direction-giving effectiveness (Bormann, 1996).

Traits, Yea: However, more recent research has led to some reconsideration. In fact, "over two-thirds of the variation in patterns of social behavior appear to be attributable to genetic sources" (Beatty, Heisel, Hall, Levine, & La France, 2002, p. 11). Too much of what we do is tied to who we are to completely ignore traits.

So, what role do you think is played by the kind of person you are born to be in determining direction-giving effectiveness? Which traits matter? Whether or not your answer is supported by research, *if you think some traits are important, it means that idea may be in play as you decide who to trust as a direction-giver.*

---

*A few of the traits identified in research as important in groups or for leaders: personality (e.g., social sensitivity, approach-avoidance tendencies, authoritarianism, assertiveness, dominance), physical characteristics (e.g., age, size, weight, height, health), vocabulary, and intelligence (see Bass & Stogdill, 1990; Shaw, 1981). Silly? Why has the shorter candidate won the popular vote for U.S. president just 33% of the time?

The problem with the traits perspective is that sometimes people who lack important traits become effective direction-givers anyway. And others who exhibit the traits identified as important do not. Recent research suggests several traits or trait-like characteristics we think are of particular importance to seek out in others and to work to develop in yourself as you age.

❖ DEVELOPING EMOTIONAL INTELLIGENCE AND RESILIENCE MAY MATTER MORE THAN YOUR IQ

IQ, or the intelligence quotient, is one of the first traits tested to see if it signaled potential as a direction-giver (is it helpful to be a genius?). However, emotional intelligence[2] and resilience turn out to be more promising constructs.[3] *Emotional intelligence* (EQ) is the ability to manage your emotions: showing resilience and reasonable optimism in the face of the inevitable pressures and setbacks involved in grouping, then adapting until you and your group can thrive.

Managing emotion requires impulse control, flexibility, empathy, optimism, and general happiness. Emotional intelligence allows you to recognize and understand your own moods, to channel your initiative, and to employ social skills needed to work well with others (Goleman, 1995, 1998a, 1998b). We think emotional intelligence is a characteristic that comes easier for some of us than for others. However, we think that any of us can work over time to develop or enhance EQ as we accrue sufficient experience and are intentional with our efforts and focus.

People who develop emotional intelligence learn to face obstacles with enthusiasm and persistence. Instead of letting their emotional responses diminish or derail their efforts, they are *resilient:* bouncing back, adjusting, and regrouping. They keep trying to achieve desired outcomes. Developing emotional intelligence is an objective in the developing field of positive psychology (Luthans, Luthans, Hodgetts, & Luthans, 2001). *Positive psychology* focuses on being happy, optimistic, content, and effective in life. Emotional maturity is at the heart of positive psychology, and both provide useful resources for you as a direction-giver.

Something to Think About and Discuss With Others

Positive psychology[4] focuses on "positive subjective experience: well-being and satisfaction (past); flow, joy, the sensual pleasures, and happiness (present); and

---

[2]See, for example, Goleman (1995), Goleman (1998b), Bar-On (1997), and Bar-On, Brown, Kirkcaldy, and Thome (2000).

[3]See, for example, Salovey and Mayer (1990), Goleman, (1998a, 2000), and Luthans et al. (2001).

[4]Positive psychology is an excellent source of information about effective doers, followers, and guides as well as about the values involved in their work as effective citizens. It also provides insight into the co-constructions involved in successful groups in general and the vision aspect of leadership in particular. If you are interested, the first core textbook on the subject is by C. R. Snyder & Lopez (2006).

constructive cognitions about the future—optimism, hope, and faith. At the individual level it is about positive personal traits—the capacity for love and vocation, courage, interpersonal skill, aesthetic sensibility, perseverance, forgiveness, originality, future-mindedness, high talent, and wisdom. At the group level it is about the civic virtues and the institutions that move individuals toward better citizenship: responsibility, nurturance, altruism, civility, moderation, tolerance, and work ethic" (Seligman, 2002, p. 3). Do you think those traits and orientations matter to group effectiveness?

Positive psychology provides a general orientation and some tactics for helping develop emotional intelligence. Luthans et al. (2001) apply these concepts to direction-giving. They explain that PAL (positive approaches to leadership) focuses on attaining realistic optimism, confidence, and hope in order to be more effective in our grouping and direction-giving. *Realistic optimism* combines "benefit of the doubt thinking" that reframes group struggles with a focus on the positive aspects of our situation in an attempt to orient to the issues that we face as opportunities rather than as problems (i.e., rather than second-guessing or casting blame, recriminations, and aspersions when things don't work out as planned). Confidence and hope combine a sense of self-efficacy (see Chapter 2) and willpower that create *motivated determination:* the ability to begin; then, the ability to maintain effort knowing you can find the means needed to adapt as necessary until you are successful over time.

Something to Consider

A popular book of advice that encourages women to make better lives for themselves and their groups provides two particularly interesting orientational tactics. These can help you keep perspective and manage emotional responses to trying times and tasks. *Glade-skiing* requires the ability to move quickly "through a stand of closely-spaced trees" (Baker & Greenberg, 2007, p. 18). Applied to grouping, this means that you try to keep a focus on major objectives so that you do not lose yourself in worry about the many brain-splintering possibilities that could happen along your way. How? One answer is *kaizen*, which is a Japanese orientation that says you succeed best over the long haul when you favor daily efforts to make "continual

(Continued)

(Continued)

improvement through small, incremental, and sometimes insignificant steps" (Baker & Greenberg, 2007, p. 38). Any task of lasting merit is likely long work. At times it will feel as though you are standing still. Small, incremental, sometimes insignificant steps keep the group moving. They can be the only difference between success and yet another unfulfilled promise. Both tactics are focal points for helping enhance emotional maturity.

EQ, and the various subjects germane to it, can help whenever you need to act as any of the five types of direction-givers. We suggest further reading about them and that you never give up on the effort to enhance your resilience. These are not ideas to learn and leave alone. You must strive for them, working with patience to practice them and to attain their fruits.

❖ SELF-MONITORING AND RHETORICAL SENSITIVITY ORIENT YOU TO THE RESOURCES AVAILABLE AROUND YOU

Emotion is an important dynamic in the life of any group.[5] In addition to your own EQ, the emotions of others affect your experience. Your ability to align your responses to what others in your group are feeling affects your direction-giving effectiveness. This means that you need to be rhetorical as you tie direction-giving efforts to the (emotional) experience of other grouping members. This raises two issues: self-monitoring and rhetorical sensitivity. Both help suggest how to use your rhetorical resources to adjust your direction-giving efforts so that they tie in well to what others experience.

Emotion can be a powerful dynamic, but it also provides rhetorical resources. M. Snyder (1974) says that *self-monitoring* is the tendency some of us have for trying to show appropriate emotional responses given what is happening around us. During many of his speeches, especially as president, Bill Clinton makes a connection to a single individual to depict his understanding of the emotions and difficulties common folks experience: "I feel your pain." A *high self-monitor* reads

---

[5]See, for example, Hochschild (1983), Fineman (2000), Waldron (1994), and Morgan and Krone (2001).

and then adjusts to the emotional state of the people in the group. A high self-monitor tries to show emotional cues that others expect, given the circumstance, whether or not that is how he or she actually feels. This requires enough acting ability to put another person at ease as he or she sees the high self-monitor responding to the emotional context in an understandable manner.

The ability a high self-monitor develops in "reading a group" affects direction-giving. For example, self-monitoring can help determine who will emerge as a key direction-giver.[6] In addition, low and high self-monitors rely differently on direction-givers: a difference that helps determine whether a group and a direction-giver are likely to be effective.[7] If you are a low self-monitor, you may need to find ways to compensate for not seeming to be in tune with the emotional climate in your group. The desire and ability to self-monitor can help you make sense of your group.

The idea is to use rhetorical resources to adjust your efforts so they tie in well with what others are experiencing. R. P. Hart and Burks (1984) say that *rhetorical sensitivity* is the tendency some of us develop to identify and use the means of communication that will provide us the most utility or influence. This is in contrast to people lacking rhetorical sensitivity who say what they feel like saying, how they feel like saying it, regardless of whether that works well for others. A rhetorically sensitive person prioritizes effectiveness over expressiveness.

Something to Consider

R. P. Hart and Burks (1984) "lay out five characteristics of rhetorical sensitivity. The rhetorically sensitive person tries to accept role taking as a part of life, tries to avoid counterproductive stylized language, is willing to adapt to existing conditions, seeks to distinguish between information that is useful and that which is not, and tries to understand that an idea may be rendered in a number of ways" (Barrett, 1991, p. 28). How rhetorically sensitive are you?

It is not dishonest to adapt your message according to the cues others in your group provide about what they are thinking or feeling. The goal is not deceit. You can adapt and remain *authentic*—honest and

---

[6]See, for example, Ellis and Cronshaw (1992); Ellis, Adamson, Deszca, and Cawsey (1988); and Cronshaw and Ellis (1991).

[7]See, for example, Anderson and Tolson (1989) and Howell, Dorfman, and Kerr (1986).

genuine with yourself and others. The goal is to make effective and appropriate what you need to communicate: to synchronize what you say and do with what you and others are experiencing. That is no more devious than dressing up when you go to work or worship. Doing so respects the context. You are attempting to help others feel at ease given their emotional state: to help them understand and appreciate what you have to say.

Learning about traits that often seem to matter provides orientational material as you build your own framework for giving direction well (see Chapter 5). Even if you reject the assumptions of the traits perspective, learning its logic is useful because it is intuitively appealing to many people. People often either explicitly or implicitly incorporate their ideas about leadership traits when making choices about whom to trust as direction-givers.

❖ SITUATIONAL, STYLES, AND CONTINGENCY PERSPECTIVES FOCUS ON BEHAVIORAL CHOICES YOU MAKE

The three perspectives in this section can all be viewed as reasonable reactions to the failure of the traits perspective to explain all that we want to know about direction-giving effectiveness. In turn, the three argue (1) that much of what matters in effective direction-giving is determined by dynamics that are outside the control of the individual (*situational perspective*); (2) that in determining group effectiveness, it matters less who the person is (the argument made in the traits perspective) and more how she or he treats others while they are grouping (*styles perspective*); and (3) that it is a combination of how a direction-giver treats others given particular situational and grouping dynamics that really determines group effectiveness (*contingency perspectives*). Again, each perspective has valuable insight and intuitive merit.

❖ GREAT LEADERS DURING TIMES OF CRISIS AND HEMPHILL'S WORK SHOW THAT SITUATION MATTERS

Historians who study the presidents of the United States sometimes say that "great times make the leader." Washington, Lincoln, and FDR are often listed by such historians as the greatest presidents. Each of these presidents had their own war and republic-threatening crises on which to stake claims of leadership greatness. Would they be so memorable without those crises? No.

In less trying times (times of "normalcy") and in less complex groups, evidence also shows that situation plays a key role in determining direction-giving effectiveness. Hemphill (1949a, 1949b) finds that effective direction-givers in one system, if moved to other systems with a history of ineffectiveness, often end up with similar results (less effectiveness). There are also cases where those who are ineffective in one system succeed in another group where there has been a history of success. This is like moving a championship coach to a bottom-dwelling team and finding that the team still struggles under her direction or putting a coach with a history of moderate success in charge of a championship team and that team continues to win.

All such cases, including great leaders emerging during times of crisis, help support an argument that the situation can be more important than who is the direction-giver in determining effectiveness. The conclusion we draw is more limited: That situation affects but does not cause direction-giving effectiveness. So, we need to understand the nature of a situation.

What matters to us from the situational perspective is our ability to identify recurring ways that context affects grouping and direction-giving attempts. In the contingencies section later in this chapter, we discuss some of those recurring situational dynamics that other experts have identified. For now, we want to introduce a few terms that help us sort out what may become important to you about a group situation. Having a terminology of situations tells us where to look for potential problems and direction-giving resources (Burtis & Turman, 2006).

A *situation* can be analyzed as a set of circumstances. *Circumstances* include anything in a grouping context that can affect grouping, but that is not part of grouping activity. The group may be aware of some of these and not aware of others. Circumstances that affect grouping choices can be clustered into three categories: supra-group issues, constraints, and contingencies. Each cluster is distinguished by the type of exigencies it tends to make manifest. These clusters represent aspects of a group's circumstances as they become something on which the group focuses. Of course, there are other circumstances, which may or may not affect the success of the group, that do not capture the attention of the group and thus are not part of group calculations.

Supra-group issues affect group action though they transcend group control (Burtis & Turman, 2006). They are important to, but beyond the direct control of, the group. Examples include the acts of competing groups, obligations of group members to other activities in their lives, and *boundary-spanning,* which is interaction the group needs to do with those outside the group (e.g., with *stakeholders* [nonmembers who are important to the group] such as a banker who loans the group money or a dying parent of a group member). Supra-group issues may enhance, diminish, or even overpower group efforts and other group-ing exigencies. They can be identified in every group situation, and they affect every grouping attempt.

The other two clusters of situational dynamics sometime originate in supra-group issues and at other times are created by grouping: con-straints and contingencies. These are the expected and unexpected aspects of how an unfolding situation affects grouping. Both are simi-lar to supra-group issues in that each tends to be the impetus for exi-gencies that affect grouping, and each may be somewhat or completely out of the control of the group.

Constraints include anything that the group can identify, which its members think may hinder or distort their effectiveness (Bitzer, 1968). Constraints include any limits, problems, or objections the group can anticipate that may twist or weaken their grouping or its effects (e.g., shortage of necessary money or time; stakeholders with wildly dif-ferent ideas of what a new president ought to do while in office). Some constraints emanate from the grouping effort, and others man-ifest outside the group as a supra-group issue. For example, as a pres-ident or governor pulls together a leadership team, a vetting process is used to identify potential issues with possible candidates that may become barriers to a successful confirmation. When an issue arises, its potency as a constraint is weighed, and the candidacy proceeds or ends accordingly.

Contingencies are unexpected issues that arise over time and then affect grouping. They may manifest from grouping or be based in supra-group issues. Contingencies limit or affect grouping but are not antici-pated to do so and, therefore, do not function as constraints. Though neglected for a time, contingencies can "explode" into the group's awareness at almost any time. If they do, they must be addressed. Some people know to set up a "contingency fund" because they have learned as a general rule to anticipate the possibility of contingencies arising dur-ing grouping, though they do not anticipate the specifics.

It is helpful to identify and figure out key circumstances in every group. What are our supra-group issues? What constraints do we fore-see? How can we be alert for contingencies and, especially, be ready to adapt? Sensitivity to these aspects of situation can help you avoid the myopia that often accompanies working with a group. It can help you watch for potential pitfalls and for resources originating outside of what people in a group naturally want to focus upon.

❖ THE STYLES PERSPECTIVE SAYS PICK THE RIGHT WAY TO TREAT THOSE WITH WHOM YOU GROUP

Style is how a direction-giver involves others in grouping processes (e.g., in problem-solving and decision-making) and in creating a group's direction. The *styles perspective* is originally based in the idea that one style for direction-giving (i.e., a democratic or participatory style) is generally superior to other styles (e.g., autocratic; laissez-faire).

Direction-giving styles can be treated as stories about your behavioral options as a direction-giver. In other words, how do you think you should treat others if you are giving direction? How do you think other direction-givers should integrate you into problem-solving and decision-making processes? What should they say and do? Your answers can help you to make accounts describing those who give direction well and of those who do so poorly. Here is some more help.

Which of the following do you most agree with? (1) It is better for key direction-givers to be directive: They should make most decisions alone and then announce to others what is expected of them. (2) It is better for a key direction-giver to make a decision and then attempt to sell his or her choice to the others in the group. (3) It is better for a direction-giver to consult with others before making a decision, then to decide, and then tell others the decision. (4) It is better for a key direction-giver to get the rest of the group fully involved in making decisions and then to go with what the group decides, even when that choice is different from the direction-giver's own. (5) A direction-giver should just trust his or her group and leave the group alone to work things out. These are the basic story line options that direction-givers tend to choose among. Compare your own preferences regarding these styles to the options listed in Table 4.1.

The choice of what kind of power to employ in your interactions also affects direction-giving style. *Power* is the ability to get things done.[8] French and Raven (1968) say that there are six bases of power

---

[8]*Politics* is any attempt to marshal the resources of power. So politics involves the playing out of power. Some of us "don't like to play games" or "hate politics," but we delude ourselves if we think we can work with others and avoid politics or the exercise of power. The question is not if we will be political but rather what kind of politics will we practice.

Table 4.1	Direction-Giving Styles

Option	*Definition and Explication*
Autocratic	Direction-giver chooses to center power and decision-making in the direction-giver; fastest; least likely to attain benefits from the group's inputs because those are de-emphasized
Selling	Direction-giver gets others to think/behave as she or he desires or requires; may be necessary when a superior tells the direction-giver what to do and that has to be passed on to her or his group lower in the hierarchy; risks feeling manipulative
Consultative	Direction-giver consults with group and then decides; tries to attain ideas and acceptance from the group but not to diffuse responsibility or authority
Democratic	Direction-giver facilitates distributed power and decision-making among group members; "participatory" processes may be very time-consuming but are most likely to accrue or enhance benefits from grouping members' input
Laissez-faire	Direction-giver takes "hands-off" approach to power and decision-making processes; some mature groups need formal direction-givers to mostly stay out of their way; for others, "delegating" is sufficient direction

Note: The autocratic, democratic, and laissez-faire style options are based on the work of Lewin (Lewin & Lippitt, 1938; Lewin, Lippitt, & White, 1939) and his colleagues R. K. White and Lippitt (1960). Likert's (1961, 1967) systems provide aspects of the selling, consultative, and participatory/democratic styles. Hersey and Blanchard (1982) inform delegating aspects of laissez-faire.

that can unfold in different stories of your behavioral choices (see Table 4.2). What kind of power will you employ? What is the coin of the realm in your group?

The search for one best style results in scholars describing a variety of combinations of choices for the direction-giver. For example, McGregor's (1960) work gives us *Theory X*, which describes a manager who is autocratic or directive and uses top-down, informative-only communications to keep employees focused on task and production. Consider Theory X one style story option. In corporate work, the style may result in employee distrust or disinterest, but such a style might

Table 4.2	Bases of Power

Option	Definition
Legitimate	Formal authority or position you occupy in the group provides power to you or to whomever serves in that position: a manager (see Chapter 3)
Referent	Influence because you are liked by others or they find you attractive in some way, e.g., you have status or provide a desired affiliation (friend; colleague)
Expert	Influence based in your competence or credibility, which is made useful by the intricacies of the task or subject matter facing the group
Information	Influence because of resources you can access or make available to others; you do not have to understand the information—only know that it is of value
Reward	Ability to provide something desirable to others or to stop something undesirable from happening to them—the key is control over what others find rewarding
Coercive	Ability to provide a negative thing (e.g., a punishment) to others or to remove a positive thing from others (also punishing)

work in military units during moments of conflict when an established chain of command is critical and decisions that may result in casualties have to be made.

McGregor's (1960) *Theory Y* managers encourage communications that flow upward and across the group, spreading decision-making via frequent and honest interactions among group personnel. Group members become resources, rather than cogs, further helping their group to thrive. This may also be an effective style in a military setting but probably under different circumstances than on the battlefield. For example, during after-action report briefings or interactions about training exercises, commanding officers may be more open to junior officers having a say. McGregor's Theory X and Theory Y are competing stories of stylistic choices.

Leader-member exchange theory provides contemporary, alternative style stories. Graen and associates suggest two general accounts of stylistic choice for the relationship constructed between a direction-giver and direction-receivers (Graen & Cashman, 1975; Graen & Uhl-Bien, 1995). The first, *LMX*, is working to make group members feel that they are an *in-group*, sharing communications and a relationship characterized by social support, mutual trust, and liking. The second option, *SX*, is to build a relationship based in exchange. Grouping personnel may feel as though they are an *out-group*, but they share communications and a relationship "defined entirely by the roles they perform and the contractual obligations" they have to the group, which results in "low trust, formal authority, low rewards, low support, [and doing solely the] tasks based on job descriptions" (Dainton & Zelley, 2005, pp. 146–147). Although it appears unlikely, we think that there may be cases where each option is preferable, based on your orientation to the group.

In sum, we think your choice of style should be rhetorical. This means you should pick and change style according to what you think will increase your effectiveness in the group. It will be easier to do so if you avoid choosing a style based just on your personal preference and if you can avoid falling into a philosophical certainty that says all people ought to always be treated a certain way all of the time.

❖ THE CONTINGENCY PERSPECTIVE SAYS YOU NEED TO ADJUST TO RECURRING "WHAT IFS" OF GROUPING

Contingency theories identify important recurring aspects of grouping circumstances that result in the need for using different direction-giving styles. They attempt to take the guesswork out of unexpected contingencies by identifying patterns of possibilities. Then, whichever pattern of contingencies arises, the various theories that comprise the contingency perspective explain the changes in direction-giving style choices you should employ as a consequence.

Typical recurring variables are (1) the nature of the grouping task, including how the group needs to approach the group's task and goals; (2) the nature of grouping personnel and/or their relationships, including with the direction-giver; and/or (3) supra-group issues that tend to recur as problems. Each contingency theory identifies the aspects of your situation its authors consider most important for you to consider when deciding how to give direction.

Fiedler's (1967) *contingency theory* focuses choice of direction-giving style on positional power, task structure, and relations between a direction-giver and the group. Positional power is determined by the group's enumeration of that power. (For example, Sue, a manager in a marketing firm, is expected to be involved in all aspects of campaign development and to make the final decision on all aspects of that development.)

The task structure is determined by the clarity of the task and of the paths that can be taken to address it, in addition to whether the quality of the group's solution can be verified as optimal. (The task, to develop a new campaign for a "buy green, buy local" exotic produce products shop, may be quite clear, but the various paths the marketing firm could take could increase their difficulty—e.g., do we focus on television, print, or new media?) The quality of relationships is a function of the confidence and trust a direction-giver and group have co-constructed from past experiences together, which is affected by the success they have achieved. (Because of their technical proficiency, Sue lets her "computer geeks" work entirely on their own to develop the "new media" part of the new campaign plan. Though Sue maintains final approval status, her approval becomes pro forma.)

Fiedler's (1967) argument is that the style of direction-giving you employ should vary with these contingencies. The variables combine into a few recurring types of situations that range on a continuum from very favorable (e.g., good relationships, high level of task clarity, and high position power) to unfavorable (e.g., poor relationships, low levels of trust and confidence, lack of past successes, unclear task structure, and limited position power). Each combination suggests a different application of direction-giving style.

Contingency theories provide a decision-making heuristic that tells you, according to each theory, which stylistic choice you should pick given the contingences you face. Their heuristics interest us less than do the recurring contingencies these theorists identify. Our goal is to help you make your own reasoned choices, not plug you into a recipe. We think that telling you some of the recurring contingencies will open up options for you in useful ways. Then, given the particulars of your group circumstances and the nature of your direction-giving type and style options, you can proceed to make your own choices.[9] Toward that end, we suggest three more recurring contingencies for you to consider: path, information, and maturity.

House's (1971) *path-goal theory* focuses your choice of style (directive, supportive, participative, and achievement oriented) on the

---

[9]However, if any one of these theories seems an ideal fit for you, feel free to consult it directly following the reference list we provide. Each has a good deal more material available once you know what theory to ask for.

nature of the goal for grouping and of the path needed to succeed. He argues people are goal driven: They want to be able to succeed in attaining group goals. To succeed, they need to know what paths are available and which to take. For example, a group of college students working on a class project may make numerous inquiries: What exactly should be done to ensure a high grade? Should they separate the task into units and have each group member work on his or her individual portion? When would it be more appropriate to work in pairs, alone, or have all members working together? Ambiguity combined with goal-driven people creates elaborations about possible nuances and choices in both path and goal. Confusion requires direction-giving input on which path to follow to succeed. When the goal and path are clear, the need for you as a direction-giver diminishes.

Vroom and Yettons's (1973) *decision tree* focuses your choice of style on various bits of the information you need to have to make good direction-giving choices. Their heuristic takes you step-by-step through a series of yes-no questions about your circumstances, such as the following: Do perceptions of fairness need to be considered in the manager's choice? Is enough information available to make that choice? Does acceptance of the decision matter? How likely is conflict as the result of the decision? Depending on your answers, you are directed to a particular one of Likert's (1961) systems/styles for engaging your group.

Hersey and Blanchard's (1969) *life cycle theory* says focus your direction-giving choices on the level of group and member maturity (Krayer, 1988). *Maturity* includes both their ability to do a task (knowledge, skill, and experience doing it) and their willingness to take responsibility for doing a task (motivation, confidence, and commitment to group and task). Every group evolves through a life cycle of increasing maturity. Various stages in that cycle are recurring contingencies that require a different direction-giving style.

Across the life cycle, the maturity of whole groups and of each grouping member can be viewed using a continuum (Burtis & Turman, 2006). Grouping members start out immature when they join any new grouping enterprise. *Immature group members* need help learning the goals, structure, and processes of the group. For instance, a new initiate into a sorority has much to learn about the customs and rituals involved in the day-to-day activities of this new group. These new members may be passive and disorganized, bring a short-term perspective to their work, have no established working history, and are fraught with tension over how to shape their experience in the group.

Average maturity members, though probably still unable to take full responsibility regarding what they should be doing, have become more willing to do so. Sorority members with average maturity may want to serve as a committee chairperson but may fail or do poorly if allowed to bite off more than they can chew, which can make them less willing to again assert themselves. *Above-average maturity members* are able, but may be unwilling, to take on greater group responsibility. They may need encouragement to step into more active direction-giving roles. *Mature grouping individuals* should be effective operating independently (signaling a use for the laissez-faire style) and are often the key direction-givers in such organizations.

The contingency perspective is valuable as a basic orientation: Be alert to contingencies as they arise and be prepared to adjust to them as they do. Further, we appreciate the focus it places on figuring out which issues tend to recur and affect your decision-making choices. (We identify additional clusters of recurring issues in Chapter 5.) As the exigencies perceived for grouping change, you should expect to have to modify your direction-giving style just as you need to change the type of direction-giving you provide.

❖ THE FUNCTIONAL PERSPECTIVE FOCUSES ON WHAT YOU CAN DO FOR YOUR GROUP

From Chapter 1 on, we argue that everyone has an obligation to help her or his group thrive. The functional perspective does not make that claim but assumes its validity. The *functional perspective* asks what it is that grouping and direction-giving activities accomplish. This perspective is not concerned with what leadership is or what managers ought to do. Instead, it focuses on how interactions undertaken by anyone may function to help or hinder a group. If what you and others do functions to help, then direction-giving is being done well. If not, it is done poorly.

Groups and individuals have certain needs that must be met in order for them to function. The human body needs protein, for example, and whatever you eat that the body can process as protein functions as protein. Grasshoppers may not be delectable, but when eating them allows the body to get needed protein, eating them is a functional response to famine. No matter how tasty, sugar cookies are hard-pressed to function as protein.

The functional perspective does not care if a theory prescribes a particular action, but only if that action allows effective grouping and direction-giving to take place. For example, you invite your group to a happy hour at your place on Friday. If that experience allows tensions to decrease and relationships to strengthen between members of your group so that the group gets along better on Monday, then your party functions to help your group to thrive. If you figure out what your group needs, you can use your own methods to provide for that need. Here are some frameworks that can help you to do so.

❖ BENNE AND SHEATS SAY EVERY GROUP MUST SERVE TASK, RELATIONAL, AND INDIVIDUAL FUNCTIONS

A number of scholars work from a functional perspective. Among the most influential are Benne and Sheats (1948), who identify three functions every group must serve. First, the group must serve its *task function:* It must do its work or play, addressing reasons members have for grouping in the first place. Every group has a task. In some groups the task is social (e.g., a circle of friends). In others it locates in self-help or therapy. In still others it involves playing a game or sport. For a group to succeed, it must find ways to fulfill its task function.

Second, to be any good at its task over any extended period of time, every group must develop and maintain itself: serve its *relational* or *maintenance function*. This requires building the relationships necessary to allow the ongoing interaction needed for grouping. Third, while serving the above two functions, the group should allow individuals who do the grouping to flourish (the *individual function*). People need to thrive along with their group rather than being ignored, worn out, ground up, or otherwise sacrificed on the group's altar.[10]

How the first two of these functions ought to be balanced plays a central role in quite a lot of management theory. The issue always boils down to what balance you strike as a direction-giver as you orient to task and relationships: which gets priority and with what consequences.

---

[10]Benne and Sheats (1948) argue that two of the three functions are necessary and that the third, the individual function, may distract from effective grouping. Burtis and Turman (2006) argue for the individual function as a necessary aspect of grouping in addition to the other two, though it can also be problematic. See also our discussion of positive psychology (above) for part of the argument in favor of making the individual function important in any effective grouping experience.

❖ BLAKE AND MOUTON'S MANAGERIAL GRID SAYS YOU NEED TO BALANCE THOSE FUNCTIONS

Beginning in the mid-1940s, work at The Ohio State University and at the University of Michigan has focused management and leadership theory and research on two basic priorities. Scholars seek to describe and measure the differences between focusing mostly on doing the task well and/or on concern for the people involved (their relationships/feelings), and they use those alternative priorities to explain grouping and direction-giving effectiveness (Goldhaber, 1986).

A focus on initiating structure and being task or production oriented creates one story or stylistic cluster. A focus on the people involved or what is called consideration or maintenance of the group is the second story cluster (Goldhaber, 1986, p. 97). For example, Blake and Mouton's (1964) managerial grid contrasts five style options. One focuses mostly on task and the others mostly on the relational function or on balancing both task and relationship.

Again, the prescriptions that result from these lines of research are of less interest to us than are the dynamics they identify as important to consider. Task, relational, and the individual functions are always important considerations. Grouping should always seek to accomplish its purposes, should always be accomplished in a way that allows grouping to continue to be effective in the future, and should always provide a benefit to those who group that is in addition to what they could accomplish on their own.

These three functions provide a test for the quality of group activity. When a group fails to serve one or more of its functions (or serves them poorly or insufficiently), the quality of group outcomes is lower than it should be (Burtis & Turman, 2006). If you and others give direction well and your group thrives, it means your group serves all three of its grouping functions.

❖ YOUR GROUPING CHOICES ALSO NEED TO EARN YOU AT LEAST ONE PROCESS PRIZE FROM GROUPING

The potential fruits of grouping should always include at least one of four possible process prizes (Burtis & Turman, 2006). The four *process prizes* are (1) getting more work done than an individual can accomplish alone, (2) getting something better done by working with others (because of improved critical processes), (3) getting something new accomplished from interactions with others (because of increased creativity), and (4) getting greater acceptance for what the group has done (because of working together).

Earning a process prize means that the choice to work with a group was a good choice (instead of working alone). If the group fails to earn a process prize, individuals would have been better served by working alone to address the exigency that concerned them. The process prizes provide a second test of the quality of any grouping. If you give direction well, your group thrives, which means among other things that it earns a process prize.

❖ EXPLICIT AND IMPLICIT THEORIES OF EFFECTIVE GROUPING AND DIRECTION-GIVING ARE IN PLAY

Most of us use a combination of explicit and implicit theories to guide our choices about how to behave well in groups and how to give direction well. A similar combination guides our assessments of the grouping activities and direction-giving attempts made by others. That is why we want you to understand the intuitive appeal people feel for one or more of the perspectives in this chapter. (Un)intentionally, those perspectives affect their choices (and yours) as you are trying to provide or to receive direction well.

Explicit theories are those we know we are using. We can explain them to ourselves and to others. For example, "I think an effective manager walks around and talks to everyone in the group." Our explicit theories are based on what we have been taught, have read, have observed, and have figured out through our own experience. For instance, a theory, idea, or research result catches your attention and becomes part of the explicit theory you use when trying to be effective giving direction to others. (Perhaps you make a nugget out of it—see Chapter 8.)

Implicit theories work the same way, helping us decide how to behave and how to assess the actions of others. However, *implicit theories*[11] are not something we can easily access, explain, or test. They

---

[11]See, for example, Calder (1977); Keller (1999, 2003); Ketrow (1991); Nye and Forsyth (1991); Offerman, Kennedy, and Wirtz (1994); and Pavitt and Sackgroff (1990).

are part of our behavior that may even be blind to us. We may not notice when they affect our choices and actions. We either will not or cannot explain how our implicit theory works for us. You can think of this as instinct or intuition. Regardless of its source or quality, implicit theory plays a part, sometimes a decisive part, in our choices and in making judgments about whether direction is given well. The fact that both explicit and implicit theories are in play whenever people are grouping helps to explain how one direction-giver can be judged as giving direction well by some people in the group while at the same time others disagree.

❖ IN CONCLUSION

Think how the implicit and explicit theories in play in your group might manifest in accounts people tell of what it is like to be in your group. Do people you work with tend to talk about grouping in terms that sound like they are using a trait or situational or stylistic explanation? What level of flexibility in behavioral choices do people you work with seem able and willing to demonstrate in the face of the constraints that concern you and contingencies that arise? Sorting out how others are thinking in these regards can improve your direction-giving choices.

5

Develop a Framework and Position Yourself for Giving Direction

❖ ❖ ❖

If you are like most of us, when you try to do something new you will stumble a bit on some aspects of the new task. You know that you can only succeed if you keep on trying, so you accept the bumps and keep after it. Your effectiveness increases as you learn from experiences, whether they are partial successes or failures. Each time you try, you adjust your efforts, making them better as you go. What you need, what you are trying to develop as you struggle along, is a formula for effective action: a framework to help you succeed almost every time you try.

The skillful practitioner has a well-developed, field-tested framework. Though he or she can make effective action look easy, ease is developed over time by trying, reconsidering, revising, and retrying. The U.S. military has protocol for performing an "After Action Report" once a mission is completed. Regardless of perceptions about success or failure, company and battalion personnel reflect on the events that transpired and try to pinpoint improvements in their approach. The results are used to develop and to refine their framework for future action.

A *framework* is an organization. It arranges and prioritizes your ideas on a particular subject providing a basis for your basic behavioral blueprints. Your *direction-giving framework* puts order to the ideas you have about attempts to give direction. It prioritizes your tactical and strategic ideas: your plans and objectives for action as a direction-giver.

This is the last of five chapters focused primarily on direction-giving processes. The remaining five focus on communicating as you give direction. In this chapter, we encourage you to build and begin to refine your own framework for giving direction well: direction-giving that others will deem to be both effective and appropriate. We also discuss positioning yourself as someone to whom others should pay attention.

❖ A DIRECTION-GIVING FRAMEWORK SHOULD HAVE A PHILOSOPHY, EXEMPLAR MODEL, AND GUIDELINES

World-class practitioners, effective coaches, and connoisseurs develop frameworks that describe how to do a particular task or enterprise well (e.g., cope with conflict, pitch a baseball, make wine). That framework can also be used to assess the efforts and outcomes of those who engage in that activity. The framework gets tested and improved with experience.

Some frameworks only work for a particular grouping effort. For example, the football coach at St. Thomas University in Minnesota has a unique approach. His players practice without pads. Other frameworks work so well that more and more folks adopt them. Over time, they become a "community standard." When college football began, players were assigned to play multiple positions. As the sport developed, coaches began recruiting players with skills specific to a position. Now, a player playing one position is the community standard. The idea is accepted by almost everyone in the community of coaches (almost all of whom practice players in pads).

When scholars develop a framework to explain how to do something well (e.g., how to communicate competently; how to give direction to troubled employees), it is subjected to years of empirical testing by other researchers before becoming a community standard. Many attempts do not make the cut. If a framework does survive tests by research, the result can evolve into a special theory (Bormann, 1980[1]). The research that goes into testing a scholarly theory is the difference

---

[1]See Chapter 3 in Bormann (1980).

between a framework accepted by a community of practitioners and a special theory accepted by a community of scholars.

A *special theory* is a coherent, consistent collection of carefully researched ideas and best practices developed over time for doing a particular act or enterprise well. A special theory has a *philosophy* that expresses the values undergirding the theory, it has an *exemplar model* that shows how the enterprise should look when it is done well, and it has *guidelines* that help practitioners make choices that are in line with the philosophy and that result in exemplary acts.

Chapter 4 is filled with conclusions based on research reports that management and leadership studies scholars use to test their various frameworks for giving direction well. Each of their frameworks matures as they build their ideas about direction-giving into a collection of hypotheses that they test, refine, and release to other scholars for them to consider and test. Each framework becomes a special theory only if it works well enough during extensive research to document the benefits they claim from its use.

The components of a special theory can provide a starting point for your efforts to set up a framework. We reason by analogy here. Your effectiveness framework will not be researched enough to become a special theory. What we suggest is that you use the parts of a special theory to inform the building of your framework. Develop a philosophy to guide your choices. Collect or create exemplars or a model of what the best practice of direction-giving ought to look like. Develop guidelines that breathe life into your framework by reminding you how you intend to behave as you attempt to give direction under various circumstances.

The two story lines we explore below should give you a sense of what a developed framework might look like. The first is called both "the classical school" and "scientific management." It is an example of a framework that achieved the status of a special theory, but it also shows how such theories get refined and change over time. It is the earliest scholarly theory we know of that tells managers a coherent, well-tested story about how to behave.

❖ TAYLOR'S SCIENTIFIC MANAGEMENT IS ONE FRAMEWORK FOR GIVING DIRECTION WELL

Frederick Taylor's 1911 book, *The Principles of Scientific Management*, describes what amounts to a philosophy, model, and guidelines for how to behave as a manager. You can get a sense of how the theory tells a manager to behave from McGregor's (1960) Theory X (see Chapter 4): authoritarian; top-down communication only. The philosophy and exemplar model in a special theory might not be explicit, but you can tease them out of what the special theory emphasizes. Economic principles, the processes of scientific research, and basic assumptions about human nature shape Taylor's framework for those who want to become "scientific managers."

Scientific management emphasizes the values of efficiency and productivity. A philosophy based in those values justifies different choices than a philosophy based in the value, for example, of creating an environment conducive to cohesiveness and long-term commitment to the group. The scientific manager's philosophy has a cornerstone concept called the *economic man*. This basic assumption about human nature is that workers are concerned only with making money (Goldhaber, 1986). A worker can "best be motivated to work by such carrot-and-stick techniques as piecework systems, bonus systems, time-and-motion studies, and cost-figuring systems" (Goldhaber, 1986, pp. 37–38). Such ideas result in scientific managers treating workers as beasts of burden who, like all beasts, can be motivated by fear and the need to be taken care of (only just well enough to function as required by the group).

Scientific managers focus on the anatomy of the organization and its processes, not its people. Aspects of its exemplar model and guidelines include *atomism,* or breaking work down to its smallest units and developing a *division of labor* that structures combinations of units so each worker achieves peak production. *Span of control* is the most effective reach a manager can have over the highest number of people he or she can reasonably supervise using *scalar processes* (top-down communications). *Functional processes* are the discouraged communications among workers ("serf" to serf—using the vernacular of the theory) and mostly unnecessary talk among managers ("vassal" to vassal). Workers are not to waste time chatting, and managers really do not need to do so either, except to be social. Communication has little importance in this framework.

Do you get an idea of the sorts of experiences people would have in a system where direction-givers use this framework? You could identify group experiences you have seen in movies, perhaps ones that you have had yourself, that fit into a basic story line that results from such stylistic choices. There is a coherence you can see among diverse experiences that lets you say those various experiences are all indicative of people who believe in scientific management. When you can identify common aspects of experiences as products of the same basic story line, you are seeing evidence that a direction-giving framework is in play.

Think of the time period in which Taylor and others in the classical school (such as Max Weber and Henri Fayol) were working: from before World War I and into the Great Depression. They developed theory for managers who worked in large organizations. This means looking for exemplar models already in existence, which at the time would include how effective armies, the church, a few monopolies, and governments are run. All tend to be top-down, authoritarian hierarchies where a direction-giver is to be followed without question. It is not surprising that scientific management uses an autocratic model and philosophy typical of such systems.

Something to Think About and Discuss With Others

What changes in Taylor's special theory would there be had his exemplar model been a family or an organic organism such as the human body? How do you think his principles and governing guidelines might change? What do you think would change if he were to base his analogy on a democratic or an egalitarian community instead of using an "economic" or "scientific" analogy?

Over time, a special theory gets modified as research tests and refines its principles. In the case of scientific management, instead of just continuing refinements, testing finally results in debunking key parts of the theory. An alternative story line emerges as a result: Elton Mayo and the human relations school. It is created in reaction to flaws in the classical framework.

❖ MAYO'S HAWTHORNE EFFECT SHOWS THE NEED FOR A DIFFERENT FRAMEWORK

Elton Mayo of Harvard Business School began as an ardent advocate of scientific management and then changed as a result of his research from 1924 to 1933 at the Hawthorne Plant of Western Electric in Chicago (Goldhaber, 1986). His studies tested, for example, what level of lighting results in peak worker productivity. The findings: Increasing lighting increases productivity. So does decreasing lighting. So does being in the control group—that is, no change in lighting results in increases in productivity nonetheless! What? Why?

The riddle is solved by an explanation called the *Hawthorne effect*, which says paying attention to people (observing them) change their behavior. Furthermore, Mayo's findings show that talk among informal groups of workers is a key motivator of human behavior (the "functional process" specifically discouraged in the classical school). Both findings demonstrate that human motivation is as much a social as an economic factor, attacking a core principle (economic man) of scientific management.

Something to Consider and Discuss With Others

Beware of connotations you have for the word *theory*. If you think of theory as something that is impractical or something that is just someone's hunch or personal opinion, you need to know that we use the term to mean something different than that. The empirical testing endured by special theories increases the level of certainty we have when embracing one of them. We are not so certain about the value of various untested hunches and opinions that people have. If a special theory is impractical or does not work when tested, it gets tossed. A scholar's theory must be testable, must be tested, and must be rejected if research does not support it. That is how scholarship gains credence. The story of how Mayo helps reject his own philosophical orientation through his research is a case in point. It is a story that demonstrates a virtue of the scholarly method.

A new direction-giving framework and second managerial story line, called *human relations,* is developed. "Economic man" is replaced by Mayo's "social man" (motivated by relationships more than by money). Dickens's classic tale of Ebenezer Scrooge is an example of the distinction between these two perspectives. After visits from the three ghosts of Christmas, Scrooge transforms from scientific manager to one who benefits from human relations, such as being nice to his employees.

The human relations framework that gives an alternative to the classical school is itself tested and soon replaced by a *human resources* framework for two reasons. First, treating people as though they are important resources in the group is not as manipulative as treating people nicely, as though they need to be handled with kid gloves, to get only positive feedback, and otherwise to be ignored (Goldhaber, 1986; also see Theory Y in Chapter 4, this volume). Second, there is an awakening sense of how a direction-giving framework that privileges communication among people in a group can help the group to thrive (instead of discouraging communications or minimizing their importance). We are still experimenting with the results of that awakening.

❖ DEVELOP YOUR OWN EFFECTIVENESS FRAMEWORK FOR EACH TYPE OF DIRECTION-GIVING YOU PROVIDE

Each of us already has some implicit and explicit ideas about how grouping and direction-giving ought to be done. None of these ideas, however, constitutes a framework until you have a coherent prioritization for how to behave in the various situations you are likely to face. That coherence is a compelling story line you can tell yourself for how you intend to give direction well. It comes from having a strong sense of your philosophy, of what you think is exemplary action, and guidelines that integrate your philosophy and exemplars into the choices you make.

We have three suggestions to keep in mind. First, develop a philosophy consistent with both the values and the preferences you have regarding how people should be treated as they group. Second, your exemplar model should make you think about what effective grouping and direction-giving ought to look like. It should include the components of thought and action you think should always be involved. Third, the guidelines you develop need to be personally useful when you give direction. What works for others will not necessarily be the best tactic for you.

Many new teachers and parents develop their framework for managing students/children by using techniques employed by their own most effective teachers/parents. They note techniques they feel were ineffective or would not be effective given their own personality and preferences. You can begin the same way.

It may be difficult to tell when your framework is sufficiently mature to be useful. The above three suggestions provide you with ways to test how well you are doing at developing your framework. (If it helps, see Table 5.1 to get a sense of our own framework.) When your framework can provide those three chunks of orientation for you, it and you are ready to go. By then, your framework should represent

Table 5.1	Our Frameworks Show the Bias of Our Values

Our *framework for giving direction well* is evident throughout this book. For example:

- *Our philosophy* includes the citizenship argument we make in Chapters 1 and 7 about everyone having the responsibility to help their group to thrive.

- *Our exemplar model* includes (1) everyone in a group (2) co-constructing the (3) grouping and (4) direction-giving needed (5) so that the group can thrive (6) in response to changing exigencies (7) that require different direction-giving types.

- Context-specific *guidelines* can be found throughout the book and complete our framework. For example, one set of guidelines is to make certain that each group we are in serves all three functions well—task, relational, and individual—and earns at least one process prize (see Chapter 4). Other guidelines are for how each type of direction-giver should credential and what they need to do to communicate well (Chapters 2, 3, and 6). We emphasize different skills in different situations (e.g., competence, initiative, credibility, adaptability, affiliative receptivity, emotional intelligence, resilience, self-efficacy, rhetorical sensitivity, marshaling resources, and articulating vision). In later chapters, we discuss how to co-construct the kinds of stories that shape future effective grouping experiences and the framing skills involved in doing so.

After taking more than two decades to build our framework for giving direction well, writing it all down now takes a book to accomplish. (In addition, our framework for grouping well requires a second book; see Burtis & Turman, 2006.) But we are trying to anticipate the needs of people in any type of group. Building your own framework can be much more specific and should take you nowhere near as long, though you will probably be refining your framework for many years.

you well enough that you are willing to share it with others. You should be able to use it to explain how you orient to grouping and direction-giving. It can be a subject for conversation if you ever interview for a direction-giving position.

❖ YOUR PHILOSOPHY SHOULD PUT YOUR VALUES INTO YOUR FRAMEWORK AND THEN INTO ACTION

A *philosophy* shows the values and preferences that undergird your framework. For example, the "scientific manager" is told to make the "economic man" assumption: not to waste energy showing concern for the feelings of an employee. Your framework philosophy should express your orientation to the direction-giving task, showing the principles and ideals you value. Your philosophy should suggest the values you want to employ as you decide how you intend to behave. Your philosophy can be useful in explanations you provide to yourself and to others when you need to sort out, explain, or justify your choices.

For example, familiar phrases from founding, governing, and ceremonial documents for the United States of America include a number of philosophy statements (e.g., all men are created equal; government of the people, by the people, for the people; life, liberty, and the pursuit of happiness; endowed by their creator with unalienable rights). Such philosophy statements undergird the grouping attempt called the United States. What philosophy do you want undergirding your own grouping and direction-giving efforts?

You can begin by trying to create your own philosophy or by borrowing someone else's. Think about the kind of philosophies others must have had whose direction-giving you admire. Think about what principles, preferences, and ideals you take with you into grouping and direction-giving interactions. How do you orient yourself to grouping and to direction-giving?

Something to Consider: Your Metaphors Matter

Do you think of the people with whom you group as beasts of burden, stepping stones, friends, competitors, or spiritual beings? Are you their boss, buddy, god, mentor, coach. Are you the bane of their existence or a resource for them? Do you think of your context as "don't take it personally, it's just business," or are you part of a team? Do you imagine that as a direction-giver you are like a gardener, chef, bricklayer, police detective, or drill sergeant? Are you conducting a symphony, being a nurturing parent, or acting as the mortar that holds the bricks together? Are you a painter, the paintbrush, the paint, or the canvas? *Words that appeal and those that do not give you signs of your philosophy.*

Your philosophy should help breathe life into your exemplar model, guidelines, and direction-giving acts, so be specific about what you value and how that should play out in your interactions.

❖ YOUR EXEMPLARS PROVIDE ASPIRATIONAL STORIES AND A SENSE OF WHAT "THE BEST" CAN BE

An *exemplar* is an excellent and useful example of something. An *exemplar model* shows what any ideal or aspirational case should involve. Both provide useful sources for reflection. Exemplars might include people you think best personify what it is you value. Perhaps you can think of someone who is gifted at a particular aspect of giving direction well or who epitomizes a balance between concern for giving direction effectively and for living life well. Your exemplars might include a teacher who helps you embrace a subject or a coach effective at making you feel like an important part of the team though you rarely enter a game.

Exemplar models might manifest in a variety of forms. They can be a chart or drawing that identifies what is involved while giving direction (see the P.I.E. equation that follows). Perhaps your exemplar model is a biography, visual representation (e.g., the pictures of model cuts in a hair salon), or something else that stokes and shapes aspirations, principles, or ideals (e.g., the visage of Susan B. Anthony or of Sojourner Truth or a key phrase such as "Ain't I a woman?"). Exemplars and exemplar models help you see how direction-giving should look when it is done well and, in particular, what ought to be involved.

Direction-giving is easy as P.I.E.		
Personal ***Passion*** about our project, which is contagious and picked up by others as you	+ gain ***Insight*** into their needs because of your willingness to spend time with them	= makes you more likely to be ***Effective*** as a direction-giver for them

It can help to identify and study people you think are exemplary direction-givers. Who do you think of as an ideal manager—someone who accomplishes great good for the group by marshaling resources within the powers of his or her position? Do you know someone who is an especially effective doer—someone whose initiative and competence is absolutely vital to a group? Who is an ideal guide—someone with credibility who your group turns to in many moments of need? Who is the best follower you know, and how does he or she translate someone else's ideas into group momentum? Can you name a leader who embodies a vision made salient by crisis? What does each of these people do that makes you think that they give direction well? In short, observing others provide direction well, reading about them after the fact, studying the theories in Chapter 4, and trying to figure out the key ingredients involved can all help inform and shape your model.

Do not make the process more difficult than it has to be. Keep your philosophy in mind and, based on your exemplars, draw a model that you think includes the key aspects of effective direction-giving and how they relate to one another. You might need one model for each kind of direction-giver, or you might be able to integrate several or all of the types into a single model. You might find it easier (and have some fun) if you imagine your model as a picture or in the form of a metaphor (e.g., grouping is a winding road; direction-giving is a plane in flight; giving direction is an improvisational dance; direction-giving is building a house). Drawing a picture or thinking through a metaphor can help you see the components and dynamics involved and how they interconnect.

❖ YOUR GUIDELINES ANIMATE YOUR PHILOSOPHY AND EXEMPLARS IN YOUR OWN DIRECTION-GIVING

Guidelines provide practical advice. Guidelines can include processes or procedures you think will help you to experience success. Any nuggets, rules, observations, tips, tactics, and strategies you collect can be made into useful guidelines. You collect your guidelines over time by (1) noticing the recurring kinds of circumstances you face in your group and by (2) keeping track of anything that works well again and again for you and for others.

As you develop your guidelines, continually compare them to your philosophy and exemplar model to make sure they are consistent and mutually reinforcing. Become a student of the process of direction-giving. Compare your guidelines to the theories others develop for giving direction (see Chapter 4). For example, consider which of your personality traits you want to emphasize as you give direction. What direction-giving style and powerbase choices do you hope to feature most prominently? Put those thoughts into your guidelines. Which contingencies concern you enough that you want guidelines on how to behave differently because of them? When do you most want to emphasize relationships and when to emphasize task? And so forth.

When you have a philosophy, exemplar model, and working set of guidelines, you have the start of your framework for giving direction well. Keep working on your framework until you become confident about it, familiar with it, and adept at using it. Heed four warnings as you do.

First, make certain that you keep your sense of values intact. Incorporate them into how you approach direction-giving. Your values are principles and ideals that you use to guide your assessments of what is important and good. Your values should manifest in how you orient yourself to your grouping and to giving direction: They should manifest in the choices you make as a direction-giver. Otherwise, the values of others or the impersonality of business, a community mind-set, or movement myopia will sweep you up into actions you may later regret.

Second, make certain that your framework is informed by an understanding of your rhetorical resources. You make choices whenever you pick between available options as a direction-giver. Such direction-giving choices have a rhetorical element to them. For example, each choice you make about how to frame the group's situation and how to explain your actions as a direction-giver is a rhetorical choice. Each is either more or less likely to be effective at influencing others than the alternative options you reject. The best choice is one that helps you give direction well, helps your group to thrive, and breathes your values into your direction-giving in an authentic way. Rhetorical resources are available to you only to the extent that you are aware of them. *If you do not see that you have options, then you will not make good choices.*

Third, your framework should be refined over time. It should be informed by new information and experiences you pick up along your way. If you stop refining your framework, you close yourself off from the next good idea and limit your potential.

Fourth, if you want to play more of a role in helping your group to thrive, you should use your framework to help advance your cause as a potential direction-giver. It takes time to develop the credentials necessary to earn a key direction-giving position (see Chapters 1–3). It takes shared experiences that show others that you can be trusted in such a role. Your interactions with others are important from the very beginning of grouping—or, starting today.

❖ POSITION YOURSELF AS A KEY DIRECTION-GIVER IN THE STORY OF YOUR GROUP

Positioning is helping others understand the resources you offer the group as a direction-giver. Positioning tells others where you want your potential contributions and talents to fit on their palate of direction-giver options. If they do not know what skills you can provide, they will not look to you as their need for direction arises.

As you are positioning, keep in mind that your potential contributions are always relative to what others put on your group's palate. When something is relative, it is judged in comparison to something else. It changes or fluctuates in value according to the comparison being drawn. If you position yourself well, others will often reach for the resource(s) that you want to provide.

When you want to make a contribution to your group, you must compete with others for the group's attention and interest. All involved have a vested interest in shaping the group's direction. Whether you are aware of it or not, this brings competition into group processes. Theater provides a context in which the competitions are easily evident. For example, the give-and-take of the audition process plays out as competitive, comparative choices made in casting decisions for minor and major characters. Actors are interested in performing well and to be perceived by others as doing so. A second example is competing for a spot in the starting lineup on a team. In both cases, group members want their contributions to be valued and to play a key role in determining audience reaction on opening night.

There is never a guarantee that others will listen to you and value the contributions you seek to provide. You have to earn attention, interest, and respect. All of that is made difficult by the fact that everyone else in the group may also have something they want to contribute. When we want to make a contribution, we enter the competition.

Becoming a key direction-giver (Chapter 1) is an unusual process because you are both a participant in it and also one of the judges or referees. For example, you may perceive yourself as an average member of your community, organization, or team. That perception results in your sense that you should not overdo your direction-giving attempts. However, the perceptions of others in your group may be different. Some may consider you a key direction-giver, looking to you repeatedly on particular subjects or under particular circumstances. Or, you might consider yourself a skilled and important member of your group only to find that others are not willing to follow your direction. What then? Well, let's understand the nature of the competition.

❖ A PROCESS OF RESIDUES HELPS US DECIDE ON WHOM WE WILL FOCUS OUR ATTENTION

Upon meeting new people and getting to work with them, we often and immediately engage in monitoring our own performances and assessing how those stack up against the efforts of others. These processes do not turn off once we come to our initial conclusions. As we continue to interact, we continue to assess others and ourselves. We compare our strengths and our faults. As we interact, we figure out who is invested in the competition and who is mostly a bystander. We develop hierarchies about whom to trust, help, seek direction from, and so forth.

To decide from whom to receive direction, we usually start by eliminating folks from consideration. People who do not contribute during grouping interactions and people whose contributions are judged to be lacking (e.g., too biased, dogmatic, or strident) are eliminated from our consideration (or given a lower priority for our attentions) until we are left with those who we trust the most or whose contributions most interest us.

The *method of residues* is the name given the process by which we figure out first who not to consider until we are left with the people we are most willing to consider (Bormann, 1975; 1996). This process is informal, a sort of interaction-based negotiation. It is usually not done in a particularly cruel or overt manner (except when children chose teams during recess). We just start paying more attention to people whose potential for giving direction we place closer to the center of our palate of choices. In office politics, everyone has a sense of who might be the next one promoted by knowing who is not likely to move up. That is evidence of this process in play.

Every group involves an ongoing swirl of thoughts regarding where to focus attention. During the initial stages of a presidential race, for example, a large pool of candidates is likely to form. Some of these individuals will appear to be reasonable candidates, and others get labeled as "long shots" from the get-go. The process unfolds with individuals getting dropped from consideration fairly quickly as party loyalists swing support to the one or a few candidates they think can build momentum.

In new groups, the method of residues is clearly necessary, but the process is ongoing in every group, even those with established hierarchies and elaborate descriptions for their key direction-giving positions. We continually assess our fellows: the quality of their contributions, whether we are willing to receive direction from them, and how they compare to us.

As we interact with others, we and they develop a sense for how to make future choices. How you behave, how you interact with others, and even the private communications you share (hastily scrawled notes, offhand comments in the restroom, e-mails, or text messages) all affect the willingness of others to trust you. *People in your group are trained by you over time, through experiences you share with them, to rely more and more (or less and less) on you as someone whose ideas and support are valuable.* You are more likely to be successful in this competition if you know it is under way, that you are involved, and play to win: It is, you are, and you can!

❖ TAKE STOCK OF THE CREDENTIALS YOU HAVE AND WHAT CAN YOU DO TO HELP YOUR GROUP THRIVE

Credentialing yourself is part of the process of positioning (see Chapters 2 and 3). Credentialing helps your attempts to position yourself and it helps others assess the resources you make available to them. By sharing information (e.g., about yourself, your experiences, your family), you work to build trust with other group members. You establish a situated identity so that others can know how to deal with you, at least in the context of the immediate interaction. The particular identity you strive to develop for others then becomes a warrant in support of your claim that you are a knowledgeable and sincere person: one worthy of their attention (Ryfe, 2006, pp. 78–79).

Take an inventory of what you have to offer your group that can help it to thrive. Then, figure out what you need to do or say as opportunities arise to credential so that others can find out what you have in your inventory of resources for the group. You may even need to figure out how to make certain that the opportunity to credential "arises."

It is a significant problem if you are unwilling or unable to toot your own horn in this way: just as damaging to your prospects and to the group's ability to tap your resources as attempts to credential that are inappropriate or that go poorly. Accept the fact that credentialing well is part of a dance that you need to learn to do with ease and grace. It is a necessary and useful process, as helpful to others in the choices they must make as it is to your own prospects. *Your credentialing task is to find ways to enhance your opportunities to serve your group.*

❖ RECURRING TYPES OF SITUATIONS CAN HELP PUT CONTEXT TO YOUR DIRECTION-GIVING PREPARATIONS

A few clusters of recurring circumstances can give you contexts for which to prepare (Burtis, 1999). You can expect to have to deal with these recurring issues at some point in your life (see Table 5.2). These are *direction-conducive* groups because a recurring problem in them

Table 5.2   Recurring Sets of Circumstances: Direction-Conducive Groups

Group type	Indicators
The confused or immature group	• Ambiguous task or immature group/members result in wheel-spinning. • People fear taking risks. • Confusion and frustration snowball into irrelevant, diverting conflict.
The inefficient or ineffective group	• Grouping activities fail to focus on key grouping exigencies. • Nobody is working effectively on grouping issues. • Unorganized or duplicated efforts diminish group outcomes.
The lazy or unmotivated group	• Work gets done poorly if at all: Satisficing/cutting corners is normative. • People are not motivated to exert the energy needed to act.
The pressured or crisis[a] group	• Pressures from a looming deadline or assessment/evaluation create exigencies that panic grouping efforts: Diversions into worry or unproductive tensions may result. • Unexpected task or contingencies reshuffle the group's deck of cards.
The struggling, divided,[a] or grumbly group	• Disagreements run deep about proper framing of the group situation, about the best way/process for proceeding, about the direction-giving roles to be played, or about where the group ought to strive to go. • Members are wary with each other if not outright upset. Attempts to act tend to renew old conflicts that derail effective grouping. • Sensitivities run high and eggshell walking limits effective acts: people fear or eschew (and avoid the risk of) trying again.

a. Communities where crisis is acute and/or those where contested communications are chronic both have their own special needs (e.g., between labor and management; in partisan politics; in competitive sports). There are also times when the group's very survival is threatened by crisis. We discuss these situations in more detail in Chapter 10 because the talents required of managers and guides change under such circumstances and because leadership can sometimes be required to address certain types of crises.

primes grouping members to desire a change in group direction. In a direction-conducive group, people want direction and are willing to receive it.

When your group faces such circumstances, it needs you and others to give it direction. Considering such recurring types of problem groups as you prepare your framework can help prepare you to face the issues they tend to create. Credentialing your abilities when facing such circumstances can help you position yourself as a key direction-giver when the need arises.

❖ SOME ADVICE THAT MAY BE USEFUL AS YOU POSITION YOURSELF

Some basics for positioning yourself are generally effective across many types of groups because they are actually also suggestions for giving direction well. You must figure out how to integrate these ideas into your specific situation, especially which are best suited to the needs of your group and to your own tendencies and strengths. We start with two general strategies that frame the rest of our advice. First, *make a decision to work for the good of the group.* Second, *exhibit a desire to be a direction-giver* (Bormann, 1975). See Table 5.3 for tactics employed by successful practitioners, which can help flesh out the strategies (Bormann & Bormann, 1996). You might decide to use some of these tactics as guidelines in your personal direction-giving framework.

Research results provide corroboration. People who attain key direction-giver roles tend to be verbally active, demonstrate communication skill, and initiate ideas. They busy themselves "introducing and formulating goals, tasks, procedures; eliciting communication from other group members; delegating, directing action; showing consideration for group activity; integrating and summarizing group activity" (Geier, 1967, p. 316). People tend to like to receive direction from those who express their own opinions and who show interest in the opinions of others. We appreciate those who get involved in helping put structure to the flow of ideas in our group and to the decisions the group makes regarding who will provide direction (B. A. Fisher, 1980).

Such lists of behaviors show potential rhetorical resources for your direction-giving choices in almost every facet of grouping. Make and refine your own list of guidelines: short enough to be easily useful. Do not try to include everything. Pick tools that best suit you and your group. Make choices based on what you know about yourself and on

Table 5.3　Tactics or Guidelines for Effective Direction-Giving

Tactic or Guideline	Example
Speak up	Make contributions that show your active commitment, but do not dominate talk time—allow others their say as well.
Don't force the group to dwell on what you think are the best ideas	State your best ideas, but do not assume you are the only source of wisdom. You may be wrong, there may be another way, and others want to be involved too—providing "the best idea" is high-status work.
Help structure the group	Understand processes that groups go through and show the group how to set itself up, to make plans, and to develop its processes.
Take readings of group opinions	Ask others what they think. Observe nonverbal reactions to the direction offered or provided by others. Ask for a straw poll.
Help the group make decisions	Note instances when the group should be moving toward resolution and help them get there. Suggest courses of action.
Do your homework	Between interactions: do research to learn about the subject and to find supporting evidence for sensible ideas. Figure out how to state your findings clearly.
Be informed about your group's work	Understand your group's purpose and charge. Stay up to date on basic issues and important interactions.
Plan for the good of the group	Keep the group charge and group members at the forefront of your concerns as you make decisions.
Put in extra time	Work as hard as or harder than others in the group.
Make personal sacrifices	Volunteer to help other group members. Do even low-status tasks with enthusiasm based in wanting the group to thrive.
Do not worry about who gets credit for work or ideas and give credit to others	Share credit and seek ways to note contributions of others. Avoid having group outcomes attributed to you alone—focus on and talk about how others were engaged.
Do not be a manipulator	Approach grouping openly, without a hidden agenda.

how you want to position yourself and to credential your potential contributions.

Figure out how your potential contributions might become compelling to other people. Start thinking about how your contributions could become part of the story of your group's experience. How could what you have to offer help shape your group? How could your contributions become part of the "group logic" others use as they make their choices? To do so, consider the reasons people have for picking one potential direction over another and for following one direction-giver over another. To do that, you need to understand how folks use reasons as they make their choices among direction-givers.

When someone offers direction to a group, that person makes a claim. The claim is that the direction he or she offers the group is worthy of their consideration. A *claim* is an idea bound with controversy. Others may disagree with a claim. If you say "let's do X," others may agree, disagree, or ignore what you say. The controversy is over which response to give to your offered direction. If you say, "Do X" and Sonya says, "No, let's do Y," the controversy is in which claim the group ought to accept (or neither), which includes the issue of from which person the group ought to accept direction. Whenever you offer direction, you make a claim (see Chapter 9).

A *warrant* is a reason for accepting one controversial claim over an alternative course of action. When you attempt to give direction, the warrant is any reason you state or that others might already have for accepting that direction. "You know me from way back" is a warrant you might say out loud (or just implicitly rely upon) to get a friend to follow your lead. "I trust her" is a warrant someone else might have for accepting direction from Sonya. "His idea was closest to my own" is a warrant a third person might find compelling. When you make a choice to follow, you are accepting a claim for some reason or warrant that is compelling to you.

Four general warrants are used to support direction-giving claims (Burtis, 1997, 2004a, 2004b). One or more of them is in play each time someone tries to give direction to a group even if the warrant is not explicit. The direction-giver's claim begins with some version of "follow me" (also either implied or explicit). The success of the claim rests on the "because" statement, provided by the warrant (see Table 5.4). Of course, you have to fill in the particulars from your group, but these four options are always available resources for you. You can refer to them when you have a concern you find difficult to focus. You can use them to help you find a way to give direction to your group.

Table 5.4	Warrants Provide Reasons to Accept Your Direction-Giving Attempt

Purgatory rhetoric argues "follow me *because* of *problems in our current system* that we must escape." This rhetoric creates energy for group action through a story of inadequacy in our status quo (a complaint). For example, what the group is or what it has accomplished is just not right. We are better or more noble/gifted than this. We have got to find a way to change this messed-up situation: to escape it; to purge our problem.

The Way rhetoric argues "follow me *this way because* it is the path to escape." This rhetoric focuses on the technique or process or orientation in play for our grouping effort to create energy and direction for the next step the group needs to take (e.g., "let's try brainstorming"; "we all need to start showing up on time"; "buck up; we can do this"; "ask not what your country can do for you ask what you can do for your country").

Vision rhetoric argues "follow me to *there, to that new place where we should end up, that goal or vision we need to achieve, because that outcome should be our aspiration.*" This rhetoric creates energy for the group from the desire we have to achieve a final product or outcome; to reach our promised land.

Savior rhetoric argues "follow me *because* of *who I am, my experiences, or my competencies; because of what I have done to help us; because of how well I personify us, our values, our process, or our vision.*" This rhetoric creates energy for following a particular group member.

These four claims and warrants provide the grouping and direction-receiving logics people use. Any direction-giving attempt employs one or more of these warrants if it is to be a serious contender. Use these warrants to frame your contributions to your group's story.

If you oppose the direction-giving someone is trying to sell to your group, you can use the same four warrants adjusted into opposition (see Table 5.5; Burtis, 2004a, 2004b). This set may be useful as you consider whether to follow (Frye et al., 2007; Perreault, 1997). It is also useful if you want to provide an elaborated alternative.

Counter-direction-giving rhetoric argues either that there is no need to heed a direction-giver or that disadvantages will come if you

Table 5.5	Counter-Direction-Giving and Alternative-Direction-Giving Warrants

Purgatory oppositional rhetoric argues "you don't need to follow anyone because we don't need to escape our current system" or "because any problem with our status quo is being dealt with adequately already" or "because any problem we have will be made worse by action." This rhetoric creates energy against change with a story of adequacy or safety about the status quo.

The Way oppositional rhetoric argues "you don't need to follow anyone because we don't need to go anywhere" or "because the means we now employ are fine" or "because changing the process we use will be dangerous or will waste our efforts so far." This rhetoric creates energy against new grouping processes by arguing we should not go down any path at all or we should continue on the same path we are already taking.

Vision opposition rhetoric argues "you don't need to follow anyone because there is 'no place like home'" or "because the new place would destroy our old place" or "because the new place is filled with bad stuff." This rhetoric creates energy against a vision from the desire to conserve the status quo or from the fear of unintended and unknown consequences of change.

Savior opposition rhetoric argues "you don't need to follow anyone because we have no reason to follow anyone if we aren't going anywhere" or "because trusting someone else instead of our current direction-givers (or making your own autonomous choices) is bad" or "because that new direction-giver has bad sense, lacks your values, or bears you malice." This rhetoric creates energy against a particular direction-giver regardless of what he or she proposes.

do. Alternative-direction-giving[2] rhetoric responds to a direction-giving attempt by arguing for focus on an alternative problem, process, goal, and/or direction-giver. Direction-giving attempts and those of opposition employ the same rhetorical resources and warrants. Learning these basics can inform your own framework.

---

[2]Alternate-direction-giving rhetoric might also manifest when someone employs the same direction-changing warrants but not with the same level of force or exigency: "I agree with all of what she is saying but think that the options she is giving to us are too extreme."

❖ IN CONCLUSION

When giving direction, the choices you make have to work well both for you and for those with whom you interact. To figure out how to deal with others, become a student of the process. Try on various tactics and strategies, observe others interacting, read books, and listen to what expert practitioners and scholars have to say. In the end, you need to sort out all of the information and experience, keeping and organizing the ideas and actions that seem to work best for you.

Develop a framework to help guide your future choices and actions. The most important ideas, including the ones that seem to work particularly well, need to be privileged in your framework: prioritized for use in similar clusters of circumstances over time. Keep your framework flexible enough to adapt to new information and experience. Adjust what you do to position yourself and to help your group given the vagaries of shifting circumstances and the people you need to engage.

Competition for playing a key direction-giving role can be as intense as it is informal and implicit. When possible, we encourage gentle discussion, seeking fulfillment from a true dialog where unencumbered minds meet without competition. But the nitty-gritty of grouping often blows right past such ideals. Gird your loins. It can be downright difficult to get others to heed what you say. Becoming and acting as a key direction-giver is an energy-intensive enterprise. The only way to get good at it is to focus yourself and your efforts. Be intentional. Develop your framework, and then climb aboard your group's particular palate of preferred potential providers.

UNIT III

Develop Your Communication Skills to Enhance Your Direction-Giving

6

Figure Out How to Communicate Effectively

To be effective as a direction-giver, you need to be able to communicate well. Even if you plan to be a sole proprietor, you will need to "sell" your business plan to a banker, explain your business to a lawyer, develop your concept into a marketing strategy, and describe pertinent details to any number of individuals who help distribute your product, provide your service, or buy something from you. You have to be able to articulate a story of something worthwhile for others to engage (e.g., a story describing anticipatory experiences of future success if they work with you). Whether you require venture capital, government licensing, a location, employees, customers, or a potential partner, all steps to success involve communication.

This is the first of two chapters in the third unit: *develop your communication skills to enhance your direction-giving.* In it, we discuss the nature of communication, including why we communicate and skills that help us be effective.

❖ COMMUNICATION IS A TOOL USED TO TRANSFER INFORMATION AND A PROCESS FOR MAKING MEANING

What is this communication stuff that is so important? Communication is a tool for transferring information (Shannon & Weaver, 1949). Communication is also a dynamic process through which people co-construct what is meaningful to them and to their group (Burtis, 1988, 1989, 1991; Burtis & Turman, 2006). We need both definitions to address the basic issues involved whenever you try to give direction to others. We discuss each in its turn.

❖ ACCURATE TRANSFER OF INFORMATION REQUIRES FIDELITY

Communication is a transfer of information. When a company is facing financial uncertainty, requiring the CEO to make significant cuts and changes in group processes, she or he must send sufficiently clear messages so that others can figure out how to think and behave as required for their work in the new realities they face. She or he must accurately transfer information about their new reality. Effective communication is an accurate transfer of information.

Information is anything that reduces uncertainty or unpredictability: for the person you address or between that person and you. The "information" that gets transferred may be data, ideas, opinions, preferences, worries, explanations: any conceivable type of message. For example, providing evidence of the company's poor financial situation and projections regarding its potential, impending demise can be scary information but it is also probably a necessary first step for reducing the uncertainty an executive committee has about the options they face.

Something to Think About and Discuss With Others: Uncertainty or Unpredictability Is Not Confusion or Ambiguity

Don't mistake reducing your uncertainty with reducing your confusion. Sometimes getting new information increases your confusion and concerns even as it reduces your uncertainty regarding the situation you now face. The second before your boss tells you that half of the jobs in your unit are about to be cut, your own job is already in jeopardy, but you do not know that is so. Your status becomes less uncertain to you when you get the new information: even as your psychological confusion about what to do and the ambiguity you sense about exploring your options both increase. Certainty correlates with predictability: The more predictable your communications make a situation, the less uncertainty in it.

In fact, parts of a message may decrease uncertainty while others parts add to your confusion. A *message* may include *verbal* content (i.e., written or spoken words, sign language, e-mail, text messages, phone calls, snail-mail, sky-writing, etc.) and will include *nonverbal* content (meaningful behavior beyond words: e.g., body movement and gestures, eye contact, artifacts and clothing, vocal variety, touch, timing, etc.). *Intentionally or not, both verbal and nonverbal content is part of the information that is transferred in a message.* If nonverbal cues do not align with the verbal message, ambiguity is introduced even as uncertainty is decreased.

If your boss Trudy tells you everything is going to be okay but is sweating profusely, refuses to make eye contact, and then, upon her departure, the office manager tells you Trudy has sold all her shares in the company and has a one-way ticket to Guam, there is a lot of information contradicting the verbal message. Something is amiss. Your uncertainty decreases as information comes in; even the ambiguous information increases your certainty.

This first definition emphasizes the important work the speaker or writer (*source*) can do to carefully consider and then to craft what he or she says, does, or writes (*message*) to give direction well to some reader, observer, or listener (*receiver*). The criterion for assessing whether this type of communication is effective is the level of fidelity that results between the source and receiver (Powers & Witt, 2008).

Messages have *fidelity* to the extent that the receiver of the message learns what the source intends. In some cases, "the most basic element of the human communication process is the degree of accuracy with which human beings can stimulate, produce, and/or reproduce within each other a specific set of desired cognitions [e.g., a mental image, thought, feeling, or orientation]" (Powers & Witt, 2008, p. 247). *High fidelity* means the receiver gets exactly the information the source intends to transfer (our company will fail unless we eliminate 2,000 jobs). *Low fidelity* means the receiver gets something other (or less) than what the source intends to transfer (if we are in trouble, I need to start cutting corners on quality control to save bucks).

According to this definition, communication is effective when fidelity is high: when thoughts in your brain as the source get transferred in pristine form to your receiver's brain. It is ineffective when your attempt does not accomplish the desired transfer of information, and it is ineffective when your attempt is entirely *redundant*—i.e., nothing new[1] is learned, so uncertainty is not reduced. Grouping people must be able to transfer information accurately in order to be effective. However, more is required.

❖ MAKING MEANING INVOLVES FINDING THE UTILITY INVOLVED

Something sometimes seems to go wrong during or after a transfer of information. In the 2008 U.S. presidential campaign, candidate John McCain said that "the United States economy is fundamentally strong." He later said his intent was to suggest that the "American workforce," the backbone of the U.S. economy, was fundamentally sound. Barack Obama's campaign used the "fundamentally strong" statement to argue that the former war hero was "out of touch." A speaker's own words are used again and again to show that he is not to be trusted on economic matters. McCain's message becomes meaningful in an entirely different way than he intends. There is no fidelity for him, though his words resonate with others in a way that they find useful. This example helps show why we need a second definition for communication.

Communication is the process of making meaning. Effective communication creates meaning that is useful, whether we intend the particular meaning or not. The question becomes, "Do we serve our own purposes when we attempt to communicate, or does our effort turn counterproductive?" It dismays us when what we intend to say gets misunderstood or twisted by a receiver. Sometimes, a receiver seems to make up his or her own meanings entirely in response to what we say. The second definition focuses on the process involved while communicating: a process that is not bound by a particular message "transferred" at some specific point in time.

---

[1]Redundancy includes when nothing new is learned in this context or nothing new is shared between these communicators or nothing expressed is accomplished in a manner that is meaningful.

Figure 6.1

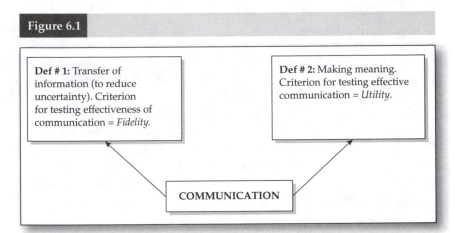

Def # 1: Transfer of information (to reduce uncertainty). Criterion for testing effectiveness of communication = *Fidelity*.

Def # 2: Making meaning. Criterion for testing effective communication = *Utility*.

COMMUNICATION

Making meaning emphasizes the creative engagement of the people involved in an attempt to communicate. At issue is not whether information gets transferred in a given moment. Rather, the issue is *what meanings get co-constructed over time as a consequence of all pertinent interactions* (including those with people whose contributions are still in play, although they are no longer present). Making meaning is much less tidy than a transfer of information.

The second definition assumes that a complex of dynamics is involved so that neither the source nor the receiver can control alone whether an attempt to communicate is successful. The criterion for assessing communication with this second definition is *utility:* Does the meaning we construct serve a function for one or more of us? If so, the communication attempt has utility (see Figure 6.1). Something useful is made of it regardless of the fidelity that meaning shares with the source's or receiver's desires. To test communication effectiveness, you do not compare the information a receiver has against what the source intends. Rather, you identify the uses or utility being put to the communication attempt by one or more of those involved.

Something to Think About and Discuss With Others

To make meaning for a word, we can attempt to attach a definition to it. If our definition is accepted by the person we talk to, we can say we share a meaning for the word. If our definition is rejected, we have not yet "made meaning" in the sense that we have not yet found a definition on which we can agree. However, we may have "made meaning" in another sense (e.g., we now understand where we disagree; each of us is now more certain about our own idea).

(Continued)

(Continued)

When we talk with someone else, each of us makes our own meanings out of the experience. If a stranger says, "I am a lion and I eat red meat," while you are waiting on a bench for a bus to Eugene, Oregon, what happens next? That experience can be meaningful for you if you develop a sense that the stranger is not safe to be around. Perhaps you walk away without speaking. You could be dismayed with yourself because of your intolerance toward strangers. Likely, the stranger will also develop a sense (if any sense remains in that head) of how to get a bench all to himself: a tale he may take to his classroom of students awaiting his report on their little "the bench and the red-meat" research project.

Making is the process for (co-)constructing something (e.g., a house; a personal meaning; an interpretation of experiences we share). Making involves pulling together resources that seem pertinent to the task at hand, from wherever we can find them. When what we are making is meaning, the making includes attaching a definition, interpretation, or framing to something. We do so by creating an association between something new and something familiar. We pull resources from past experiences and from our aspirations for future experiences. We consider ideas we create ourselves and ideas that others share with us. We draw the context and our personal preferences into the making. *We do not work alone in a vacuum filled only by the information someone wants to transfer.*

Meaning is the significance we attach to something because of experience we have with that something. A new business owner might save the first dollar she earns to mark something important (success; future prosperity; self-employment after years of working for others). To others, the dollar may have no meaning beyond its exchange value. When we claim that "X means Y" or that "X is meaningful" to us, we attach significance to X. We give it meaning.

Making attachments and associations is the process we use to make meaning. A meaning could be the definition we associate with or try to attach to a word. A meaning can be a word, idea, feeling, story, or action that we associate with a behavior, person, or event. For example, each meaning we have for an experience is an interpretation we associate with the experience because we think it helps frame and explain the experience. What is meaningful to us includes whatever cluster of attachments we pull together as our interpretation of the experience. The words, stories, and feelings we include in our cluster of attachments all comprise our sense of the meaning of the thing.

Rarely is the meaning we make solely the product of a bit of information some source just tried to transfer to us.

That is the nature of *process:* It involves a complex hierarchy of interrelated and meaningful attachments we have already made and are continuing to develop, which trickle into our present and future group experiences. *Process* is a word that represents ongoing, unfolding, dynamic, nonlinear meaning making. The meanings we make are often not complete or fully worked out. They are rarely static. They are subject to change in the initial moments of an experience, immediately after an experience, as we compare one experience to another, as we share stories of our experiences with others, and on into the future as we have time to reflect.

Whenever we communicate, new message content is always subjected to integration into our preexisting hierarchy of what is meaningful to us. When someone sends a message or talks to us, we experience that event as part of an ongoing process. We interpret the verbal and the nonverbal content of the message. We integrate aspects of the context into what gets communicated (are we in a good mood? has it been a long day?) along with past experiences we have had with the source (has she been trustworthy in the past?) and with other people on the same or related subjects (is this new message consistent with what our co-workers are saying?). We do all of that as we interpret what is meaningful about the message. So, the message may be relatively simple, but the cluster of attachments that result is likely more complicated.

Something to Think About and Discuss With Others

Which do you think matters more, the ability to transfer information with fidelity or the ability to create meanings that have some particular usefulness for the people who are communicating? Sometimes your efforts to communicate can accomplish both—you can accurately transfer information that has utility for both of you. But sometimes the two (fidelity vs. utility) are at odds with each other. Sometimes you have to decide whether you are more concerned with getting your own point across and accepted or more concerned with the ongoing relationship you need to accomplish your shared task. Sometimes an attempt to transfer information might fail to reduce uncertainty but still will be appreciated because the source "made an effort" to reach out. At issue: Which approach to communication do you emphasize in your direction-giving? Under what circumstances is it more important that the other person understand exactly what it is you want him or her to know? Under what circumstances is that less important than that you and the other person come to some level of understanding that may prove to be useful to one or both of you, even if you do not come away from your chat thinking the same way or the same thing?

The second definition changes our perspective. Through its lens, we understand that *direction-giving communications are ongoing, intricate, integrated, interactive, improvisational dances* that sometimes work out well, sometimes flow in our favor, and sometimes are strained or go poorly. All such outcomes are possible even when we are doing as we ought when attempting to communicate.

To assess the effectiveness of your own communications, focus on how what you are doing affects grouping. What matters most to a group is whether communications function to enhance group direction (see Chapter 4). Figuring out how communication functions is easier if you understand why people communicate in the first place.

❖ PEOPLE COMMUNICATE FOR PURPOSES OF INQUIRY, TO INFLUENCE OTHERS, AND TO BUILD RELATIONSHIPS

People feel the impulse to interact with others for three basic reasons. We feel the need to understand, the need to influence, and the need for relationship. These needs are so fundamental that we call them imperatives. As long as we are healthy and thriving, we are motivated to inquire, to influence, and to relate (see Table 6.1). Communicating is a process that helps us to address these imperatives.

Television shows and motion pictures often appeal to the needs created by one or more of the imperatives. For example, our need for inquiry—to ask questions and get answers in order to understand—is catered to by the news, by mysteries and whodunits, by the History and Discover channels, and by shows such as *MythBusters*, *Jeopardy*, and *TMZ*. These scratch our itch to know what is going on, who is doing what (with whom), and how we might get involved.

Other shows focus on our need to assert ourselves—scratching our influence itch through vicarious participation in how others get what they want from one another. We like the feelings of competence, power, and triumph when our team prevails or our proxy makes a winning argument (e.g., sports; *Survivor*, *The Apprentice*; lawyer and law enforcement shows; superheroes and others with mysterious powers). We can get extremely upset if our proxy is denied the spoils of victory or influence-corroborating prestige we feel is their due and ours.

Many movies and shows cater to our need for relationships with others. We feel a kinship to those on our favorite soaps and serials. We are fascinated with how other people manage to relate well or poorly

Table 6.1	Imperatives Goad Our Communication, Interaction, and Co-Constructions

Imperative	Description
Inquire	The imperative to make sense of what is happening to us. To wonder; to ask questions; to seek answers; to sort things out. Who am I? Who are we? How do I fit in? What are we doing? What should we be doing? How do I measure up? Why/how did that happen? How can I make it better? What choices do I have? What do you think? Why are you acting like that? What is next?
Influence	The imperative to get others to see things our way or to do what we want. When I speak or act, I do so watching for confirmation or support or compliance from others. I adjust what I do in order to gain your consideration or support. I may need or want you to understand or appreciate or accept or corroborate my idea or behavior. I may need or desire a change in your own thoughts or actions. I use contact with you to make myself feel good or whole or right.
Relate	The imperative to have social contact and to get along with others. To require social contact as its own end or to gain something beyond my ken (beyond the limits of my own knowledge; capacity; comprehension). For example, to desire safety or other good fruits from the power of numbers. I want you to include me; to like me; to respect me. I enjoy or like or respect you and want to affiliate. We must get along well enough to work or play together.

with one another, resulting in lots of movies and shows about families, friends, doctors and patients, and romantic couples. We are even fascinated by stories of the dysfunctional (*House, Scrooge, Hancock*): cut off from the rest of humanity, hoping for them what we hope for ourselves, some sign of a connection to others. We appear almost endlessly interested in stuff like this.

What is an imperative and why does it matter? An *imperative* is something that goads us. It seems to be demanded of us: something we perceive that we must do. The three imperatives are basic impulses that spawn communication. The communication that results often leads us to create groups and to attempt to give direction to our groups.

Understanding these imperatives can help us make judgments about how an individual's communications might be functioning for him or her beyond the actual substance or content of the messages that are sent. If, for example, Fred feels the need to have some influence, to make a difference in the group, the particulars of his message may be less important than whether he feels as though he has had a say, that his voice matters, that he is heard.

Of course, each communicative attempt is spawned among particulars. For example, "I talked to you because I need a loan" or "when she said hi I answered because I do not want to seem unfriendly." However, the millions of possible particulars can be overlaid on the three basic purposes we try to serve through our interactions.

These purposes are part of the reason we try to communicate. Whether these imperatives are served in a given episode, the particulars of the episode might be served. Whether the particulars are served in a given case, one or more of these imperatives might be. That creates some of the mystery in communication. And, consequently, knowing the basic purposes people serve by communicating (in addition to the particulars of a given instance) helps explain why people can seem pleased, or not, with how their interactions are going. It can help you figure out how to interact with others in a manner they appreciate even when you cannot respond to them as they seem to require given the particulars. Understanding interaction at such a basic level can help you give direction well.

In Chapter 1, we said that people group because of exigencies. Well, imperatives are like master exigencies representing clusters of universal human motivations. Throughout our lives, if we remain mentally healthy, we experience these imperatives. Parents who are frustrated with how their child's sports league is managed may feel an exigency to create a new organization that better meets their needs. While the initial exigency for this new attempt to group may stem from something minor and specific (e.g., the cost to participate, the rules in play, the lack of opportunity to participate, and so on), a basic imperative could also be involved. So, each of our communications is based in exigencies that spawn it and in imperative it helps us to serve.

Our ability to communicate enhances our effectiveness for responding to these imperatives: So does our work in groups. We seek the certainty wrought from inquiry. In addition to the particulars in play in one of our groups, we fear lack of influence and loss of relationship. As a consequence, we are motivated by those who seem to know what is going on: to have reasonable answers. We like someone who seems to appreciate our need to make a difference or who seems to like us and to want to affiliate with us. We give such people a lot of leeway for disagreeing with us, as they help us satisfy one of the general imperatives we feel as we group together.

❖ INQUIRY IS THE IMPERATIVE TO MAKE SENSE OF WHAT IS HAPPENING TO YOU

The inquiry imperative manifests in questions you have about what you are experiencing. It stimulates your attempts to make sense of the world (at least the parts of it you care about). When your attention is engaged by something, you want to know more about it: how, who, what, why, when, and where. We need to make something meaningful out of an experience to gain some sense of ourselves in the experience. As we begin to answer our questions, as we form our interpretation, we frame what is happening and what we should do about it. We become more certain and less restive: more comfortable having scratched our inquiry itch.

Inquiry is a part of any situation. When faced with a new grouping situation, you may think, "What is this group?" "What should I be doing in this group?" "Who are these other people?" "How will we get along?" When everything is familiar, we still inquire. We want to know about how we are doing in the eyes of our colleagues. "Are they influenced by us?" "Do they want to keep or to change our relationship?" Every bit of news sets off an inquiry impulse. For example, a co-worker got a raise; a new branch office is going to open up in the next city over. Each starts the mind spinning. What we say and do as we interact in response begins to address our inquiry itch. We scratch out a sense of direction on the subject matter in response to our inquiry.

The imperatives are inherently interrelated as are our responses to them. As we attempt to make sense of and to frame a situation, we are figuring out how we should respond to it. That means we are also shaping an attempt to influence: first our own emotional responses, soon the responses of those with whom we share relevant relationships.

Do you remember the "why" game little children play with an increasingly exasperated parent? A little boy answers every statement or direction given by Dad with an innocent, "But why?" This wonderful case of the inquiry imperative also demonstrates the relationship and influence imperatives. Even at such a young age, the child's questions indicate he is responding to all three imperatives: inquiry (wanting to know the answer), influence (getting Dad to do what he wants him to, which is to keep on talking to him), and relationship (the desire that it be his Dad's work to focus on him, to dialog with him, and to be in relationship with him). The child enjoys continuing to arouse the parent until something is done that makes him reconsider future attempts to communicate in this maddening fashion.

❖ INFLUENCE IS THE IMPERATIVE TO GET OTHERS TO SEE THINGS YOUR WAY OR TO DO WHAT YOU WANT

The influence imperative involves the need each of us has, at times, to get others to do what we want (e.g., you should be buying me a pizza or going on a date with me or working harder or smarter). When we seek to give direction to a group, we are attempting to exert influence. When others agree or comply, we get support for something that we need done. If we "sit on" our ideas and do not allow them to influence others, we remove ourselves from the direction-giving enterprise in a way that probably hurts the group. We have to *go public* with our ideas in order for them be influential.

Going public involves the influence imperative in an even more basic need than getting something we want. We have a need to get others to help us make sense for ourselves of what we are experiencing. We seek this help by asking them to corroborate our views of the experiences we share. For example, "It sure is hot today, isn't it? We probably should cancel the festival." Or, "That S.O.B. crossed the line today—we should do something about it, don't you think?" Both of these are attempts to have influence by receiving corroboration. The influence we exert varies to the extent others *corroborate* or share and support our views regarding what is happening now and what should happen next.

Getting corroboration is a potent concern behind many of our communication attempts. It is as though someone who corroborates our idea or action is somehow confirming who we are in addition. That feels very good. It also explains why we feel hurt (ego-defensive) if someone critiques our ideas or acts, even though criticism is required for improvement. Confirmation is a powerful potion. We seek it for its own sake. It also indicates our influence, which can add to our status and effectiveness. Giving confirmation is a way others indicate we are behaving in a manner that makes sense to them. Their act of corroboration says they are willing to accept our influence on this subject and to affiliate with us in our choices.

❖ RELATIONSHIP IS THE IMPERATIVE TO HAVE SOCIAL CONTACT AND TO GET ALONG WITH OTHERS

Relationships are an imperative both because social beings need to be in contact with other social beings and because the other two imperatives inevitably lead us into contact with one another. Yes, we want friends and acquaintances just because we like being with other people, but we also need them to help us scratch our inquiry and influence itches.

When we seek relationship with others, we immediately invoke the other two imperatives. We ask them questions about themselves and their life experiences, including about other relationships they have. We want to influence them and begin trying out our conceptions on them in the process of seeking corroboration. From time to time, we decide to work together with other people on something, and we often turn to our friends or to other people with whom we already have a relationship to get started. Whenever we start grouping with someone else, it means learning about them, trying to influence them, and developing (more of) a relationship through our grouping activities.

Something to Think About and Discuss With Others

In *Castaway* and *I Am Legend*, our heroes are completely without human contact for a long period of time. Tom Hanks is marooned on an island after his plane crashes, and Will Smith is in a city where every other human (it appears) is dead. In each case, our hero "creates a companion" to talk to, to develop a relationship with: Hanks with a soccer ball he calls Wilson and Smith with a dog he calls Sam. Each responds to the lack of human contact by seeking relationship. It doesn't even seem odd to us that they behave this way. We all know people who treat pets as members of their family. We each feel a relational imperative. The activities we engage in as a result bring us into contact with other people. How does your own need for relationship affect your willingness to try to offer direction to your group? How does it affect your choices about whether and from whom to receive direction?

In sum, the three imperatives provide some of the motivation that is in play during many communication attempts. People will push back against you if you appear to them to be someone who blocks their ability to address their imperatives. For example, others will struggle with you if you keep secrets from them or if you perceive you as denying them access to relationships or to influence they feel that they need or deserve. Consider the lesson of scientific managers who told their "serfs" not to talk and found, as a consequence, that informal groups (relationships) had more influence over productivity than did their own directives (see Chapter 5). As you consider the processes of communicating and of direction-giving, do not ignore how impulses to inquire, to influence, or to relate may play out in ways that shape how people behave.

Every communicative episode, including every direction-giving attempt, has a dual track of assessments going on. One is how well the episode is going on its own terms (the particulars), and the second is how well the episode is helping to satisfy underlying imperatives. You can get a better understanding of resistance you get from others if you consider how what you are doing affects their ability to address their imperatives. They may feel that their words carry too little influence, given how you respond. They may feel that the way you treat them hurts them relationally, perhaps making others in the group look at them with less favor. They may feel that your direction-giving limits their ability to find out what is really going on. Pay attention to these basics as well as to the particulars in your group.

❖ ATTAINING A SYMBOLIC CONVERGENCE OF TERMS, MEANINGS, AND STORIES REQUIRES EFFORT AND SKILL

Your approach to leadership and to other types of direction-giving (see Chapters 2 and 3) should change when you understand that direction-giving communication is always a process and not just a particular event during which a bit of information is transferred. Broadening your horizons this way means lowering expectations for a particular direction-giving act. We understand attempts to provide direction as helping to grow a web of co-constructed meanings around which the group converges over time: a web of meanings that create and sustain the group's direction, processes, and fruits.

Communication makes meanings that range between an individual's idiosyncratic ideas and the co-constructions people share about their experiences together. *Idiosyncratic meanings* are one person's views or ideas that are not shared by others. *Idiosyncratic* means somewhat different, unusual, and peculiar. Though there can be benefits to such differences, it is difficult to base joint, coordinated acts such as grouping and direction-giving in meanings that are held by just one individual. In any communication, there are aspects of the meanings made that are idiosyncratic and aspects that are shared. The key to utility in direction-giving communication is for people to converge around sufficient shared meaning that their communication enhances grouping.

The process we discuss above for making meaning and the imperatives that spawn so much of our communication behavior both begin with idiosyncrasy. However, for grouping to be effective over time, people must begin to converge upon a shared set of words and meanings that they think represent their common concerns, grouping experiences, and desired outcomes (see Chapter 1). These manifest in the group's stories about its past, present, and future experiences. These become a part of what is called the group's symbolic convergence (Bormann, 1983[2]).

Achieving some level of symbolic convergence through their interactions over time is what allows a group of people to move together in the same direction. A symbolic convergence results when our group begins to share meanings about the nature of our joint grouping activities and enterprise. We know we have co-constructed some level of *symbolic convergence* when the people in our group all start to use the same particular words, definitions, and stories to describe who we are as a group, what we are doing, why we are acting as we are, what we hope to achieve, and whether we should make changes.

Co-constructing a symbolic convergence requires skill and patience. Our advice for your attempts concerns both when you are sender and when you are receiver (see Table 6.2). Both creating and receiving messages comprise your competence as a communicator.[3] *Communication competence* is your ability to communicate well. It requires you to interact in a manner that is both effective at serving your purposes and deemed as appropriate by others as you do so.

❖ CREATE MESSAGES THAT GAIN ATTENTION, ENHANCE UNDERSTANDING, AND ENCOURAGE IDENTIFICATION

You will not communicate or give direction well, if you fail to command attention and be understood. More is needed, of course, but

---

[2]We are borrowing a term from Bormann's symbolic convergence theory without using the same definition for the process of symbolic convergence that he applies in that theory. We believe our "extrapolation" of the concept is consistent, however, with his original meaning for the term, which is based in how the process of dramatizing and sharing group fantasy leads to a sense of cohesion, shared group consciousness, and rhetorical vision (see Bormann, 1983; Bormann, Cragan, & Shields, 2001).

[3]See Powers and Witt (2008), Powers and Bodie (2003), Powers and Love (1989), and Powers and Lowry (1984).

Table 6.2	Effective Message Creation and Reception

Creating Messages	Receiving Messages
• *Consider now and later.* Your effectiveness rests both on the quality of message you construct (do the best you can with it) and on what others do later with your ideas, after they have heard your message.	• *Prepare yourself to work hard.* Listening to or making sense of someone is not like cracking an egg. You have to keep working at it. If at first you (seem to) succeed, try, try again. Develop defenses against distractions.
• *Figure out what is meaningful to others.* Focus your energies less on insisting what others should think based on what you intended to say and more on gleaning over time the meanings that they actually take from their talks with you.	• *Test the meanings others intend.* Ask probing questions about their ideas and paraphrase those ideas until you both explicitly agree on your interpretation
• *Emphasize activating others.* If they become primary symbolizing agents, creating ideas in support of your own, they become the future of your direction-giving attempt of today.	• *Focus on the big issues.* Place less priority on remembering details until you know the big issues that concern someone as they communicate. You might first have to help them figure out what concerns them most.
• *Be patient.* Co-creating shared meanings requires a joint effort that probably has to unfold over time through many different messages and shared experiences.	• *Find something useful.* Try to connect with a message, applying it to your own needs. Do not make a source do all the hard work.

Advice elsewhere in the book is not repeated here.

nothing else much matters if you fail on these basic levels. Once heard and understood, your effectiveness will vary according to how much a receiver identifies with your message.

Try to think of your direction-giving as a process in which you get others in the group to identify with your story about the group: your story of the issues facing the group and for how the group should respond. Furthermore, think of your job as helping them to help you create and tell the story of your group's experience. Accomplishing this requires identification and the advice on both sides of Table 6.2. It requires a reorientation regarding what it means *to communicate and to give direction well: less something that you do and more something that you engage others in helping you do.*

Instead of thinking that you must persuade everyone else to do what you want, orient yourself to helping others identify themselves with the story of a group experience that you are trying to tell. To create *identification*, you must show that you share common values, common experiences, and common substance with your receiver, all of which become the basis for a common ground of shared meanings between the two of you (Burke, 1969). With identification, it becomes possible to communicate well, to converge on a set of shared meanings, and to co-construct the direction for your group (see Chapter 9).

A focus on creating identification puts you, the direction-giver, in the position of figuring out what it takes for you to help activate the receiver's sense that he or she already shares in or agrees with what you are saying. The concept of identification fits nicely within the context of the advice we give in Table 6.2. We try to shift your focus from traditional prescriptions for how to communicate effectively (though those can be helpful in crafting a message that carries you as far as a single utterance is ever able) to a broader concern with the ongoing process of creating shared meaning over many messages and points in time.

The person who is most responsible for creating and manipulating the symbols integral to the success or failure of a communicative episode is the *primary symbolizing agent*. We usually expect the source of a communication attempt to be the primary symbolizing agent. However, when the source says all that needs saying, the receiver remains passive: waiting to be told what to think, perhaps ignoring the source entirely. It can be a mistake to leave a receiver passive: It invigorates the potency of your direction-giving if others in the group help you co-construct it.

Help others in your group become active symbolizing agents. Help them identify with the symbolic convergence you work together to co-construct as the story of your group's experience. Barack Obama relied on the symbol of "change" during his presidential campaign in 2008; his supporters filled in the blanks about the nature of the change they imagined. George W. Bush emphasized "security" during his reelection campaign in 2004; his supporters filled in the details about the kind of threats facing them and the country.

Getting others to be primary symbolizing agents is tricky but necessary. Think of a time in the future when people must make sense on their own out of your long-ago direction-giving message. If they cannot adapt what you said as contingencies arise and circumstances change, they will either cease to be effective or they will diverge from the shared path. *Direction-receivers can become as adept as direction-givers at sorting out how the shared meanings in our group tell us we should behave when we face a point of ambiguity.* Helping others co-construct the story of your group's experience is the subject of Chapters 7 and 8.

To co-construct meanings that are shared, to attain the meeting of the mind needed for identification and symbolic convergence, you are going to have to "grade your own work" by determining how what you say and do is playing out over time in your group. After you have said something you think is important, you need to find out to what extent the message you want to get across to the other person actually has legs in the group. What meaning did they make of what you had to say? You can do that, in part, by asking about the meaning made by the other person. This puts you in the role of receiver in order to test the quality of work you did as a source. This involves asking probing questions and following up with even more questions.

Here is how an interaction using this orientation might play out. When you attempt to communicate because you have something important to say, follow up your message by asking, "Have I made sense?" When they say yes (which people often do just to be polite or to get you to leave them alone), thank them. Then, say something like, "I'm not sure I was clear. What do you think I was trying to say? Just tell me in your own words" Asking them to *paraphrase* you means they have to put your thoughts into their own words. Do not let them just quote back to you what you said. It may sound good to be quoted, but using your words allows them to remain passive. Asking them to put your thoughts into their own words requires interpretation. It opens the possibility of finding where the two of you might not be on the same wave length. You are asking them for feedback and you are asking them to help you co-construct your message to them as they reflect on their understanding of what they think you mean. Good for you!

❖ RECEIVE MESSAGES REFLECTIVELY, ORIENTED TOWARD UNDERSTANDING IDEAS AND FINDING UTILITY

Seeking symbolic convergence also requires your focus as a receiver. Effective communication and direction-giving are often more about interacting and listening than about being the one who does the best talking.

Being reflective means turning an idea over and over in your head: to return to it over time and not just in the moment. Receiving messages reflectively means that you orient yourself, through future reflections, to squeezing the most you can out of communication opportunities. *Finding utility* is an orientation that says, "If there is something of use in what this other person is saying, I am the one who is going to find it." This is an alternative orientation to focusing on, as some of us do, what we would like to be saying ourselves when someone else is talking (or worse, focusing on how boring or otherwise unhelpful the talk is that is being sent our way).

Something to Think About and Discuss With Others

You have more capacity to listen effectively than you probably realize. Most folks think faster than anyone else can speak intelligibly: something experts call a *speaking-thinking gap*. Taking advantage of this gap allows you to be reflective as a communication episode is unfolding. Instead of going on a mental vacation when you think you understand what the other person is trying to say, use the extra time your quick brain provides to mull over what is being said, looking for something useful in it. For example, reflect on how the information could be applicable to you personally and develop questions you can ask to learn more.

Finding utility is an orientation that says "I seek something of value in the words of others." If we commit to being reflective, we give ourselves a better chance (and more time) to find utility.

Attempts to be reflective and to find utility are enhanced if you *look for the big picture and take notes of necessary details.* "Looking for the big picture" means trying to establish what the basic idea or two might be that underlies the many details in a given message. This can be tricky if the person creating the message is not sure what his or her big picture is, which happens more often than you might think, especially if this person communicates with a powerful voice. It is even more difficult when people know what they intend but it keeps morphing on them as they talk. Making the process more interactive (at some point in time) can help you (and them) figure out "what's it all about."

"Taking notes" means conceiving of the possibility of needing what you are hearing at some point in the future. Developing a retrieval system or file for keeping track of notes whose purpose is not yet clearly understood can prove useful over time. But more important than whether you can ever actually find your notes when you need them is the orientation that says from the get-go, there is going to be something in this interaction that will be worth capturing. An orientation toward "taking notes" reinforces your ongoing efforts to find utility.

To further improve your understanding, you need to avoid distractions from others and from yourself. For example, if you are too tired or too preoccupied, you should try to reschedule the interaction. Being irritated or too full of your own ideas and their merits can also distract you, as can allowing someone else to pull your attention away from the source. The point of committing yourself to avoid distractions is not that you will always succeed but rather that it too reinforces the goals of trying to be reflective and to seek utility.

❖ IN CONCLUSION

It is rare that what a leader or manager says is most of the communication taking place on an important subject. Much of the direction-giving is actually accomplished as others interact, contributing their ideas, biases, and bits of information to the ongoing process of meaning making. Whatever information a leader (or manager, guide, or doer) conveys, the interactions that follow will likely be at least as important in determining the final effects of a direction-giving attempt over time. Over time is when the process and effects of communication always unfold.

In sum, communication is both a tool we use to transfer information and a process by which we make meaning. Successful communication evolves as we work together to co-construct a shared understanding of the particular issues and general motivations that are in play. As we communicate, we co-construct the experience we are having and what we hope will become our future group experience. Doing this well is more likely as grouping members get on the same wavelength.

7

Shape Effective Experiences and Expectations for Citizenship in Your Group

In this chapter, we finish our unit on communication by explaining how we use it to create and shape experiences. This chapter is about the role your communication can play co-constructing effective group experiences and group direction. Then, in Chapters 8 through 10, we explain how your stories and framings can help a group to thrive. Direction-giving efforts as a doer, follower, guide, manager, or leader are attempts to affect a group's experiences. When you give direction to a team, organization, or community, you change the unfolding story of that group.

❖ HELP SHAPE STORIES OF EFFECTIVE GROUP EXPERIENCES FOR YOUR GROUP

Groups maintain themselves and are effective in part through stories members share. These stories describe and shape experiences the group has had, is currently having, or hopes soon or someday to have. You can give direction by helping shape three types of experience stories: ones that create a sense of who we are as a group, ones that give direction to our group, and ones that create an expectation for citizenship action in our group (see Table 7.1).

Table 7.1	Three Types of Experience Stories You Need to Share as You Group

- You need experience stories that constitute and shape the group's sense of itself as a group.
- You need experience stories that enhance your group's sense of direction and effectiveness.
- You need experience stories that create an expectation of citizenship in your group.

Communication functions to help us create and structure our own personal experiences as well as experiences we share with others (Burtis & Pond-Burtis, 2001).

❖ A HUMAN EXPERIENCE IS A CONSTRUCTED UNDERSTANDING OF WHAT IS MEANINGFUL

Imagine that you and a few friends are asleep in a tent on a camping trip one night. You are awakened by a loud bang outside. "What was that?" you exclaim, disoriented. "I think it's a bear," moans your first buddy, awakening reluctantly but fast. A second buddy charges out of the tent brandishing a rifle, then falls to the ground shooting into the night. More bangs follow; the night is briefly bright. "You shot my car!" screams your first buddy as she stumbles out of the tent. "Where is the bear?" you ask, peaking from the tent to see the last of the fireworks display fading from the sky over the nearby town.[1]

---

[1]Burtis and Pond-Burtis (2001) use this illustration to discuss how communication relates to experience.

Your actual experience was sleeping while camping, being awakened in the dark by a bang, and then hearing your buddies and a gunshot and seeing light. Communicating, or making meaning about the nature of the experience, is what allows you to make some sense of it. Your meaning-making process begins even as the experience is unfolding. You struggle to interpret and to frame the experience. You use communication to decide what is meaningful.

There is little doubt that you will talk about this experience. That talk will likely continue and evolve over time. After you return from the camping trip and over the years that follow, you may still find opportunities to recount the story. You may use it as a teaching tale to warn your child about the dangers of loaded guns. You may use it as an inspirational story about the patriotic fervor of a small town that shoots fireworks off in the face of marauding bands of bears. Your recollection and retelling of the story may turn what started off as a scare into a humorous anecdote. When a friend remarks, 10 years later, "I would have been scared if I was with you," you may or may not recall your own fear. Both your talk about the experience and the experience itself evolve. Your "actual experience" is transformed into your account and into the uses to which you put that account.

Where does the actual experience begin and end? Is experience just what your body goes through? Is the evolution of thought and talk, the making of meaning that accompanies and continues after the experience, part of the experience as well? We think experience encompasses all these things. Were we to limit our conception to just what the body goes through, then people who have blacked out from excess drink or a blow to the head would be judged as having a more meaningful experience the night they were unconscious than did the person who was with them, trying to keep them alive. Too much focus on what is and is not an "actual experience" can skew or diminish the uses we can make out of an experience.

Something to Think About and Discuss With Others

Experience matters to us only if it is meaningful. The "actual experience" of the body of the dead drunk, Alzheimer's patient, or trauma accident victim can be less meaningful than the symbolic constructions of others who observe and interact with that person. If awareness ever returns to the recently unconscious or briefly lucid, does having had their actual experience give them a better sense of what is meaningful

(Continued)

(Continued)

than does the account given to them by the observer of what has been happening? A TV show tells about a rape victim who experiences no ill effects because she does not recall her attack. She seems totally unaffected by the trauma, until some lawyers convince her she really is a rape victim (who can testify for them in court) by telling her the story of what happened to her and then showing her footage of something that looks like her attack. Finally, she feels traumatized by an actual experience from years earlier.

Experience is something in which we engage: a focus of our attention and/or energy. Experiences include events where we participate and those where we observe. Experiences include what we get told about, read about, or see on the silver screen. As long as we can sense it and are engaged by it, we are having an experience: firsthand, secondhand, virtual, vicarious. Experiences help us figure out what we think is meaningful. We engage our attention in something and it becomes an experience as we find it meaningful.

The experiences that become meaningful to a group help shape the group's story. The experiences that concern us in this book range from the most mundane of grouping matters to the life changing: anything that affects the ongoing story of the group's efforts to thrive. We start by discussing your individual experience and then sort out how you make something meaningful out of experiences you share with others.

Communication is how you construct accounts of your own meaningful experience. When you have an experience you think is meaningful, you develop a story or account that frames the experience for you. Your accounts probably focus on what has happened, is happening, or will happen. You are engaging in a normal human process: You translate experience into a symbolic representation you can make use of and share. You construct and make use of accounts.

Meaningful experience requires an account. We symbolically reconstruct experience into an account. An account helps to make sense of our experience. Attaching words to experience is what we do when we need to interpret and frame something meaningful. As we attach words and other framings, we create an account or story that makes experience useable (see Table 7.2). We attach words to an experience so that we can think about it and interact with others about it.

Table 7.2 How Shaping Accounts Integrates Experience, Meaning, and Communication

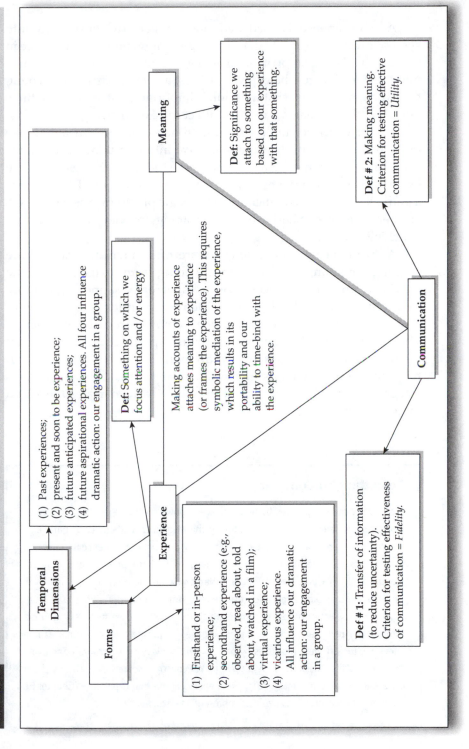

Temporal Dimensions

(1) Past experiences;
(2) present and soon to be experience;
(3) future anticipated experiences;
(4) future aspirational experiences. All four influence our engagement in a group.

Meaning

Def: Significance we attach to something based on our experience with that something.

Experience

Def: Something on which we focus attention and/or energy

Making accounts of experience attaches meaning to experience (or frames the experience). This requires symbolic mediation of the experience, which results in its portability and our ability to time-bind with the experience.

Forms

(1) Firsthand or in-person experience;
(2) secondhand experience (e.g., observed, read about, told about, watched in a film);
(3) virtual experience;
(4) vicarious experience. All influence our dramatic action: our engagement in a group.

Communication

Def # 2: Making meaning. Criterion for testing effective communication = *Utility*.

Def # 1: Transfer of information (to reduce uncertainty). Criterion for testing effectiveness of communication = *Fidelity*.

Any experience is mediated once it gets (re)constructed into symbolic form. Such mediation is an intervention into the experience in order to make sense of it or to make use of it in some way. Such intervention changes the experience. Yes, as we construct an account, the experience affects what we think is important. But at the same time, our ideas about what is important affect the experience.

As we construct understanding from experience, meanings we make become part of the experience. We interpret things even as we experience them: making and sometimes sharing meanings about the experience (e.g., about why it matters) even as it unfolds. For example, a journalist provides commentary on a tragic plane crash as passengers are being rescued. She is shaping meaning for viewers as they are watching events transpire.

As we develop an account, we are often unaware that we are creating something new. What we are doing seems to us to be just the making of an objective account of "what is really happening to those involved in the crash." However, each intervention is a creation of something new: something somewhat removed from the experience. The journalist might interject her own experience in a plane that nearly crashed, which has little to do with the current event, but can help her frame what is meaningful about it. Her frame gets integrated into our experience of the crash as she narrates the action in her report.

Something to Consider

We *analyze* our experiences by breaking them down to the parts that seem most interesting or relevant to us and then by thinking further about each part (e.g., about how each relates to the big picture). We *critique* experience by creating descriptions, interpretations, and evaluations of it. Both analysis and criticism require *applying words* and *definitions* that *frame* our account of an experience. Analysis, criticism, and application of symbolic forms (words, definitions, and framings) are all selective processes during which we *filter* what we think, say, and do: through our personal values, attitudes, knowledge, perspective, and other experiences. We top off these processes by *constructing our version or account* of an experience. In each of these ways, we intervene: We construct something new out of our experience as we communicate or make meaning about that experience (Chapter 6). Our symbolic constructions begin to represent the experience for us.

To experience is to be enveloped in a process involving perception, interpretation, and adaptation. The thinking about, critiquing, and acting on what is perceived all become part of the experience. *What is meaningful about human experience is less the event than it is a constructed understanding of the event.*

By creating an account of an experience, we strive for what Gregg (1984) calls *fixity:* a somewhat stable and useful representation of experience. Gregg explains that words were invented in the first place to help simplify experiences: "holding them still" enough for us to make sense out of them, to make use of them.

It is difficult to find a moment when there is any separation between an experience and the symbol(s) used to represent it. Communication about an experience and the experience itself are sometimes nearly synchronous. Once the first word or phrase (any symbolizing) is applied, the processes of fixity begin.

Because of fixity, experience is intrinsically tied to communication. A meaning is the significance we give to an experience. It is the interpretation we decide to make of an experience. Interpretation is selecting words we think explain and frame experience. What we interpret and extract as meaningful from experience is whatever engages our attention as the most interesting or useful aspect. *Our account becomes the residue of our experience.* The meanings that we have for anything that we hold dear are a residue of our experiences with that thing. When someone matters to you, it is because of experiences you had or hope to have with this person. When group choices matter to you, it is because of experiences you had or hope to have with the group.

In addition to constructing your own accounts, you also negotiate or co-construct shared accounts for group experiences. When you experience something with someone else, you have to "negotiate" what "really happened" with those who share the experience. That is the case as you discuss the experience, especially if you want to use the shared experience to shape aspirations for the group. Coming to a symbolic convergence in which you agree about interpretations of key group experiences is a basic aspect of direction-giving (see Chapter 6).

The words and framings you personally apply to an experience are your own account. A group uses similar processes to develop its symbolic convergence: shared terms and framings, which comprise the story of the group. These become the group's "official account": negotiated meanings, memories, and aspirations that shape the group's experience story.

For example, groups share accounts of their past[2] in celebrations, dedications, memorials, and commemorations. They do so to honor the past, to shape the group's story about the past, and to use accounts of the past to serve the group in its present and future. Stories that become official accounts are rhetorical resources for grouping and direction-giving activities.

When two people engage the same something, each likely has a slightly different experience. They attach slightly (or substantially) different meanings. They have to interact to find or create any meaning they share. A group is a co-construction of meanings that people figure out how to share. Nuances and competing interpretations are sorted out. Meanings become shared over time as groups tell and revise (negotiate) stories of past, current, and aspirational experiences. Individual interpretation becomes part of group experience.

By sharing accounts, experiences that interest us get integrated into group experience and begin to provide direction. Experience stories are told to help us form and maintain groups. Experience stories are told to help us provide knowledge and insight that helps our group thrive. For example, existing military strategy evolves from a process of using experience stories to shape future operations. D-Day involved the successful landing on beaches in Normandy due largely to what was learned by the failure of British and Canadian forces to land at the port of Dunkirk years earlier. Failed experience became useful as Allied forces framed a story for future experiences involving attempts to attack unfortified landing zones. Beyond the information they transfer, stories integrate otherwise isolated experiences into the story of our group. *When we create a shared account, we make experience portable,* which allows us to carry the residue of our experience with us into the future.

When you "negotiate" an experience with others who end up disagreeing about what is true or meaningful about the experience, you keep your own interpretation from the interaction. However, if you want to group and to give direction well, you need to understand what your group shapes as its account or experience story. Remember from Chapter 6 that what we say when we attempt to communicate or to give direction is not all that the other person hears. The other person hears you through his or her own accounts and sense of the group's experiences. You need to *consider the likelihood that your message is but a few drops in the flow of the other person's experience.* Crafting your messages well is important for any direction-giver. However, it is at least as

---

[2]See Phillips (2004), Bodnar (1992), Hess (2007), Hasian and Carlson (2000), and Hauser (1999).

important for you to have a sense of the unfolding story of your group's experience as others understand it.

Communication allows you to have vicarious experiences and to bind time. You can put experience stories to excellent use in shaping your direction-giving attempts. You can go so far as to use experiences you have not actually had, at least not personally or directly. *Vicarious experiences* are the actual experiences of others that we manage to make our own. We can learn from such experiences, even dread or enjoy them as though we ourselves are participating.

Each of us benefits from vicarious experience, probably beginning from the time a parent or teacher reads us a story or tells us an account of his or her own life experience. For example, firefighters "swap stories after every fire, and by doing so they multiply their experience; after years of hearing stories, they have a richer, more complete mental catalog of critical situations they might confront during a fire and the appropriate responses to those situations" (C. Heath & Heath, 2007, p. 18). The capacity to make use of vicarious or extended experiences is a marvel.

In short, you can have an experience, even if you are not physically present when it happens. Over time, that is how humans preserve and perpetuate civilization. We accomplish something called *time-binding* whenever we transfer an experience from one place to a different place and, by definition, different time (Korzybski, 1933). As we experience something in the moment, we employ time-binding. We use the past to help make sense of the present. To test our current group direction (to decide if we are on the right track), we extrapolate an account from what is happening now to where we will end up in the future. Society is a manifestation of time-binding. What is learned by one generation is passed to the next. Sharing accounts of experiences is how we make experience useable, how we save a residue of the experience and make it portable, and how we bind time.

Groups that maintain themselves over time are stronger according to their ability to time-bind stories of grouping experiences. Think of your family as a continuous grouping experience. Consider its traditions and the time-binding heard during holiday gatherings. What ends a family or group is the loss of any sense of its past. Then, if any remnant of it survives, it is a new group having a fundamentally different experience story because of the loss of its time-bound anchors.

It is difficult to overstate the importance of our abilities to have vicarious experiences and to bind time. They allow us to stretch our understanding beyond limits established by our normal perceptual capacities. Superman might be able to see through a wall, but your sight can be extended by listening to someone from the other side of the wall describing what is happening there or by reading a story told by someone about what happened there 40 years ago. If the one who tells the story is gifted or we are suitably engaged, we can find our own present and future experience affected by their story. Think of the most effective direction-giver you know. Take away his or her abilities to time-bind (e.g., to learn from his or her own experiences; to share accounts with you) and you disable them.

❖ STORIES OF PAST, PRESENT, AND FUTURE EXPERIENCES ARE HOW YOU GIVE DIRECTION TO YOUR GROUP

Current, past, and future constructions of what is meaningful are integrally related aspects of the experience story we shape for our group. Effective direction-giving involves framing and reasoning "from experience—from prior cases—and we make new decisions by abstracting the essentials from an appropriate prior case. . . . The case from which we reason leads to the framing of our experience" (Fairhurst & Sarr, 1996, pp. 71–73). We would not do or say what we are now doing or saying if the past and future were completely separate from the now.

There are past, present, and future aspects to every experience. For example, when we interpret and analyze our present and recent experiences, we do so in part by using words, meanings, and stories that are already familiar because they are meaningful parts of our past. We frame our future according to what is already meaningful. As new experiences change our perspective, we revise interpretations and accounts of our past as well as our framings of the future. The three temporal aspects of experience are integrated throughout the story of any group (see Table 7.2).

Something to Think About and Discuss With Others

The Tennessee Volunteers have one of the most successful basketball programs in the past 35 years under Pat Summit, the "winningest" coach in NCAA history (men or women). As her team competes each year, their present experience is affected by past success (e.g., their ability to recruit top players; expectations for excellence shared by team members, fans, and donors; responses to the team by pundits, opponents, and officials). Both past and present influence the future story for the team (e.g., chances of and aspirations for a ninth national championship or Summit's

1,000th win; ability to recruit a coaching successor). A loss in the first round of the NCAA tournament means something different to the Vols than to a first-time qualifying team.

How do past successes affect your own group's present experiences and aspirations? How do past struggles? In what ways do your group's aspirations for the future affect its present?

People use experience stories to justify and adjust grouping activities. The direction-giver at any given moment is probably the person who is describing, interpreting, or evaluating some salient aspect of past, current, or future group experience. The potential set of past, recent, concurrent, soon-to-be, and long-term future experiences is mined for information and guidance. We decide which exigencies for grouping are salient based on a combination of past experiences, current experiences, and anticipated or aspirational future experiences.

Many effective direction-givers are people with talent for making use of time-binding and vicarious experience to help shape the story of their group's unfolding experience. Effective direction-giving tends to be a future-oriented activity: a stream of answers to questions about what to do next or how, describing anticipated experiences, and getting the group to consider aspirational experiences.

To tap the rhetorical resource based in future experiences, we need to distinguish between what is anticipated and what is aspirational. Both anticipatory and aspirational experiences can motivate current action, shape or guide current experience, and help us to put past experiences into context. They are also useful in assessing group outcomes. Did we actually accomplish what we said we hoped to accomplish? But they are also different.

Anticipated experiences are future experiences that appear to be within our grasp. They have been projected or planned for and seem to be in sight. There is more certainty attached to these the more closely we come to achieving them. As they become more and more inevitable, until they are finally current and then past experiences, they lose some of their rhetorical force.

Aspirational experiences are future experiences that excite our interest and motivate our actions. They portray improvements we want to try to attain but have not yet got a handle on. A company struggling to land its first major account may motivate employees by emphasizing that a desired client is "within their grasp" or "close enough to taste."

Aspirations, to be compelling, must be different from current, antici-pated experience: different enough to be attractive enough that folks feel inclined to stretch themselves in efforts to attain them. The aspira-tional experience can provide substantial rhetorical force for direction-givers who wield its potential attractions in ways that engage the group. Over time, however, the aspirational, as it is attained, can become anticipated. It can lose some of its rhetorical force, potentially skewing the bar by which future aspirations are set—championships you win can lead your group to start to expect to win.

To tap the rhetorical potential in either sort of future experience requires a compelling and realistic story of that future experience. Then, our future experiences can start to help shape what we do now: what we experience now. When we aspire and then set *goals* that include the substantive, measurable steps needed to attain our aspira-tions, we can be strongly influenced by our future experience. We can also strongly influence our future experience through our actions intended to breathe life into them. With sufficient time and attention paid to making it a reality, an aspirational experience can become a guiding light for grouping choices.

We evaluate the quality of our grouping efforts and of the direction we have been given by comparing what we are experiencing to our anticipated and aspirational experiences. When we compare our pre-sent to our potential for something else, we consider and explore the options that face us. We rehearse the possibilities as we tell stories of future group experiences (Scheibel, Gibson, & Anderson, 2002).

Aspirational stories are rehearsals. Aspirational stories give us a chance to vicariously experience what is not yet: binding time from present to future to back again. Doing so helps us to decide whether we want to partake of a particular future: in particular, whether we want to expend the energy necessary to co-construct that future group expe-rience. Aspirations require change. When they require us to exert more energy than is our norm, they may lose their appeal and our attention unless something spurs us on.

When someone tells a group what they should be doing, that per-son describes the present experience relative to an alternative. The equation may be as simple as "We are not working; we should be." Or "This is not how we ever did our inventory before. What is up with you people?" Or "The deadline is upon us and it looks like we will exceed our goal and win the week of free vacation time on the island." Our response to the experience we are having is filtered through our expectations for that experience. When stories of what we want are not matched by the stories of what we are now experiencing, we become troubled and begin to wonder how to get back on track or to start to move in a new direction.

If the experience we are supposed to be having, according to our expectations, is not aligned with the experience we think that we are having, that violation of expectations will elicit arousal. Arousal might be energy creating—for example, a group that exceeds its goals for yearly fundraising when it finds out how close it is to doubling the money it expected to raise. Arousal can be dampening or frustrating. Either way, current experience unfolds in an ongoing comparison to anticipated and aspirational experience. We are almost always able to assess current experience as "better than expected" or "not what we imagined" or "worse than our darkest nightmares."

Try to think of any direction-giving attempt you provide in terms of the experience your messages suggest grouping members ought to be having right now or in the future. Of course, there are particulars you need to convey, but those particulars need to be understood as part of the ongoing, unfolding story your group is already experiencing.

We all know that one set of circumstances can be interpreted and framed in two or more entirely different ways (e.g., as evidence of effective grouping; as evidence of a challenge the group faces; as evidence of impending disaster for the group). So, we have a choice about which account of past, current, and future experience we choose to engage. Whichever way we engage a group creates different dramatic action in the group as the experience story unfolds through the efforts and interactions of group members. Your account of the group's experience as a direction-giver helps shape the experience that follows. As you attempt to provide direction, the group will be hearing your potential contributions through the filter of how they think what you suggest will affect their experience.

If you do not continually assess, interpret, and frame grouping experiences, you leave that opportunity and rhetorical resource for someone else to use. The group's experience story will be told. The only question is how you are involved in its co-construction. If you are charged with the responsibility to manage the group or if you are convinced of the need to help provide direction to your group, it is a mistake to absent yourself from the work of shaping the stories of your group's experience. They can become a group's official representation of its experience.

If in your opinion all is going well, you should find ways to reinforce existing activity. Your account of what is happening now is part of how you accomplish that task. You cannot simply set an experience into play and expect that it will continue to unfold as you hope. Such a laissez-faire style is too limited. People talk (as Elton Mayo found with his Hawthorne studies—see Chapter 5). They modify their experience based on the stories they share as they talk.

❖ CONSTITUTIVE RHETORIC IS HOW YOU CO-CONSTRUCT A SENSE OF YOUR GROUP AND OF "THE OTHERS"

Sometimes we intentionally use a story to try to provide direction. Often, however, sharing accounts unintentionally provides direction. Stories influence cohesion and group climate. They affect the attraction we have to aspects of our task and to desired outcomes.

One of the foundational functions served by telling the stories of grouping experiences is shaping who we are and what we do as a group. *Constitutive rhetoric*[3] represents whatever we do in the attempt to create or shape who we are as a grouping entity, what it means to be part of our group, and how we connect who we are to our efforts to act like a group. In short, constitutive rhetoric is how we co-construct our sense of ourselves as a group: for ourselves and for the consumption of interested others.

Constitutive rhetoric places special focus on who we are as a group of people. As we interact together, co-constructing and sharing stories of our grouping experiences, we constitute a sense of ourselves: who we are, what we are, why we are, and how we are. Constitutive rhetoric is employed when a grouping member or direction-giver "projects onto the audience an image of the idealized 'people' to whom [he or she] is speaking. This . . . provides the audience with a set of characteristics to value and a set to downplay in identifying with this constitution of a 'people.' . . . They are invited to see themselves as a collective with common qualities, experiences, and values, and significantly, a common enemy" (Morus, 2007b, p. 6). We constitute our group by inviting each other to behave "as our people" ought to behave.

---

[3]For information on constitutive rhetoric, see, for example, Charland (1987) and McGee (1975). For examples of constitutive rhetoric, see, for example, Charland (1987) and Hahner (2008), who provides a cultural criticism of the "Americanization" practices used to acculturate young immigrant girls into the cultural values of the United States during the period surrounding World War I: a process accomplished through CampFire Girls and Girl Scouts. See Morus (2007a, 2007b) for a discussion of the attempts to create national identity for the Serbian people, and see Roy and Rowland's (2003) explanation of Hindu nationalism.

Constitutive rhetoric can help shape what we experience by putting a particular framing on what we are and do. It is one thing to face the world as you and another to face it as a freedom fighter, Marxist, feminist, environmentalist, Moslem, Christian, or Jew. Such "idealized people," constituted by stories of their experiences, provide framings accompanied by pride and preference.

Rivalries between competing schools or sport franchises are formed in such a manner. During the Olympic Games, countries rally around their teams and feel national pride (e.g., in 1980, the United States rallied around its hockey team as it upset a dominant Soviet team). Countries marshal their resources against attack in such a manner—for example, how the United States responded to 9/11 (2001), the Gulf of Tonkin (1964), Pearl Harbor (1941), the sinking of the *Maine* (1898), the Alamo (1836), or when "the British are coming" (1775). Rhetoric used in such situations appeals to your role as a member of the idealized group. It raises then praises the identity of your group. It sings of love and duty: for your team/country and to your team/country. It can have a tremendous effect on the engagement people have in their grouping experience, which affects the dramatic action that later unfolds in the life of the group.

Constitutive rhetoric is also how we co-construct "the others" (e.g., a hated rival, terrorists, communists, the Western democracies, etc.). A key to figuring out who we are is to figure out who we are not. To do that, we need someone, anyone, we can identify as "other than us" or as "an outsider" to our group. The "other" may be fabricated: an idealized other, created as a strategically useful attempt to help us constitute ourselves. Regardless of its source or substance, we need a counterpoint against which to shape our sense of ourselves. (How do you constitute your group's other: as enemy, competitor, or loyal opposition?)

"Who we are" is constituted in part by what constraints and challenges we face and in part by who opposes us. Every culture, religion, or "founding philosophy" has constitutive aspects, describing who its adherents are as a people. Every such perspective includes a story of struggle and probably of heroes in the cause, as well as enemies. There is always something to battle, always something that pushes against us and makes our progress difficult. Attempts to constitute an "us" are often easier to articulate as we construct the "other than us." We define ourselves and we define who we are not. Such constitutive rhetoric helps us figure out how to behave.

❖ HELP SHAPE STORIES OF EXPERIENCE THAT CREATE AN EXPECTATION OF CITIZENSHIP IN YOUR GROUP

Effective groups must co-construct experience stories that engage people sufficiently for the group to succeed. One type of experience story needed in every long-lived group is a story that helps create a sense of our duty to our group as citizens.

The obligation of citizenship is for members to help co-create the direction a group takes. This means helping others in the group figure out what we need to do so that our group can thrive. One person's efforts to help a group thrive tend to stimulate interactions among other grouping members. The success of groups, what makes some of them thrive as others wither, is always, fundamentally, the result of *human engagement*. People engage a group by trying to create a successful experience through their attention, action, and interaction. As others engage the group, their efforts manifest as shared dramatic action created through engaged interaction. A group is effective because engaged citizen-members co-construct the experiences that make it so.

❖ CITIZENSHIP EXPERIENCE STORIES STIMULATE PARTICIPATION, CRITICISM, AND REASONED CONFORMITY

Citizenship is a term traditionally used to represent enumerated obligations and privileges that come from being a "member of a country" (e.g., for male U.S. citizens, residency, registering with selective service at age 18, voting, habeas corpus, and free assembly). Formal citizenship is of less interest to us than is the social contract we explain in Chapter 1.

A social contract is an informal calculation. If you are able to move along in life in part because of the power and flow of a group, then you owe that group. In this sense, *citizenship* is your duty to "give back," to help your group thrive. To do so, you must engage your group.

Your engagement should always include some form of (1) participation, (2) constructive criticism, and (3) reasoned conformity (Gastil, 1992, 1993). These are acts of citizenship regardless of the type of direction-giving you provide the group, including if you act as a follower (see Chapters 1 and 2). Who is better situated than group members to criticize and to create improvement in grouping processes and objectives?

What becomes of a group if its members do not participate? How can a group succeed if members refuse to blend their efforts: to conform in reasoned ways so they can work with each other? Participation, constructive criticism, and reasoned conformity are necessary aspects of your engagement in a group (i.e., conforming by blending your own ethically appropriate, authentic, and functionally necessary energies and actions with the efforts of others). These acts help give direction to your group (Burtis & Turman, 2006). They are the heart of your ability to behave as an engaged and effective citizen.

A social contract obligates people to each other. It obligates the members to the group and the group to its members. A group member should not act entirely as an independent or sovereign agent because grouping people are *interdependent*. Each member's acts affect the others. We all give up some of our autonomy to blend our efforts into the group. That sacrifice obligates others in the group to contribute as well. None of us should be deprived of or spared from the efforts and fruits we should be able to reasonably expect from our group experience.

Understanding recurring types of poor citizenship refines our understanding of what citizenship requires. The obligation for each individual to try to help the group is why we judge poorly any social loafers, passive members, and saboteurs. The social loafer's *nonfeasance*, or failure to perform expected acts, takes energy from the group. The passive member's *acquiescence*, or meek and mindless submission to others, takes quality from the group. The saboteur's active attempts to unravel the work of the group are counterproductive to the shared processes and purposes of grouping. *Malfeasance* is doing acts that cannot be justified because they are contrary to grouping processes or goals. *Misfeasance* is the abuse of supposedly good grouping acts or supposedly good grouping processes to accomplish one's own ends. All of these reduce the ability of the group to thrive by depriving the group of an appropriate contribution.[4]

Think of your life experiences as a worker, boss, family member, or student: in whatever role you play on a team or in an organization or community. Your experience will show you that you are better at what you are supposed to do when you are surrounded by others trying to do what they are supposed to do. You and your efforts can be diminished or even hurt when others are not interested or are distracted.

Regardless of the reasons, each of us is enhanced in our own efforts by others in the group, or we are diminished. So, if someone is not willing

---

[4]In Chapter 2, we explain that a follower, an active and important type of direction-giver, is neither a passive member nor a social loafer.

to fulfill the social contract, it can be better to divorce our efforts from theirs rather than to let their actions become our model or our group norm. We may struggle along without everyone always providing what they ought. But no group can handle too many social loafers, passive members, or malcontents.

Intentional efforts to help a group to thrive do not happen spontaneously. Taking citizenship seriously requires a group to indicate how its members ought to engage. The issue will probably be raised indirectly in the stories grouping members exchange about their experiences. Such stories share a sense of expectations for the citizen-member.

More direct approaches are also in order. This entails experience stories constructed specifically to create an explicit expectation of citizenship. You will hear such stories shared among members of any team that expects to win. You will hear them shared in any family that tries to be supportive. You hear a version in any organization that seeks to create a product and make a profit. No group attains its best fruits through efforts of only a few. Stimulating the engagement of many requires stories of responsibility that the group experience needs to entail.

If this sounds complicated, remember how communication helps us create and shape experiences. All that is needed to begin is to show a positive orientation toward this obligation. We create expectations of citizenship by sharing accounts and experiences that show our social contract is in play. When we share experiences and stories that demonstrate that we share a social contract, it helps create a sense of accountability for co-constructing the group experience. By shaping and sharing experiences that help the group thrive in the moment, we help the group to be effective and to continue to thrive over the long haul.

❖ HOW GROUPS PERPETUATE THEMSELVES SHAPES THE EXPERIENCE OF CITIZEN-MEMBERS

Groups perpetuate themselves through processes members engage for doing so. Bormann (1983) explains that you need to help your group attain three key types of convergence. *Consciousness-creating* experiences help constitute the group's sense of itself (e.g., who we are as a group; why we matter as a group). If the group survives long enough for its members to create a symbolic convergence around their shared sense of the nature and importance of the group, it becomes harder for the group to be undone and easier for grouping members to continue their efforts.

Consciousness-raising is accomplished through experiences that inculcate new people into what is meaningful in the group. This includes recruiting and/or socializing new members and, if necessary, shaping experiences that help nonmember stakeholders understand why the group is important to support. *Consciousness-sustaining* experiences help established members celebrate successes and recall why it is important to them to continue to group. Taking part in the co-construction of these three key types of symbolic convergence experiences is an aspect of your citizenship participation. It is also a way to strengthen your engagement in the group and to help provide direction to your group.

We find examples of these experiences writ large and small in most groups. Whole countries use formal systems of education to inculcate values into the young that can perpetuate the culture of the country when the young mature and take over. Smaller communities use parades and other celebrations to instill and perpetuate their sense of what is important to them about themselves. Organizations house offices of communications or hire public relations firms to shape their narratives for various internal and external publics. Families share stories across generations. Teams retire numbers, field mascots, and otherwise attempt to shape stories that their various publics will find sufficiently compelling to engage. All seek to perpetuate, to time-bind, the values and processes their group has converged upon as "us."

❖ PLAY YOUR PART AS A CITIZEN OF YOUR GROUP

Effective grouping requires "articulate advocacy" and coordinated action so citizenship does too. *Advocacy* involves expressing your concerns or ideas. It is accomplished by developing your position: developing your reasoning and finding evidence that supports your idea. Making and stating your case gets your advocacy articulated to others for their consideration. Advocacy can also manifest as a follower's support for or promotion of the concerns or ideas expressed by others (see Chapter 2).

Advocacy is not limited to making speeches or formal written messages, though those certainly can be useful. Much of our advocacy is found in the day-to-day interactions we share, including in the interpretations, framings, and stories we select and try to use to shape our grouping experiences. Advocacy is affected by the impression we create of ourselves, which lends weight to or detracts from what we have to say. Advocacy is found in the words we choose to use and the definitions and meanings we seek to get others to share.

A citizen is an advocate who is putting a part of himself or herself into whatever case he or she makes while engaging a group. The phrase *articulate advocacy* represents the well-reasoned and supported parts of your case that you present to others. But your advocacy includes all of how you try to get your sense of things integrated into grouping activities, group direction, and the story of your group's experience.

How well you succeed in your advocacy is based in part on how well you understand your group's story. That, to an extent, is a function of how fully engaged you allow yourself to become in the group (see Table 7.3). Ignorance makes it hard to appropriately engage the values the group struggles to sort out. Ignorance is not stupidity. Ignorance about aspects of the group's story may simply mean that you need to hear more stories and share more grouping experiences. You have to deeply engage a group to play such an important role.

Table 7.3	Engagement in the Group and the Ignorant Citizen[a]
The "ignorant" citizen has a deficiency in some aspect of his or her engagement in the group. Citizenship is the obligation to help your group to thrive. This includes engagement in the co-constructions and reconstructions of your group's story/experience: past, present, and future.	
Citizen engagement ranges from lower (most ignorant) to higher levels	
Lower levels of group engagement	Level 1: Affiliate with group or with a member of the group
	Level 2: Behave according to a primary group ideology (e.g., voting): Following the ideology is a citizenship shortcut—it does not require you to really engage the group or understand, gather, and test information on group issues
	Level 3: Engage at a beyond-the-surface ideological level (i.e., engage ongoing decisions about what should be done and what would be meaningful to the group)
Higher levels of group engagement	Level 4: Help co-construct the group's ideological soup (i.e., engage the ongoing struggle, sorting out what should be the most basic of group values)

a. This terminology is informed by research in which scholars attempt to develop journalistic practices that will inform and engage a citizenry (Porto, 2007).

If you do not, an ignorant but effective advocate can do as much damage to a group as a saboteur.

Everyone in a group works for or against the group. Among grouping people, neglect is never benign. A *citizen-member* is someone who intentionally attempts to help co-construct a thriving group. We use terms such as *duty* and *social contract* to frame the orientation of this person, distinguished by the sense that she or he is a co-creator of the story of the group's experience.

❖ IN CONCLUSION

All group members should think of themselves as having both the duty and opportunity to contribute to their group. To do so is an act of humanity because we share the imperative to develop relationships with one another and because we sometimes share exigencies for action that we can only address together. Any experience story that gives a group the direction it needs is an important story. This includes stories that help constitute who we think we are as a people, stories that help us succeed and thrive, and stories that create an expectation of citizenship for our group. Who will do that work if you do not?

UNIT IV

Use Stories to Unite Your Group's Efforts

8

Help Shape the Story of Your Organization, Team, or Community

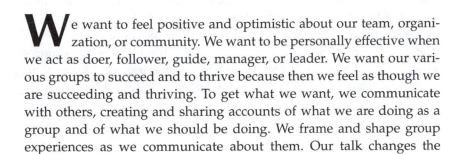

We want to feel positive and optimistic about our team, organization, or community. We want to be personally effective when we act as doer, follower, guide, manager, or leader. We want our various groups to succeed and to thrive because then we feel as though we are succeeding and thriving. To get what we want, we communicate with others, creating and sharing accounts of what we are doing as a group and of what we should be doing. We frame and shape group experiences as we communicate about them. Our talk changes the group's experience story.

The final unit of the book explains how you can use stories to unite your group's efforts and help your group to thrive. In this chapter, we focus on how you can help shape the story of your group. In Chapters 9 and 10, we discuss framing skills that help you shape direction-giving stories and the special sort of story called leadership vision.

Your stories can help to transport people from where they are now as a group to a new understanding of what it is they should or could be doing. Your ability to shape the story of your group's experience is enhanced by understanding the power of narrative, knowing the kinds of story that animate group life, and your connection to the story of your group's experience. Helping you with the first two is the work of this chapter, and the third is the focus of this book.

❖ YOU CAN USE STORIES TO UNITE YOUR GROUP AND TO GIVE IT DIRECTION

People are distinguished from other animals by being the storytellers or *Homo narrans* (W. R. Fisher, 1978, 1984, 1985a, 1985b, 1999). Stories are a portable resource. We take the residue of our experiences along with us by creating accounts of them. We bind time with our stories. We can transport ourselves back to previous and much older experiences by retelling accounts of them. We get transported to future, aspirational experiences by stories we share of them. Our narratives become real to us as we experience them (Harter & Bochner, 2009). While experiencing a story, we mine it for lessons. We use stories to figure out how to shape present and future action.

Stories are sometimes the most useful resource you have to make your direction-giving effective. "History is written by the victors," is Winston Churchill's spin on the subject, or, as Plato puts it, "Those who tell the stories, rule society." Both acknowledge that group direction is provided by people who shape the group's symbolic convergence: its shared terms, meanings, and stories. Groups converge in their interpretations until they have a sort of "official framing" of the group's experience story (see Chapters 6 and 7). By shaping accounts of their group's experience, people sort out what is meaningful to the group and how members ought to behave.

Something to Think About and Discuss With Others

What stories would there be of the Holocaust if Allied forces had lost World War II? Remember, Hitler's Germany would help shape those accounts. As just one example of change: Eisenhower's directive that a sizable number of American servicemen tour the camps (so future generations could not deny them) would not have been made. It often takes decades, even a century or two, before accounts are balanced by historical perspective (if that ever is accomplished).

The story we shape for a group includes its past, present, and aspirational experiences. We test our understanding of current and past experiences by telling stories about them. Stories help us shape our future group experiences. We share accounts as we decide how to behave both now and in the future. When you give direction to a group, you change its story. If you give direction that helps your group to be effective, you are constructing an experience story in which your group thrives. You can choose to become a seeker and shaper of stories that will unite and give direction to your group.

Do not be put off by negative connotations you have for the word *story*. You may think stories are a waste of time and frivolous at best. Perhaps you frame them as recreation: germane neither to the task nor to your work as a manager or leader. Many experts disagree. Scholars[1] who study direction-givers often focus on how story is useful in their work. Narratives are as real and useful as any type of communication.

❖ FIND COHERENCE IN CO-CONSTRUCTED STORIES OF YOUR GROUP'S EXPERIENCE

Story is found in coherence of meaning. Coherence is created in two ways. A *narrative* is a coherent story with a plot and characters. In this sense, narrative is a story you might try to tell. *Narrative* is also the coherence of meaning you pull out of the various messages others send your way. In this sense, narrative is a story you hear. Actually, within a single person, the two processes of telling and hearing narrative are almost seamlessly integrated.

Whenever we communicate, each of us is trying to construct a coherent narrative out of the experience. We try to do so as we listen to the accounts others share with us. We try to do so as we are making and telling our own accounts. It is coherence of meaning that makes a story. Without coherence, a plot is just confusing and characters make no sense. With coherence, even if we are confused about the plot and unfamiliar with the characters, we can follow the story. As something told or something heard, a story is the coherence of meaning: "put into" or "pulled out of" narrative.

For meaning to be *coherent*, its elements must combine in a credible way. The credibility of a story is a judgment made by the person(s) who

---

[1]See Kouzes and Posner (1993), Ryfe (2006), Ricoeur (1980), and H. White (1980).

hear or use the story (W. R. Fisher, 1984; West & Turner, 2004). The judgment that something is coherent is based on whether the story seems to hang together in a consistent manner as it unfolds. Does it include the details we think we need to make sense of it? Are characters believable, and do they behave in a manner we understand? Whether telling or hearing a story, we test coherence of meaning in the account.

Coherence of meaning is something people try to put into accounts they are constructing. Even more important to direction-givers is the coherence of meaning people create as they receive messages. In this case, coherence is pulled out of messages others send. The story you create for yourself as you interpret the messages other people send to you may not have much fidelity with what those others are trying to say (see Chapter 6). After all, you are putting together your own account of what is happening. So, you pick the bits and pieces of what they say that you think are meaningful given the story you are constructing. To some extent, the story you are constructing probably began for you before the direction-giver's talking did.

> Stories are powerful leadership tools. "The ancient art of storytelling is perhaps the major way that leaders teach." Stories serve as "a mental map that helps people know . . . what is important . . . and how things are done in a particular group."
>
> (Kouzes & Posner, 1993, p. 197)

It is not always obvious that narrative is involved as people give direction to a group. Every story and every account is a narrative. However, *some narratives and accounts do not sound like a story.* Why call them a story, then? Because, as we interact, we make stories out of information we share. Evidence of a story becomes evident when you look for coherence of meaning, and you need to be able to do that well to be effective over time as a direction-giver.

Narrative is directly employed or indirectly invoked in almost all communications. We do not have to hear a whole story to know that it is "there": that there is a "more complete story" than what we have just heard. Sometimes a whole story is indicated by bits of information. An analogy might help. DNA allows a crime scene investigator to discover who was at the scene of a crime from just a small bit of hair or bodily fluid, piecing together the whole story in just 42 minutes! A crook who does not know how bits and pieces of info help others create a story is likely to end up in the hootchkow.[2] A direction-giver who is blind to the stories others shape from tidbits of interactions will just be less effective and more befuddled.

In your group or in a relationship, you can sometimes tell when there is a broader story than what is said. You can sense it from bits of a message or from aspects of behavior. For example, a smile or a frown from someone when a new idea is introduced is a subtle unit of information. From it, we construct a story of what the individual who smiles or frowns is thinking. Your effectiveness as you interact with others is affected by how well you can read such cues as evidence of a broader story that is implicit but in play.

Details you are given about how to do something when you are new on the job generally get translated in your mind into a story for how you can employ those details. You imagine how to act as you try to do the thing that should help you to be effective. If you cannot make sufficient sense of what you ought to do, you will be anxious until you get more information that helps you form a more satisfying account about what is expected. If something goes wrong as you attempt to play out your experience, the basic narrative you constructed no longer works, and you need to create a new account to explain your current experience and what to do next.

The key is in how we treat information when we receive it. If we can tie something new to our already existing accounts of our past, present, or future experiences, we can integrate new information into our own unfolding narratives. We are eager to make new information interesting and useful to us. "Oh, you are from Topeka; I was there once. . . ." or "Do you know Bruce, he is at Firestone too?" New info is hard to remember until given the context and coherence of story.

As direction-givers, we need to be concerned with how the information we provide a group gets translated into stories of the group's experiences. If we do not translate the ideas into the group's narrative ourselves, the ideas we need to share with others will get translated into story by the person we talk to. Or, a third party may provide them a story that frames our idea. These are ways that fidelity is diminished. Your idea is less likely to work well for your purposes if it gets framed by someone else as part of someone else's version of the story of your group.

---

[2]Note the aspects of story that begin forming in your mind as you try to make sense of a single, nonsensical term: the second employed so far in this book. Did you notice the first one? What do you make of it?

Consider the strategy employed by Jon Stewart as he provides background for stories presented on *The Daily Show*. He and his staff are skilled at using limited excerpts of what politicians say or do to support their own comedy and point of view. Their reframing removes or diminishes the original contexts. This creates entertainment value for the audience in ways that people who are quoted might not like. The reframing lets audiences try on Stewart's point of view as a possible interpretation of what is going on in their world (Waisanen, 2009).

As we interact with other people, they try on our ideas. They become convinced by what we say when they think our ideas pass muster in their own accounts for what is happening. As a direction-giver, your effectiveness can be enhanced by the extent to which you can figure out how your messages are getting translated by others into their accounts of group experience.

❖ NARRATIVE PROVIDES A POTENT TOOL FOR SHAPING EFFECTIVE GROUP EXPERIENCES

Narratives can help us and our groups in at least three ways. They can be persuasive or informative and they can help create energy and enthusiasm. Research documents the potency of all three of these effects (Green & Brock, 2005).

Traditional persuasion attempts to motivate someone to change his or her actions or attitudes by using an argument, which may be supported by logic, evidence, or some form of emotional appeal. Stories also motivate a person to change his or her actions or attitudes. In fact, the persuasive effects from a narrative sometimes last longer than effects from traditional persuasion. And persuasive effects of story manifest whether the story is fiction or nonfiction, whether the person affected by the story is male or female, and sometimes even when a story is contradicted by reality.

The process of persuasion is different in stories than it is with traditional persuasion (Green & Brock, 2005; Ryfe, 2006). In traditional persuasive attempts, we hear the argument and weigh any evidence or emotional reaction as we consider what we want to do in response. Our consideration constitutes a testing of the message as we think about whether to make a particular response.

When listening to a story, we suspend such testing. Instead, we are transported[3] to wherever the story takes us. When we get swept along with a story, we are "psychologically transported" away from wherever we are, into the realm of the story. Instead of testing the story, we "take part" in the story: perhaps as one of the characters, as the narrator, or as an invisible bystander. As we take part, we get a new experience. When we return, we bring that experience back with us. The process can be similar as people share accounts of group experiences.

Even when we are not necessarily "persuaded" by a story, we can learn from it in ways that enhance our grouping effort. Stories can be informative and sharing them can help us solve problems in our group. When we are perplexed or frustrated, we tend to share stories about what is frustrating us. The interactions that surround such talk often help a group address their own issues either directly or indirectly (Bormann, 1996; Ryfe, 2006).

Finally, stories tend to create energy and the enthusiasm we need to renew our efforts as a group. We get excited by accounts of aspirational experiences. We measure our progress against a compelling outcome and redouble our efforts to achieve. Both excitement and determination can be put to work in renewed grouping efforts. Effective direction-givers try to harness a variety of the rhetorical resources that can be found in the stories a group uses to shape its experiences.

❖ SEEK AND SHAPE STORIES THAT SHOW OR START SOMETHING SPECIAL IN YOUR GROUP

During the only full season of the award-winning television show *Boomtown* (2002), one of the two main characters, a police detective named Bobby "Fearless" Smith, carrying an unmarked gun, accosts his childhood coach, Mr. Baker, in the man's own home, alone, late at night. Fearless intends to kill his former coach, who had sexually abused him as a young boy. Near the climactic end of the episode, after an extended emotional exchange with "Coach," Fearless storms out of

---

[3]See Brock, Strange, and Green (2002); Bruner (2002); Gerrig (1993); Green and Brock (2000, 2002); Oatley (2002); and Polichak and Gerrig (2002).

the house to find, much to his surprise, that his partner Joel had followed him and is lurking in the dark yard. They speak:

Fearless: How'd you know I was here?

Joel: A little bird told me.

Fearless: I didn't do it.

Joel: I know that.

Fearless: What if I had?

Joel: You wouldn't.

Fearless: What if I had?

Joel: That's not who you are.

Fearless: What if I had?

Joel: *I brought a shovel.*

The close bond between the two partners rings forth, solidified by a single, simple final line.

This brief dialog gives evidence of the power of story. In commentary for that episode, the author, Graham Yost, says that the "shovel line" is the one he is most proud of in his whole life as a writer! Yost and Mykelti Williamson, the actor who played Fearless, explain that, after the shovel episode and from that moment forward, the group of writers and actors asked of each new script, "Do we have a shovel moment in this story?" It became their rallying call.

Note the uses made of the story. The account, "I brought a shovel" (instead of handcuffs to arrest or verbal reprimands to scold), informs observers about the relationship between the partners. The shovel story is a critical incident shared by the two characters as it affects their relationship from that point forward. The shovel story is a memorable message for the group of players and writers whose collaboration on *Boomtown* incorporates it as an indication of the quality to which they aspire through the rest of their work on the show.

People tend to do such things: tell, repeat, and make use of their accounts. Some stories help to shape us or our groups. They change, sustain, motivate, warn, warm, or worry us. This part of the chapter is about types of stories we use to show or start special things in a group. We discuss story types that ameliorate direction-giving efforts: improving their potency. First, some terminology (see Table 8.1).

Table 8.1	A Nomenclature for Story
Sensemaking	The meaning-making aspect of communication
Narrative	A story; the coherence of meaning extracted from messages or experiences
Account	The version a person gives of what has, is, or ought to happen; their story or narrative
Frame	A construction of meanings used to make sense of something (see Chapter 9)
Defining stories	Accounts we make of particular instances we use to decide and describe who we are, what we do, and what matters to us
Master narrative	The whole or gestalt of the grouping story from its foundation to its aspiration, including its saga of shared struggle and sacrifice

Some narratives are intended to do more than just tell a story. Some are used intentionally as an attempt to influence others, perhaps to change specific aspects of their future behaviors. Other stories may have a moral to them that provides general guidance for living life well. Some stories actually become "defining" experiences by which other experiences are measured.

❖ MAKING ACCOUNTS, SENSEMAKING, AND DEFINING STORIES ARE FOUNDATIONS OF NARRATIVE

Much of grouping behavior is spent making accounts and sensemaking. *Accounts* are the narrative/version a person gives of what has, is, or ought to be happening. Making an account helps us make sense of an experience (see Chapter 7). As we group, we need to make sense of the salient events, ideas, or activities we experience. We do this by comparing what is new and unknown with terms that are familiar so that the new something starts to make sense to us.

Regardless of where we find ourselves in the hierarchy of an organization, community, or team, Keyton (2005) says each of us helps make sense of our environment and of our grouping activities and interactions. She says sensemaking and defining stories are evidence of this involvement. *Sensemaking* is the meaning-making process (Weick, 1995). *Defining stories* are those accounts that help us decide and describe who we are, what we do, and what matters most to us (Brown, 1990). As we make sense of our experience, we integrate our spin and ideology into our account. The meanings we apply to our co-constructions become our *framing* for the details we decide are most important to us as we figure out how we ought to behave as a result.

❖ CHARACTERIZATION, IDEOGRAPHS, AND RHETORICAL DEPICTION ARE POTENT FORMS OF NARRATIVE

Scholars identify several key frames (characterizations, ideographs, and rhetorical depictions[4]) that often make their way into group accounts. *Characterization* is how we portray the nature of something or someone we frame. For example, "Better watch out when Fred is friendly; it means he's out to get you." The characterization of friendly Freddy probably colors future interactions with Fred. Lucaites and Condit (1990) use Malcolm X characterizing every Black American as an "ex-slave" to highlight his combative orientation and ideology. They say characterizations can manifest as an emotionally charged label, phrase, or other depiction that creates connotations and evokes emotions that prime the listener for action.

Something to Consider

Characterization should always be of interest to direction-givers: both when selecting your own characterizations (a process to be undertaken with great care) and when listening for loadings in characterizations made by others. They provide evidence of a larger narrative that might be either useful or worrisome. They might be

---

[4]Rather than expend much energy trying to distinguish among the boundaries of these interconnected concepts, we suggest focus on the essential nature of each. Can you identify aspects of a grouping story that might function as one or more of these concepts? If so, you know you are onto something.

found in any story of group experience. They may also appear outside of narrative structure, but when they do, they are shorthand for a larger narrative. Characterizations may show the orientation of a speaker, including his or her values and preferred action. They may also signal group ideology and vision. Shared group characterizations are used as a guide and as an authorizing agent when sorting new information and accounts. Characterization may be the route by which one individual's framing becomes integrated into the broader group story. They develop currency and authoritative weight in a group as they chain out and become shared by others, integrated into group stories, activities, and direction. You can locate characterizations in formal communications and in small talk.

Ideographs are the value-laden aspects of a group's shared vocabulary (Delgado, 1995; McGee, 1980). Ideographs are tips-of-the-iceberg evidence of the group's *ideology:* its dogma or philosophy of basic beliefs, values, and attitudes. Ideographs include ideologically approved words that represent members of the group. For example, *comrade* represents a person and a relationship among members of a communist community. Ideological priorities guide political attempts to shape group identity. For example, consider how preferences can turn into angry confrontations about [mis]use of terms such as bailout vs. loan; victim vs. survivor; Latino vs. Hispanic; African American vs. American vs. ex-slave. Ideographs appear frequently among the recurring terms group members use when sharing their symbolically converged accounts.

Rhetorical depiction illuminates or compresses key aspects of the group's story into a brief, potent portrayal (Osborn, 1986). Just as a sculpture can capture the essence of struggle in a marble portrayal, the direction-giver might use characterizations, ideographs, and other framings to create a depiction that captures the essence of what we hate about our enemy or love about ourselves. For example, communists have their rhetorical depiction of capitalists and vice versa; Republicans have their rhetorical depiction of Democrats and vice versa. A rhetorical depiction includes the key frames groups use to reference and describe each other.

Something to Consider

A rhetorical depiction can be at the center of what moves a group. When invoked, a shared depiction transports grouping members into their common framework for

(Continued)

(Continued)

responding to basic issues they have already figured out how they want addressed. Osborn (1986) explains that "we experience the world either directly or through depiction, and even direct experience can be mediated and predisposed by previous depictions that prepare us for the experience" (p. 81). "Depictions are lenses that can color what we see" (p. 86). They have the "capacity to facilitate identification, the sense of closeness or oneness that can develop among those who participate in social communication." Such identification "determines what we shall do, or at least what we shall attempt" (p. 92). "Rhetorical depiction typically does not arise from any single technique or moment in discourse. More often it is a controlled gestalt," (p. 80) co-constructed over time that insinuates "itself into our consciousness" becoming "difficult to dislodge" (pp. 80–81).

A rhetorical depiction can begin with a single characterization, framing a person, event, or behavior. However, over time it can become a complex of representations we share about what is meaningful in our group story, especially about the nature of us and/or of our primary competitor or enemy or problem. It likely includes the ideographs and characterizations that matter most to our group.

These three framing devices provide shortcuts to stories of shared group experiences. When we use a characterization, ideograph, or rhetorical depiction, we quickly access the interwoven set of shared meanings in the broader narrative. We hear one and quickly grasp the struggle and which side of it we are on. These are among the most potent portable parts of a master narrative of our group.

❖ THE MASTER NARRATIVE IS THE OVERARCHING STORY OF YOUR GROUP'S EXPERIENCE

If someone introduces you to his or her group, that person probably will tell you what he or she thinks are "high points" about the group's experience. "There are over 1,000 members in our temple" or "We have the number one recruiting class in collegiate soccer at Akron."

A master narrative, however, is more than just the "high points." A *master narrative* is a gestalt or overarching story of experience: past, present, future. The master narrative of a group involves all of what is important or meaningful to the group. It includes how each meaningful aspect connects with and shapes other meaningful parts of the group's ever-unfolding experience story.

Do you have a master narrative for your own life? (No? Really?) If you have had more than one job or have been in more than one committed relationship, how well did each seem to fit into the rest of your life? If one job or relationship is more fulfilling than another, it could be because it fits better with your own sense of who you are and what you should be doing with your life. If you ever find yourself wondering, "Why am I doing this?" or "Why am I so unhappy?" or "Is this really all there is?" you have a master narrative for your life. You use your master narrative to orient yourself and to decide if your expectations are being met by the experiences you are currently constructing.

Groups, once they mature enough to have a sense of themselves, have co-constructed a master narrative. A group's master narrative includes the key framings we discuss above. It also includes the group's foundational myth, its saga of shared struggles and sacrifices, and its aspirational stories of future experiences.

The *foundational story* is the myth of who we are and how we got started: our "once upon a time." Our *saga story* tells of past experiences, especially of the struggles and sacrifices of our heroes since our founding. The anticipated and aspirational aspects of future group experiences are our *vision/outcome story:* the "happily ever after." All effective groups need such stories as a basic part of their sense of themselves. These recurring stories are renewable, reusable, and recyclable rhetorical resources for direction-givers.

Such stories are portable experiences you can employ when you need to give direction to your group. When your direction-giving account taps a foundational, saga, or an aspirational story that the group has already converged upon as meaningful and authoritative, it adds rhetorical force to your attempt.

Something to Think About and Discuss With Others

A master narrative takes time for a group to develop. Some relationships and groups may not last long enough to develop one. Some may develop a master narrative without being fully aware that they have constructed such a high level of shared meaning. A master narrative may be deeply embedded and difficult to access. You might only get whiffs of it in the background of stories people share. Try listening for coherence across stories of past, present, and future experiences. When aspects of a master narrative are clear to you, they can help you make sense of new episodes and information. What is the master narrative in your group?

It is easier to give direction when you are well versed in your group's master narrative. This is especially true for those who become engaged by it and connected some way with it in the minds of other grouping members. What it means for us to be in this group, what we should do, and how we should respond to a new episode are questions much easier to address through the filter of the master narrative. If people know your place in the story of their group, they will better understand how to receive the direction you offer. If you know the story of the group, you will better understand your rhetorical options for asserting influence. Getting in touch with and connected to a master narrative happens as group members share stories and accumulate shared experiences with you over time.

❖ CREATE COHERENCE IN MEMORABLE MESSAGES, CRITICAL INCIDENTS, TEACHING TALES, AND NUGGETS

Memorable messages are accounts or incidents that help us understand how to fit into a group (Stohl, 1986). They are remembered for a long period of time and have a major influence on our life in the group (Barge & Schlueter, 2004). They can be rhetorical, or unintended. Memorable messages can be behaviors we observe or accounts that we hear (e.g., someone stealing paperclips; a story of an unpleasant experience; an order or command—do this; don't do that). They provide us information we think helps make sense of a group and its culture.

A *critical incident* is an act that supposedly creates a turning point in the life of a group. A key direction-giver says or does something. Afterward, the group's story unfolds in a way that is significantly different than it would have otherwise. In 1961, John F. Kennedy said the United States should put a man on the moon by the end of the decade. In 1969, Neil Armstrong took the stroll. That is the way the story goes: Kennedy's speech was a critical incident.

In the moment, it is probably hard to tell what is/is not going to be a critical incident. Indeed, critical incidents may not actually be empirically demonstrable at any point in time. However, critical incidents can be found in the stories by which grouping members attribute cause for changes in their group (Cohen & Smith, 1976; Flanagan, 1954). Although a president helps develop public policy, Kennedy was not a significant figure in NASA, nor did he have a foundation in science or aeronautics. With the perspective of history, however, those who tell the story make his contribution clear. Kennedy's address to Congress advocating increased funding so we could go to the moon is cited as the critical incident that made it so, though he was 6 years dead before the deed was done.

Someone who has not been a key direction-giver becomes one simply by stimulating a critical incident (see Table 1.3 in Chapter 1). Critical incidents are what grouping members believe about their experience in the group, and they provide insight into those who tell them. Such a story places the act's originator in the role of key direction-giver. Many of the best stories for shaping group direction "come from the critical moments" direction-givers confront (Kouzes & Posner, 1993, p. 197). Such moments are likely to become part of the group's saga story.

Teaching tales are accounts told to change someone's behavior. These rhetorical attempts try to influence present or future behavior: to help someone learn how to behave in the group. A teaching tale can be based in a *mundane moment* (e.g., a parent tries to impart basic knowledge to his or her child; an employer trains a new employee), a *teachable moment* (trying to help someone learn from something that goes wrong), or a *crisis moment* (trying to encourage transformation of self or system in response to significantly shifting circumstances). Any account intentionally employed to teach something to someone is a teaching tale, including types of stories we discuss above and below.

A *nugget* is a brief bit of information that interests or intrigues you (Pond & Burtis, 1998). It is an encapsulated idea you want to try to remember and to use later (e.g., a verse, quotation, or pithy phrase—brief, succinct, concise: yet forceful and to the point). It can capture an essence or evoke a delight or desire. In *Dead Poets Society*, Robin Williams plays the character of John Keating, a teacher who inspires students with the admonition: "carpe diem" or "seize the day." When you hear a nugget, it tugs at you, intrigues you, and makes particularly good sense to you. That is probably why Keating selected this nugget to share. Regardless, it makes particularly good sense to a group of students who approach their final year of school differently because of it: Keating's nugget becomes their memorable message.

"Mining for nuggets" is a metaphor that borrows from the process of mining for gold. You may have to dig through mounds of moldering material to find the small something(s) that might be useful to you. A shiny bit of gold in a huge pile of debris is still a treasure. Direction-givers can be helped by finding nuggets to share with a group or by locating such nuggets among group experiences.

Something to Consider

Reading a book in search of nuggets is different than reading a book to find out what the book has to say. What makes something a nugget is that you have use for it or interest in it. It could be a bit of info about a skill you wish you had. It could express a philosophy. When you search for nuggets, you are looking actively for something of utility (see Chapter 6). You might find a whole nugget or you might have to make one: taking sprinklings of gold dust as you accumulate them over time until you have enough shiny material to mold your own. When you find a nugget, write it down, pick it up, and find a way to save it so that you are sure to stumble across it again and again over time. What nuggets do you already carry about with you: What pithy ideas do you hold near and dear?

Nuggets are sometimes found in *familiar phrases* or cultural clichés such as "don't cry over spilt milk." Examples include mottos, proverbs, and sayings. *Mottos* are rules a person or group tries to live by (e.g., "What would Jesus do?"—Sheldon, 1896; Karl Marx's "From each according to their ability, to each according to their need"—Walicki, 1995). *Proverbs* are pithy phrases expressing something that is obviously true and suggestive for how to behave. *Sayings* are personal, family, team, or workplace phrases repeatedly invoked and meaningful only to those in the group. Nuggets you note that others have put into play can give you a sense of the group and of its members. Nuggets you use that engage the group can help you shape the story of the group.

Something to Consider

Familiar phrases, though clichéd, truncate the need for a full telling of a framing or story. Among the most portable accounts, they are meaningful across many groups sharing the same culture. Experiments show that such phrases can be quickly and easily understood and can be influential in situations where their content is not carefully tested because the receiver gets transported by the account they evoke (Howard, 1997).

As a direction-giver, you need to seek stories you can use to help shape the group's experience. Many sensemaking and defining stories are accounts of when something memorable happened or began for a group. Other stories are special because they shape an individual in ways that change his or her experience in a group. Still others are important as they add rhetorical force to a direction-giving attempt. All such stories can be used to help show or to start something special in your group.

❖ FIGURE OUT WHAT OTHERS WILL HEAR IN THE EXPERIENCE STORIES YOU TELL AND HELP SHAPE

Using story effectively involves more than just telling a story. Telling stories does not serve a useful function for your group if you tell them simply because you like them or the attention they bring you. To be effective, symbolic convergence must result between storyteller and listener.

Co-constructing a symbolic convergence about the story of your group's experience requires negotiation regarding what will become your group's shared meanings. We work together to construct a story about issues we face (W. R. Fisher, 1987; Gouran, 2003). We search group experiences and our own for missing pieces until we feel we have a reasonable account. "If it were me, I would . . ." and "nobody does that unless . . ." are common formulations.

Remember, when we hear a story, we experience it. It is not surprising that we exercise influence over how a story unfolds for us. The stories you tell have to be "picked" by the group as part of the mix of meanings they use to explain how they experience the group. Your stories need to be used by them to guide what they want the experience of the group to become.

An *official account* of group experience is arrived at through a process similar to the method of residues we use to negotiate who will play direction-giving roles in the group (see Chapter 5). People decide which stories are meaningful by paying attention to some stories and not others. People act differently as a result of having heard some stories. Many stories and story fragments are posited only to be ignored; the ones that matter are the ones that remain over time as an aspect of how the group engages their experience. New stories, in order to matter, must get integrated into the ongoing story the group is constructing of its experiences.

Something to Consider

MBSA (managing by storying around) argues that "storytelling is an effective leadership practice. It's simple: anyone can tell a story. It's timeless: stories are fadproof. It's universally appealing: everybody, regardless of age, gender, race, listens to stories. Its fun: stories are enjoyable. It's also a useful form of training, a good method for empowering people, an effective recognition device, a strong recruiting and hiring tool, a useful sales technique, and an excellent way to pass along corporate traditions" (Armstrong, 1992[5]).

Using story to give direction does not require you to be a masterful storyteller any more than being a good storyteller means you are an effective direction-giver. However, the ability to use story as a direction-giver can involve several skills. One skill is constructing stories well or, better yet, co-constructing them with others. Another skill is collecting stories as they happen or as they are being shared by others. This provides you with narrative content that is authentic and has already been judged as meaningful and authoritative by folks in the group. Story skills also include figuring out how and when to tell a story.

Something to Consider: Some Story Skills

When you have a story to tell, commit to telling it well. "If you are feeling truly excited . . . show it. If you are deeply concerned . . . show it. Allowing your emotions to surface brings excitement to your voice and increases your natural tendency to use gestures and to smile. . . . Start your story by relating an heroic deed. . . . Give your story a theme, and be willing to repeat it. Keep the story short. Use people's names. Verify all facts. Be sure to end your message or story with its moral: a conclusion that demonstrates concretely the intended message or lesson to be learned. . . . The stories you tell should be about others, about what constituents are doing to put shared values into practice, and should demonstrate their commitment . . . Telling stories about others gives you the chance to reinforce that everyone is a . . . [direction-giver]. Hearing a story about people . . . with whom they can identify . . . stimulates them to learn how to take such actions themselves. Talking about heroes encourages everyone

---

[5]This is Kouzes and Posner's (1993, p. 10) synthesis of Armstrong's work.

to do the right thing. Besides, people seldom tire of hearing stories about themselves and others they know. Such stories tend to get repeated, and the moral of the story gets spread far and wide in the organization" (Kouzes & Posner, 1993, pp. 210–211). Who are effective direction-giving storytellers you admire?

❖ IN CONCLUSION

The ongoing story you are experiencing as "your life" affects your interpretation of any new story you hear. And any new story you hear can affect the ongoing story of your life. To be effective as a direction-giver, you need to help shape the story of your group's experience: past, present, and future. Nest your direction-giving efforts in and into the accounts others share about their group. Your effectiveness is linked to your ability to keep up with the experience story that is engaging other group members. In Chapters 9 and 10, we discuss skills for framing stories and a special sort of story: leadership vision made salient by crisis.

9

Develop the Framing Skills Needed by Every Direction-Giver

We want to present ourselves well to the world, and our clothes help us do so. The clothes we wear should keep us warm in winter's blusters and safe from the sun's rays. They also hide our private parts and bulges. We want items that fit, but color and style are often as important to us as length and width. Which cloth brings out the color in your eyes, and which makes you look robust and healthy? Which pattern makes you look plumb nifty and which, just plain plump?

Clothes serve two functions. When we pick out what to wear each day, we consider what we think will look good on us and the situation we will be in (e.g., the weather; the work we do). Some days, both functions matter to us; on others, just one. When you pick the clothes you wear, you shape part of the impression you will make on others. You are framing yourself. In fact, *you frame yourself by what you wear, by how well you groom, and by what you say and do.*

In Chapter 8, we work on communication skills needed by all types of direction-givers. That work continues here with a discussion of the framings that direction-givers use to shape their accounts of grouping experiences. We discuss the nature of framing and explain five framing skills.

You can tie this material to your own group by asking, "Who does the framing in my group?" In particular, "Who shapes what our group eventually co-constructs as the most meaningful parts of our experiences?" "Who shapes what our group is doing now, and who frames how group members view that activity?" "Who shapes what our group decides it wants someday to accomplish, and who shapes what each of us should be doing toward those ends?" Each of these is a framing: part of the experience story co-constructed by and for your group.

All direction-giving involves framing. Of course, some talk seems devoid of frames (e.g., "do x to y"). But communications play out within a contextual framing that is co-constructed by interacting parties. There is a relationship between the source and receiver. There is also some (clear or clouded) sense of the general nature and purpose of their joint activity. Certainly, if there is a direction-giving attempt, it is framed by the context of the ongoing group experience. Absent a contextual framing, even the simplest sentence ("do x to y") makes little sense. "Who are you to tell me that?" "Why me; why should I?" "What is x, and why should I think so poorly of y?" Without a frame, we react by searching for coherence by providing our own.

Frames help you with every aspect of your direction-giving attempts. You use framing to define problems, diagnose causes, make moral judgments, and suggest remedies (Entman, 1993). You use framing as you are *positioning* yourself as useful to the group in certain circumstances (see Chapter 5). You use framing if you *prime the pump*, trying to "ready someone" for an upcoming event (e.g., being especially nice before they go to vote in an election between you and someone else) or to get them prepared to behave in a certain way (e.g., a bartender puts a $5.00 bill in the tip jar so others feel they should tip). You use framing if you do *agenda setting*,[1] which is telling folks what to think about for an upcoming meeting, without telling them what to think. Regardless of the direction-giving you offer, your efforts are enhanced by skillful framing.

---

[1]McCombs and Shaw (1972) coined the term *agenda setting* to explain how mass-mediated sources of information (e.g., journalists) affect their audience: by getting them to think about a subject, not what to think on that subject. We think that agenda-setting is put in play in most groups by their direction-givers.

❖ FRAMING IS BASIC TO ALL COMMUNICATION: YOUR FRAMES SHAPE YOUR DIRECTION-GIVING ACCOUNTS

What is framing? Well, think about the work done by the frame (see Table 9.1). A frame, in a building, is the skeleton of a house (or backbone of some other fabrication). The frame supports everything else that matters. A frame holding a painting or blackboard separates that item from its surroundings. The frame provides a line of demarcation. The frame for a window or door is the place in space that holds the door or window. The frame allows a particular tool or activity to work. But frames do not just go around, between, or through an object, space, or idea.

Frames can affect the nature of what is framed: affect how it is perceived, affect its shape, and affect its composition. For example, the clothes you wear (and the frame and mat surrounding a painting) make certain features more readily apparent to the eye. How a frame of film or video is constructed leads the viewer's eye through the resulting visual form material. Framing can suggest speed and progress of the character or car. It can suggest struggle and impending

Table 9.1	Consider the Rhetorical Resources You Can Dig Out of the "Frame" Metaphor

Each of the following suggests rhetorical options for your own direction-giving attempts. A frame is something that goes around the outside of something on display (e.g., a painting). Such a frame ought to "bring out" or "turn up" essential and interesting aspects of what is framed (e.g., a particular color in the work of art might be brought out by including a like color in the matting or framing material used to encompass the painting). A frame on a chalk or bulletin board provides a sense of completion and of quality crafting. The potency of potential in a person or animal is suggested by its frame. For breeding animals, the frame is their skeletal structure on which desired meat or muscle will grow—or some other desired characteristic such as ability to be a fast horse or durable bull moving over rough terrain. For people, what do you think is suggested by the Timberlake lyric, "that pretty little face on that pretty little frame"? To frame someone is to make them appear to be guilty when they are, in fact, innocent. With eyeglasses, the frame holds the key part of the tool—the lens. That frame helps you focus on aspects of whatever is out there, but it also creates blind spots where you cannot see. In short, as metaphors go, "framing" is loaded.

failure. Ads in magazines are laid out to frame the material so that the viewers' experience is anticipated and guided. The quality of such a framing can be measured by how well it leads your pupil through the ad and whether it does so in the order desired by the advertiser. In short, we use frames in many ways, each with potential applications in direction-giving. In particular, we use frames to shape each and every thing that we try to communicate.

Something to Consider

What is the difference in your experience when viewing a DVD presented in widescreen compared to the full-screen version? Consider the fact that approximately half of the visual material is lost in the full-screen version. Film editors make selections for you, as they reframe the original film.

Frames are basic aspects of the messages we share and of the stories we tell. Frames are basic to our understanding of the context in which we communicate—for example, of the experience stories in our groups (see Chapters 7 and 8). If you receive a message but do not understand the frames in the message, you are more likely to misunderstand and even to make mistakes, especially if an issue arises that requires your interpretation. If you receive a message but do not understand the contextual framework in which your interaction is unfolding, you are just as likely to misunderstand and make mistakes. When two people operate from perspectives informed by entirely different frames, there will likely be some very creative misunderstandings. The mistakes you make may baffle the both of you.

Frames help us make sense of what we are doing together and to blend our energies well. The person whose sense of the group is shaping the story of the group is the one who frames the focal point of the group's attention. Direction-givers struggle if they are not able to frame the context in which they offer direction. They struggle if they do not know how to frame their direction-giving effort.

Something to Think About and Discuss With Others

On May 1, 2003, President Bush held a press conference on board the USS *Abraham Lincoln* in which he declared the end to "major combat operations in

Iraq," 41 days after the war began. The president, in full flight gear, co-piloted the U.S. Navy Viking S-3B jet to the carrier. He spoke to a world audience. A banner behind him proclaimed "Mission Accomplished." This phrase was later appropriated by opponents of the war and of Mr. Bush who argued that it showed he was wrong-headed and would not come to grips with the reality on the ground in Iraq. How many framings can you identify from this description and context?

❖ FRAMES, LIKE DEFINITIONS, ARE HOW WE ATTACH MEANING TO THINGS

A *frame* is a constructed meaning. When we construct a frame we make a meaning. Using a frame is attaching a meaning to something by attaching a frame. So, a frame is a meaningful construction. We share our frames when we include one or more of them in our account or story of something (e.g., a recent group experience). If we develop or negotiate a frame in our group, it is a meaningful co-construction. Because communication is the making of meaning, and a frame is a constructed meaning, *communicating is the process by which we create and apply frames.*

We name and define things in order to understand them. We define a word by attaching a meaning to it. We define a situation by attaching meaningful words and more elaborated descriptions to it. In fact, *to frame* and *to define* are often synonymous and simultaneous. We define a situation by selecting terms that fit our perspective on the situation. In a group, we struggle until we develop a shared sense for how to frame our situation. We need to develop a symbolic convergence of frames for what we are doing.

Framing is the act of constructing meaning. Framing is also the act of attaching meaning to something. Sometimes we need to articulate and elaborate on the connections among several frames so we develop a framework, showing how they are related, including how to use them together. A *framework* is a coherent organization of related ideas and frames. In Chapter 5, we encourage you to develop a framework of your own to organize the ideas you have about which actions will work best for you as a direction-giver given various circumstances. Your framework organizes your ideas for how to give direction well.

Something to Consider

Framing is a natural, human process. "We frame reality in order to comprehend it, negotiate it, manage it, and choose appropriate repertoires of cognition and action" (Gitlin, 1980, pp. 6–7). However, your framings must work in conjunction with your receiver's schemata. People with whom you interact already have psychological categories and stereotypes as part of their own clusters of meanings. In other words, they have their own framings (Entman, 1993). Your framing has to behave in a manner so that what you say to them makes sense given their own framing. Frames provide clues about how we think the group should orient to its experiences. Frames show motives through "the presence or absence of certain keywords, stock phrases, stereotyped images, sources of information, and sentences that provide thematically reinforcing clusters of facts or judgment" (Entman, 1993, p. 52). People focus on what we consider actionable aspects of a group situation. We experience these as exigencies that we perceive will make grouping with others in particular ways into good choices. The exigencies we perceive are affected by the frames we have of our grouping. The frames we have for grouping are affected by the exigencies we perceive. Our frames show our subjective sense of a situation and of our group experience (Goffman, 1974). "Situations are shorthand terms for motives. . . . We discern situational patterns by means of the particular vocabulary of the cultural group into which we were born" (Burke, 1965, pp. 29, 35). "To comprehend an exigence[2] is to have a motive. . . . Exigence must be seen neither as a cause of rhetorical action nor as intention, but as social motive . . . : a set of particular social patterns and expectations" (Miller, 1984, p. 158).

Frames can be found in any persuasive message, organizational audit, or strategic plan. Whenever you need to construct a particular and compelling sense of your situation or how to respond to it, your effort will involve framing.

❖ FRAMES SHOW MOTIVES, SHAPE EXPERIENCES, AND PROVIDE AUTHORITATIVE WEIGHT IN THE GROUP

When you are framing, you translate group experiences, as well as the exigencies you perceive for additional action, into meanings you want others to consider. Frames give clues to the motives at work. Your frames tell the group about you, and their frames tell you about them.

---

[2]*Exigence* is Bitzer's (1968) original term, which we replace with *exigency.*

In groups, motives manifest in our basic communications, and as we interact, we negotiate the shared frames that get integrated into the story of our group experience. For example, if someone opposes your group's choices, you might hear that disagreement in his or her framing of the group's action. "This risky scheme we are using gives me pause" or "It is interesting how what we are doing is changing the basic mission of our group."

The frames we use help shape the experience of our group. Our choice of terms always affects what we foreground and what we ignore. *Foregrounding* represents the parts of our situation that are given priority by our having named them (or by some other indication that they are meaningful to us). Each frame we use draws attention to something by taking that attention away from other possibilities. Other possibilities get backgrounded. *Backgrounding* represents the parts of the situation that are diminished or ignored by being left out of a frame or by being pushed to the side. We foreground what matters most to us, making it salient, as we background what we are not attending to, making it appear unimportant.

Direction-giving involves a series of attempts to foreground some issues and ideas while backgrounding others. Simons (2001) says that anyone selecting a frame "must decide what will be intensified and what will be downplayed" (p. 117). Burke (1989) extends the concept of framing to almost every word because such symbols magnify (foreground) what they represent while reducing (backgrounding or even excluding) what they do not focus upon.

In some cases, what is not in the frame is as meaningful as what is included. The same is true for what is implied by the frame and for what can be understood to be just outside of the frame. Entman (1993) says the process of framing includes selecting what is salient. To frame is to select some aspects of a perceived reality and then to treat them as important.

When we develop our frames, we use terms and definitions that we think give us a tactical or strategic advantage. Since the frames we use are never free of motive, neither is the terminology we employ. It is not objective. It is based in the needs we have to make sense of our circumstances and to profit from our grouping efforts.

Our most extravagant efforts to influence others begin with the basics: the selection and definition of terms. Schiappa (2003) says that our choice of definitions should be guided less by what a dictionary says and more according to the politics of the context. His criterion: Which terms and meanings work best for our group? As we negotiate group frames, we seek symbolic convergence around terms and meanings that meet group needs and earn group approval.

When a group agrees on what is meaningful and how to represent it, the group puts its stamp of approval and authoritative weight on its interpretation (Clark, 2005). A meaning has authority in a group when it is co-constructed into community consensus. Consensus develops through interaction. People contest meanings in front of each other. As they interact, members begin to use a frame and then rely on it and support it until it is normative. They select preferred terminological and definitional framings from among those offered as direction for their group.

Groups converge around a key term as reasonable to use, a definition as appropriate to attach, or an interpretation as necessary to make. As we attain sufficient symbolic convergence, we can succeed as a group. Framing attempts that follow get authoritative weight from our past choices (to the extent that the new framing attempt plays well among existing group frames).

❖ DEVELOP THE FRAMING SKILLS YOU NEED TO USE TO BE EFFECTIVE AS A DIRECTION-GIVER

Effective frames attract attention, enable comprehension, and influence acceptance. How can you be intentional about becoming more effective in your own framing attempts? First, understand five interwoven framing forms and skills: naming, faming, blaming, claiming, and taming (see Table 9.2). Second, know the territory that is available for framing: available to you and to any direction-giver. We start by discussing the framing skills, and then, in the last section in this chapter, we address the territory direction-givers frame in every group.

❖ NAMING, FAMING, AND BLAMING ARE BASIC ASPECTS OF THE PROCESS FOR MAKING MEANINGS

In Chapters 6 and 7, we discuss the nature of communication: how group direction is co-constructed by grouping people as they share accounts of their past, present, and future experiences. Basic processes in shaping these accounts are naming, faming, and blaming.

Naming, faming, and blaming are fundamental framing activities. We use these three to create and shape the composition of important messages we want to share. We use them to try to manage the perception

Table 9.2   Five Interwoven Framing Forms and Skills

Basis for Clustering	Framing Skill	Description
Create basic meanings = name, fame, and/or blame	Naming	Putting words or labels (e.g., characterizations, ideographs) and their definitions onto meaningful aspects of the group experience.
	Faming	Putting values and evaluations onto some aspect of the group's experience. Determining and describing what or who is good and bad; what is and is not effective; what is and is not appropriate.
	Blaming	Making attributions of causality for key aspects of grouping. In particular, who or what caused a good/bad, (in)effective, or (in)appropriate thing. Can stimulate *shaming* or *maiming*.
Create elaborated, meaningful constructions = claim or tame	Claiming	Making a cogent argument. An elaborated case, position, or idea becomes powerful and influential because it is well reasoned and supported and then gets centrally processed by engaged others.
	Taming	Creating a sense of identification (or other emotional connection) between yourself and others so that you or your idea is influential if peripherally processed by opposing or disengaged others.

others have of the accounts we share. These framing forms provide the most basic of meanings. However, the most elaborated meaningful constructions and framing activities also inevitably involve a fair share of these three forms. So, the first three forms of frames are always in play as we co-construct accounts of grouping experiences.

We are naming, faming, and/or blaming whenever we attach words, definitions, or an attribution of quality or of causality to the ideas, events, actions, or people that comprise our grouping experience. Naming attaches a label and/or definition to something, faming attaches a value or evaluation to something, and blaming attributes causality for something. We use these frame forms to shape perceptions of what is important or insignificant, good or bad, progress or frustration, success or failure, and who is to blame for anything on that list (see Table 9.3). Though inextricably interwoven (use of one almost always triggers the appearance of the others), for purposes of clarity, we discuss each of these three framing skills as though they are discrete.

Naming is attaching words and/or definitions to an aspect of our group experience. You do this as part of any account you create. You do this by attaching a loaded or evocative word, label, or other symbol to the thing of interest to you. Whenever we attach a word, label, or other symbol to something, we attach the meaning we have for it as well. That meaning is probably some combination of the formal definition and informal connotation we associate with the word, label, or symbol. We can attach our meanings explicitly, or we can provide a bit of information (e.g., just a word, short phrase, or image) and leave meanings for others to infer (for example, wearing flight gear and co-piloting a fighter jet). To name is a most basic act of communication and of direction-giving.

Naming is accomplished by attaching meanings and often involves just putting a word or definition onto something. *Definitions* are shared meanings for symbols, including words or labels. *Labels* are meaningful words and phrases, including, for example, any time you employ characterization or ideograph (see Chapter 8). *Symbols* are anything that represents something else.

So, all words are symbols, but so are use of space or time to show your power, use of touch to show your concern or sexual interest, and architecture such as targeting the Twin Towers and Pentagon as symbols of America's power and influence. Additional symbols include the artifacts with which we adorn ourselves or our group (e.g., gang or university colors; flags; sexy scents or piercings; clothes; **ink**) and emblems—nonverbal acts with cultural definitions (e.g., the okay sign; flipping the bird; moving the head to indicate yes or no).

Once something is named, it has a definition for those who accept the term that has been applied. "The 'primary definition' sets the limit for all subsequent discussion by *framing what the problem is.* This initial framework then provides the criteria by which all subsequent contributions are labeled as 'relevant' to the debate" (Hall, Critcher, Jefferson, Clarke, & Roberts, 1978, p. 59). She or he who names a thing, defining what is meaningful about it, frames that part of the group's experience. With sufficient symbolic convergence, terminology

Table 9.3	Examples of Naming, Faming, and Blaming in Action (+ Shaming and Maiming)

Naming, faming, and blaming help create basic meanings for things: in the following case, about a "new plan" designed to "save" a company that has "fallen on hard times."

Framing Device	Sara	Jess	Parker
Naming = labels and definitions are applied to aspects of the group experience.	This could be just the chance we have been waiting for to shake things up around here. We can make money off this. Maybe the pain we feel now can be used for gain over time if we just hang together.	Brother, I can't believe it! We are giving up, that's all this "not really new plan" really means. This is our going out of business sale. We are waving the white flag. What a travesty. We need to start looking for new jobs.	We are just doing some retrenching to stay ahead of the curve. This new plan lets us act now and address issues that present challenges to us for the next few months. So chill out, dude.
Faming = value or evaluation is attached to named elements of the group experience.	Things are not as rosy or as bleak as some folks think. We are struggling, but we have not failed, and we may soon turn the corner. This is a good, steady plan for a vigorous effort to build a better future for us all.	This awful mess is evidence of the cancer on the heart of this outfit. We are sick, and this risky scheme is like throwing us an anchor. Hello: we are drowning here! We should act like our hair is on fire because it is. Brother, a bunch of fools is in charge.	The fundamentals of our e-company are basically sound. It is good to cut the fat once in a while. We need to shake off the rust. That is all we are doing. We are a family. We take care of our own. So chill out, dude.
Blaming = causality is attributed for what has been named or	Folks, we are not alone. The whole economy is struggling$_3$. I don't care who or	Our management is a joke$_1$. You are a joke$_4$. Can you spell hara-kiri; seppuku$_{4,5}$?	Dude! Our management team has been working hard to keep us within

Table 9.3 (Continued)

Framing Device	Sara	Jess	Parker
famed. Blaming may also involve scapegoating[1], mortification[2], or transcending[3]. Blaming may lead to shaming[4] and maiming[5].	what was the cause[3]. In fact, just blame me; the buck stops with me[2]. What matters now is action. The plan has flaws, but we cannot give up. This plan might be able to get us to a better place by next year. Let's try.	That's what they do in Japan if they screw up like this[4]. We might as well have George W. Bush or Nancy Pelosi in charge[5]. The bunch of you should be fired, beginning with you, doofus dude[1], because it is your mess[1,4]. And don't call me dude.	the margins of profitability. They have kept us in the top tier versus most of our competitors to this point. You should be ashamed of your attacks[4], Jess. Get on board, or resign, you damn crybaby![4,5]

What frames do you see in each message? Do not spend much energy deciding if a frame is only this form or that. A single frame might incorporate, in part or whole, two or three of the forms. Subscripts in the above dialog indicate examples with matching numbers in the "framing device" box.

becomes a tool we use to accomplish high-level integrations of our energies.

Faming is attributing value or evaluation to some aspect of grouping (e.g., to an aspect already deemed worthy by having been named or, perhaps, something given a name by getting famed). Faming is an attempt to sort out and shape group values and evaluations. For example, faming says what matters to us, assesses how well we are doing, or suggests the better course for what we should do next. Faming frames may describe what or who is good or bad, what is or is not effective, which of our acts have or have not been successful, what is or is not appropriate, which actions we should do, and from what ought we abstain. All of these involve valuations, assessments, and evaluations. They are frames that suggest what our group ought to value.

There are two sides to fame: the bright and the dark; the "we should" and the "we should not"; the "we have already" and the "we have not yet." Both sides are faming frames. To point to some aspect of grouping and say "that is an abomination" fames that aspect of the group's experience as notoriously bad, just as saying "what a blessing" fames something as incredibly good. Fame, you see, can be good or bad or both good and bad; the fame metaphor is inclusive, representing both sides. When we fame, we proclaim our praises or post our protests, creating sides. To create sides is making one valuation relative to another. We say her, not him; this, not that; we should, should not; we have, have not. We fame to shape our sense of what is well and what is poorly done, what is well or poorly considered, well or poorly presented, and so forth.

Consider the faming that plays out as two candidates seek your vote. Both try faming aspects of themselves and of the other candidate. Both paint themselves and their own planned policies in a positive light. Often they do so while faming their opponent in less attractive colors. It can be hard to separate one fame frame from the other. As each describes what is good about his or her plan, it calls to mind what might not be so good about the opponent. As both describe and disagree over particulars, their fame framings tell us the values and evaluations they want us to attach to those particulars. They seek to shape the sides, setting the agenda for which fame frames we ought to consider relevant. They try to tell us how aspects of grouping that concern them stack up against the alternatives also painted in their fame frame.

Naming and faming are so closely integrated that we usually need not try to pry them apart. They can be simultaneous, when the same term or phrase both names and fames. For example, credentialing is you creating a fame frame for yourself. It tells the group when you are the one they ought to follow (see Chapters 2, 3, and 5). A credential names a capacity or experience you have, framing it as an important aspect about you as part of this group. As you name a credential, you simultaneously ask others to accept your faming frame: that the capacity or experience you name is important and ought to be considered for use by them.

Something to Consider

Faming allows a functional equivalent of credentialing to be accomplished by others. When someone says something that fames someone else, it provides a credential to that someone for the group to consider. Sometimes such faming statements are actively sought—for example, endorsements designed to shake a little fame off a popular person (e.g., a film star) and on to a candidate de jour. Faming shapes reputation. He or she is naive; an agent of change; a liar; an infidel; speaks truth

(Continued)

(Continued)

to power. Such faming names an aspect of the person's character and potential. A credential names and fames, whether it provides pretty paint (e.g., "I am the decider" or "a fixer"; "he is a national hero") or poisonous paint (e.g., "he thinks the fundamentals of the economy are sound"—used to paint John McCain; "I have a life-time of experience" and "he has a speech he made in 2002"—used by Hillary Clinton to paint Barack Obama).

Blaming is attributing causality for an aspect of grouping: for any past, present, or future group experience. It includes any framing for *what or who causes* the good or bad, effective or ineffective, or appropriate or inappropriate things we experience. Blaming also has two sides because what you cause can end well or poorly.

It is human nature to attribute cause. It is part of our inquiry imperative (see Chapter 6). Inquiring minds want to know—what is causing our group happenings? Turman (2005) finds that coaches typically employ blaming in the teaching tales they put into postgame speeches. Regret-inspiring messages combine antecedents (Sarah missed the last-shot) and outcomes (causing us to lose the game). Positive attributions tie a player's efforts with the team's successful performance. Coaches almost always assign cause to team success or failure. Blaming is a common aspect of the calculus of coach commentary.

Whether we are explicit with our blaming or not, our other frames tend to be biased to fit our attributions of cause. Blaming ascribes either an internal or external locus of causality for our group outcomes (Kelley, 1967, 1973). The internal-external locus of control affects our sense of power to respond to the exigencies facing our group. For example, blaming helps the group sort out whether we are victims— does our fate rest in the hands of others, or are we skilled folks temporarily beset by difficulties that we are able to overcome? When we blame, we pick either an internal cause (something we control) or an external cause (something we do not). Constructing our own sense of self-efficacy can be one manifestation of the blaming frames we build into our accounts.

Blame framings shape our sense of how we are involved as causal agents in our groups. For example, in this book, we say that you have the ability to help shape your group. We use a blaming frame that describes you as someone with power and volition. If you act well, we say you should be blamed for the good that can come of it: helping your group to thrive. If you act poorly, we blame you for the struggles your group endures as a consequence. If you think that you are not a causal contributor to your group, you may shoot angry blame frames back at us, thinking that other people or circumstances are really the cause of what happens in your group.

Attributions of causality can stimulate additional framings in reply. When faced by an attribution that you caused good outcomes, you need only take a bow and share the credit. Replies to a blame frame for negative, inadequate, or bad outcomes tend to require greater elaboration. It comes in the form of a message called *apologia*,[3] the basis for and process of apology. Apologia tend to include an explanation for the cause of the problem, a statement of regret, and a plan for making restitution, though forms vary by culture (Park & Guan, 2009).

Other specialized and elaborated forms of blaming can also be constructed: shaming and maiming. Both shaming and maiming get others involved in co-constructing your blame frame. *Shaming* is a blame frame that suggests someone should *mortify:* to take blame upon themselves for a bad outcome. For example, in March 2009, Senator Grassley of Iowa suggests that AIG managers who drove their company into the ground (so American taxpayers ended up bailing out the insurance giant) should commit a ritualistic form of suicide called hara-kiri or seppuku: self-disemboweling that shows remorse for serious offense or failure—the way a samurai could die with honor under such circumstances. (Some say Grassley should apologize for his remarks, but attempts to shame him fall on deaf ears. He stands by his remarks, though he explains that they are not literal.)

Maiming is a blame frame that hurts someone's potential contributions by attacking his or her character. This form of frame is an attack on the person called mudslinging or ad hominem. A direction-giver is effectively maimed when the group perceives her or him to be so wrong-headed, silly, or dangerous that the mere mention of her or his name can draw a chorus of boos or hisses. Evidence of maiming in play is found in the case of Muntadar al-Zeidi, a broadcast journalist whose reports often focused on the plight of widows, children, and orphans in the Iraq War. He became a hero to those who shared his maim frame of George W. Bush when he threw his shoe at the visiting president during a press conference, calling him a dog. (He was sentenced to prison for his act.)

---

[3]See Ware and Linkugel (1973), Kruse (1981), Ryan (1988), Goffman (1971), and Lakoff (2001).

Maiming can be so effective that any position or argument receives scorn in response if it is associated with a maimed member. The scorn may not be justified on the basis of the merits of the idea under consideration. However, by generalization, it plays out that way. The idea is discredited because the maimed member suggested or supported it.

Long-term shadows on reputation can result. In 1938, Joe Kennedy served as U.S. ambassador to Great Britain and helped orchestrate the Munich Accord, which resulted in European appeasement of Hitler. After the outcome of the accord helped facilitate the start of the Second World War, this Kennedy's potential bid as a future presidential candidate was tarnished. Even years later, those effects continued to play out. John F. Kennedy was told to make accommodations with Russia during the Cuban Missile Crisis. Instead, mindful of the price his father paid, JFK maintained a stance of strict adherence to the idea that all Soviet nuclear weapons be out of Cuba.

❖ CLAIMING AND TAMING ARE ELABORATED CONSTRUCTIONS OF WHAT IS MEANINGFUL

The more time and energy you spend developing your frames, the more ways you will find to express related and supporting versions of them. As you do, your frames will become more elaborated and intricately developed. Two approaches to such elaborations are (1) to focus on logic and evidence to build a powerful case supporting what you want (claiming) or (2) to focus on emotion and relationship to create a situation conducive to close affiliation with you or with what you want (taming). These two approaches can be closely integrated and work in tandem or they can be kept largely discrete. Either may also employ naming, faming, and blaming frames.

People use both claiming and taming to make themselves or their ideas more influential. With claiming, we seek support directly, explicitly: developing and explaining our ideas for the other's consideration. With taming, we seek support indirectly, often implicitly, by cultivating emotions and/or relationships that create a context conducive for people to want to affiliate with us or with our idea. The people who receive these frames are likely to process them differently. They will tend to process a claiming frame directly, thinking through the argument and coming to a conclusion. Processing a taming frame tends to be done indirectly, while experiencing the emotion or relationship: Little careful analysis is made of any argument.

Research on how attitudes and behaviors can be changed shows that two approaches can work. One approach encourages what is called central processing, and the second encourages peripheral processing.[4] Claiming encourages careful consideration of the details of the ideas and evidence in our message from a receiver who is both engaged by the subject matter and mentally capable to do the careful thinking involved (central processing). Taming frames create a general impression that is favorable to us or to what we think. Those who are less motivated by the subject matter or who are less able to engage its details can still like or support us (peripheral processing). Each approach works in some cases, depending on the context and people involved.

Claiming is making a cogent argument: one that is compelling. This requires your claim frame to consist of three parts: (1) making clear what you want the other person to think or do (your claim), (2) making clear the reason(s) that support(s) your claim (your warrants; see Chapter 5), and (3) providing evidence that supports those reasons (e.g., examples, statistics, testimony—preferably from an expert or eyewitness). Evidence should function to enhance parts of your argument that need support in one of three ways. Use evidence to clarify, lend interest, or add authoritative weight to your ideas.

Providing claim, warrant, and data puts a claiming frame on your direction-giving attempt. When you use claiming, you frame your idea as a position others ought to adopt after they analyze it (assuming that they are thinking clearly and able to process such thoughts).

There are necessary conditions for claiming to succeed. Claiming is influential only if your idea is well reasoned and supported. Then, as you present it, your idea must get centrally processed by engaged others. Those conditions are not, however, sufficient. When someone whose support you need is dead set against your ideas, you might find that even a superior quality claiming frame is inadequate for the task. In such cases, taming may be necessary in addition or as an alternative.

Energies spent working on the emotional connection you develop with another person may allow that person to act as you would like, even though he or she disagrees with your idea. In such cases, this person may do what you would like him or her to do because of his or her

---

[4]See Petty and Cacioppo (1986a, 1986b), Gass and Seiter (1999), and Petty, Cacioppo, Strathman, and Priester (2005).

Something to Consider: To Claim or Try to Tame; That Is the Question

Central processing results in specific elaborations of issue-relevant thinking. Peripheral processing results in a general sense or inexact impression, probably based in emotion. The distinction matters[5] because people will respond to your framings based on how they process your messages: in the moment and over time. Central-route processing requires others to elaborate on your message on their own, attaching additional meanings of their own to the thoughts you send their way. When they have an open mind or already subscribe to positions consistent with what you advocate, claiming is a very effective way to give direction because it is likely to succeed if done well. So, in those circumstances, a claiming frame provides a potent way to exert influence in your group. When you are effective, central-route persuasion tends to last longer and to be more resistant to counter persuasion attempts made later by other potential direction-givers.

Those for whom your message is discrepant (meaning that they already have strongly held views at odds with your own) are much less likely to hear your claim as a rational, well-supported argument (though it no doubt is). Though they may elaborate on what you claim, their elaborations will likely run counter to your own position. This means that there is a risk that, the more you claim, the more reasons they construct for not agreeing with you. If so, you will fail in your attempt to influence them and may, in fact, strengthen their resolve against your ideas. (Arguments sometimes fail to work because people can be ego-defensive about their own position and are likely to judge discrepant ideas as emotional or biased.) For such cases, peripherally processed messages through ongoing taming attempts are more likely to be effective (e.g., using your likeability, credibility, or ability to identify your values with theirs).

For which of the folks in your group and for which of the subjects that tend to recur in conversations in your group, should you employ claiming; taming?

relationship with you or the emotion she or he is feeling, rather than because of the reasoning and evidence you provide in support of what you have to say.

Taming is creating a sense of identification or other emotional connection between you and others. *Identification* is when two people begin to view something in the same way (Burke, 1969). Instead of you trying to enact something on or extract something from them, identification is when people see your ideas as consistent with or in balance

---

[5]See Petty and Cacioppo (1986a, 1986b); Petty et al. (2005); Gass and Seiter (1999); Benoit and Strathman (2004); Stephenson, Benoit, and Tschida (2001); and Benoit and Smythe (2003).

with their own. Identification manifests in finding common substance between the two of you. Shared experiences and values combine to provide common ground on which you begin to move in the same direction and to seek to support each other as you go, even at times when you might disagree about some details (see Chapter 6).

An alternative to identification is to develop a particular type of relationship. For example, behave in ways that get the other person to like you (referent power), treat you as an authority (expert power or ethos), or acknowledge that you have positional authority over them (legitimate power). Liking and authority (either based in position or in expertise) are aspects of influence that are typically processed peripherally (Cialdini, 2001).

Other connections you share with others can be created in a variety of ways even if you do not develop a relationship. You can start a dialog in which the other person appreciates being included. If you do not have time or ability to develop identification or such a relationship, other emotional connections provide additional taming options (see Table 9.4).

Table 9.4	Taming Frames That Can Enhance Your Influence

Research indicates that the following dynamics will tend to increase your influence if you can put them in play. This does not mean that they will always work to get others to do what you want. However, they can help create a readiness in others to be responsive to you/your ideas.

- Create social proof or a bandwagon effect by showing that others are already on board/in agreement with you (Cialdini, 2001).

- Seek appropriate opportunities for propinquity, or to "bump" into them often enough that they become familiar with you, lose any fear they might have about you, and become comfortable with you, *though they share no particular relationship with you* (more than 500 studies show this effect).

- Create a sense of obligation: give something they value today so that, in the future, they feel a sense of obligation to reciprocate when you have a need (Cialdini, 2001).

- If you already have credibility (see Chapter 2) with someone, use of intense language can enhance your influence (M. Burgoon, 1995; M. Burgoon & Miller, 1985; M. Burgoon & Siegel, 2004). If you lack credibility, intense language is counterproductive, making you seem immature or out of control.

- If you already have credibility with someone and can give him or her details for dealing with the resulting angst, you can (1) use fear appeals or you can (2) invoke a sense of scarcity to enhance your influence (Burgoon & Siegel, 2004; Cialdini, 2001).

- If you already have credibility with someone, violating his or her expectations for your nonverbal behavior in a positive manner (e.g., through how you use touch, space, time, or glance) can enhance your influence (J. K. Burgoon, 1978; Dainton & Zelley, 2005).

Using frames will not make you effective, but frames are essential to your effectiveness as a direction-giver. If you use them well, so that your frames get integrated into the evolving story of your group's experience, you will provide direction in the most fundamental of ways.

❖ FRAME YOUR GROUP'S PURGATORY PUDDLE, WAY/PROCESS, VISION/ OUTCOME, AND SAVIOR COMPLEX

A second way to be intentional about improving your framing skills is to know the territory that is available for framing in every group (see Table 9.5). Four terms outline that territory: your group's purgatory puddle, the way/process, vision/outcome, and savior complex (Burtis & Turman, 2006). You can help to frame key aspects of the territory represented by each term.

Table 9.5	Group Terrain for You to Frame With Your Direction-Giving Attempts
Aspects of Grouping That Need a Frame	*The Potential Focus for a Framing Attempt*
Your group's purgatory puddle	The task we do; who we are as a group and as individuals in the group; the situation in which we work i.e., our supra-group issues and constraints
Your group's the way/process	The techniques and procedures we employ; the norms, roles, interaction patterns, and orientations we create for ourselves; how we co-construct any confusion, conflict, conformity, and sense of group consciousness we share
Your group's vision/outcome (see Chapter 10)	Our promised land, which is both what we hope for (anticipate; aspire to) and what we actually co-construct; the fruits of our grouping labors
Your group's savior complex	The improvisational dance, based in our conceptions of appropriate direction-giving activities, in which we decide: from whom we accept direction; how to give direction to others; whether we encourage and support direction-giving; how we transition through direction-givers

The direction-giving work in every group includes the need for frames that make sense of (1) the group's situation, its personnel, and its task (the purgatory puddle); (2) its potential processes and preferences (the way/process); (3) its purposes and desired products (the vision/outcome); and (4) its various direction-givers and their interactions (the savior complex). For a complete discussion of these four terms and the kind of recurring pitfalls you can expect will tend to get in your way as you attempt to frame the territory they represent, see *Group Communication Pitfalls: Overcoming Barriers to an Effective Group Experience* (Burtis & Turman, 2006). For now, though, what matters is for you to realize that someone in your group frames each of these aspects of your group's experience.

The parts of this terrain you choose to engage will help determine the nature of your direction-giving. The parts someone else frames will affect your direction-giving. Ask yourself, "What role will I play?" "Which aspects of my group's terrain do I think that I am best suited to help to shape?" "Where does our group need additional framing in order to thrive?" Use the four terms to help you analyze your group and your direction-giving options.

❖ IN CONCLUSION

Framing is a natural aspect of human engagement in any new or compelling situation. Your choice is not whether to frame but whether you will be intentional about trying to be effective as you frame.

Acknowledging the fact of framing, that it is both a natural and a functional part of your response to a situation, can help you focus on trying to be more dexterous, adept, and effective in your framing efforts. When you frame an aspect of the group experience, you are the one shaping that part of the story of your group. You are giving direction to your group. As you do, are your framings helping your group to thrive?

10

Leadership Vision Can Be a Crisis-Based Direction-Giving Story

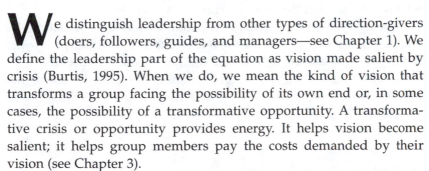

We distinguish leadership from other types of direction-givers (doers, followers, guides, and managers—see Chapter 1). We define the leadership part of the equation as vision made salient by crisis (Burtis, 1995). When we do, we mean the kind of vision that transforms a group facing the possibility of its own end or, in some cases, the possibility of a transformative opportunity. A transformative crisis or opportunity provides energy. It helps vision become salient; it helps group members pay the costs demanded by their vision (see Chapter 3).

But there are other conceptions of vision and crisis to consider. We say that all five types of direction-givers may be needed by a team, organization, or community because every type of group faces different exigencies over time. Crisis is just one of those types of exigencies, and vision is just one of many possible direction-giving responses. You have options, and discussing them is the work of this chapter.

Something to Consider

Thomas Jefferson said that, "During a crisis, we . . . hope that strong or heroic leadership can save the republic. Thus, while we are suspicious of strong leadership, we also admire it" (Genovese, 1994, p. 23).

Vision is a buzzword: fashionable in contemporary explanations for what managers, leaders, and groups need in order to succeed (Hart, 1995). The fourth edition of the encyclopedic *Handbook of Leadership* (Bass & Bass, 2008) includes numerous entries on the subject of vision. The third edition, published in 1990, has just one index entry for vision: a brief segment on the importance of intuition that mentions imagination, vision, and foresight as "closely allied" to insight (Bass & Stogdill, 1990, p. 103).

Vision is a loaded term. Saying that a leader "has vision," implies either incredible insight into how a group ought to behave now in order to succeed years from now or fantastic foresight into what a group will someday encounter. Saying that a group has a vision suggests a special sense of purpose. Our group is important as is our work—we have a vision. What the first President Bush disdainfully referred to as "the vision thing" seems today to be considered a prerequisite for anyone who would be a key direction-giver (see Chapter 1).

Vision is a useful heuristic or explanatory tool for translating the "magic" of leadership into understandable terms. By magic, we mean the aspects of leadership that are the most potent and difficult to explain (see Table 10.1). The vision metaphor helps put a handle on the mystery and mythos of leadership. But doing "the vision thing" *defies prescription:* It is not easily taught.

❖ DO YOU NEED VISION AS A PLANNING TOOL OR DO YOU NEED A VISION THAT TRANSFORMS YOUR GROUP?

As use of the vision metaphor spreads, so do its meanings and the circumstances to which it is applied. Experts have a wide range of definitions

Table 10.1	The Mythos and Mystique of Leaders and Leadership

Magic stretches the point, but we use the term because of how people often respond to leaders and the term *leadership:* as though special beyond the constraints of normal reality. Leadership and leaders are held in such high esteem because their groups are transformed and escape a crisis that threatens survival, and they are associated with extremes of emotion and energy, and they are so difficult to study.

(1) *Stories of transformation* result in mythos and mystique for leadership and leaders. Leaders become mythic through tales of the feats they accomplish. Leadership is treated as something to be universally admired and desired, though difficult to attain: lending mystique. Mystique is enhanced by the energy and efforts it takes to support or oppose a leadership vision. The mythos of leadership is connotative baggage evoked when the term *leader* is bandied. People use conceptions of leadership to divide others into those who have and those who do not have "the right stuff."

(2) The *extremes of emotion* during crisis add more mythos and mystique. The crisis itself is a catalyst for emotional concern and response. The vision that spawns leadership usually creates grossly divided opinions that further inflame emotions. Transformative vision is not neutral. It demands decision, action, and change. It is a catalyst: a force that divides as it directs. It tends to create powerful divisions among affected people: a very strong, loyal support and vociferous opposition that is equally adamant and dedicated, though fewer in numbers or lesser in power (for the time being). Opinions and issues captured by and surrounding a leader are emotionally loaded and intensified by the stakes associated with following or opposing. People who embrace a vision are emotionally and cognitively responsive to its pull. To support the leader is to value vision-expressive activity. They may overlook eccentricities and ignore errors and contradictions in what the person who personifies their vision (their leader) has to say. To indict the leader is to indict self. A corollary is that people who follow a transformative vision sometimes give 110% of themselves and their energies in pursuit of what they believe. When these folks clash with those who oppose them, stories of the results fuel the mythos and mystique of leadership.

(3) Beyond transformation and emotion, mystique is added by *how difficult it is to study leadership vision:* What is it exactly? How can we identify and measure it? When does it begin? In what form(s)? How does it play out in group interactions? When is it a causal force? (Douglas, Burtis, & Pond-Burtis, 2001; Kouzes & Posner, 1995). The answers are often elusive and confounding (or overly-simplistic).

for vision[1] and conceptions about its use. We use the term *vision/outcome* to cover that range (Burtis, 2004a, 2004b; Burtis & Turman, 2006).

❖ VISION/OUTCOME REPRESENTS ALL YOUR GROUP PRODUCTS AND PURPOSES

We pull vision into focus by using the term *vision/outcome* to represent the range of grouping and direction-giving phenomena called vision. *Vision/outcome* represents both the purposes for and the final products from grouping. It includes any accounts we share about the importance of our group and the purposes for our grouping (e.g., stories that constitute our group; stories about our aspirational future experiences; see Chapters 7 and 8). It also includes any potential or actual fruits borne of our grouping: task, relational, and individual effects from working together.

Outcomes are whatever the group may achieve or co-construct. Such products can be anticipated and measured. Outcomes include work that gets done (the group's productivity or other measure of success at task), relationships and group consciousness that grouping people develop, and individual effects on members from their shared experience (e.g., friendships; professional contacts; a thickened skin—"thanks for making me a fighter" "life ain't easy for a boy named Sue").

Vision is more difficult to define and measure. Synthesizing purpose and aspiration, a vision involves the group's sense of itself. A group's *vision* is a story the group shares about its desired future experience (vision is aspiration). This could include a team's desire to have a winning season or a sales division figuring out how to win its company's productivity prize. In addition, a group's *vision* is a story the group shares of its fundamental values: what gives it purpose and that "for which it stands" (vision is constitutive). Both definitions are part of how a group comprises its sense of self. And sometimes there is tension between the two. Can the team win and keep its integrity? Can the division stay cutting-edge if it focuses on short-term objectives?

People tend to measure a group against both their expected outcomes for the group and against their vision of the group. Our process and progress are tested against our stories of desired outcomes and of who we are and why we matter as a group. Consequently, we may be

---

[1]See Mumford and Strange (2004), Strange and Mumford (2002), Bogler and Nir (2001), Conger (1999), Boal and Bryson (1988), Yukl (1994, 1998), Holmes (1993), and Bell and Harrison (1995).

pleased by our recent outcomes while still disappointed in our group because it does not measure up to the vision we have of ourselves. Or, we may be pleased by our authenticity, even while our productivity is slipping.

Direction-giving attempts that use vision/outcome rhetoric employ stories, such as those about our potential as a group, to frame and motivate grouping effort (e.g., stories that encourage anticipation of the fruits available from grouping well and stories that anticipate regrets from failing). Attempts that direction-givers make to stir a group by invoking its purpose or pride are vision/outcome rhetoric. This includes any attempt to attract the group to a promised land. Such rhetoric serves several framing functions for a group (see Table 10.2).

❖ CONCEPTIONS OF VISION RANGE FROM LOW- TO HIGH-INTENSITY FORMS OF DIRECTION-GIVING ACTION

Two clusters of contemporary conceptions of vision deserve consideration. One cluster treats vision as a planning tool: necessary for managing ongoing operations[2] of any long-term group planning tool (PT vision). The second cluster treats vision as group-transformative when a group faces extremes of crisis or opportunity (GT vision). The clusters are related by type of action but separated by the intensity of the dynamics they involve, as are leadership and management (see Chapter 3).

Something to Consider

There is nothing "better" about GT or PT vision except in how well each fits grouping exigencies given the perceptions of those who are doing the grouping. Folks may disagree about what, if any, vision is required for their grouping enterprise. If people want their group to continue to operate effectively, they may want PT vision to be part of their process. There may be times when a group is so fundamentally shaken that even excellent management does not seem sufficient. When exigencies are so extreme that "textbook" answers and managerial approaches do not seem to be up to the task, cries for GT vision may be heard.

---

[2]See, for example, Quigley's (1993) process of vision co-construction developed for use in complex organizations to modulate institution-wide change.

Table 10.2	Framing Functions That Vision/Outcome (V/O) Rhetoric Can Help You Serve

Framing Function	Process by Which Vision/Outcome (V/O) Rhetoric Helps Serve the Function
Name Define Focus	V/O rhetoric is how we co-construct the nature of our V/O: name, define, focus, and refine it. V/O rhetoric is used by direction-givers to orient the group: helping establish the shared assumptions, values, and terminology used by the group and where it is headed.
Interpret Explain Instruct	Direction-givers use V/O rhetoric to guide grouping choices and action. This includes frames that help the group understand how both new and existing phenomena are relevant to the group and so how they ought to be treated.
Organize Control Develop Persuade	When faced with many issues and options for action, V/O provides a framework of criteria for direction-givers to use to suggest a particular choice of organization for our actions (justified as necessary to effectively serve the V/O). V/O is invoked to control, develop, and motivate efforts to go in a desired direction or to a desired destination.
Legitimize Authorize	As we co-construct our V/O, direction-givers use it to clarify and legitimize the premises, practices, uses of language, and stories that attain the group's authority.
Imagine Anticipate Aspire	There is creative force in attraction to change and to future promise. Direction-givers use V/O rhetoric to tap this creative force, getting us to imagine, and then to aspire to, or at least anticipate, new group experiences and outcomes.
Document Evaluate Feedback	As we co-construct a shared sense of what we value and anticipate, our direction-givers use our V/O to document, assess, and evaluate our actions, process, and progress and to suggest changes in our efforts and in group direction.

We portray the two conceptual clusters on a *continuum of vision intensity* (see Table 10.3). Levels of intensity vary across five dynamics in the continuum: in (1) the strength of *exigencies* perceived for grouping that support the need for vision, (2) the *rhetorical resources* available to potential direction-givers who feel they should try to use vision, (3) the *rhetorical force* created by the messages used by those direction-givers as they actively attempt to employ vision to give direction to

| Table 10.3 | Continuum of Vision Intensity: Varying Levels of Force Perceived in Exigencies, Rhetorical Resources, Direction-Giver Rhetoric, Member Engagement, and Salience |

Planning Tool (PT) Vision	*Group-Transformative (GT) Vision*
Lowest to moderate levels of intensity and energy required ←→	Highest intensity and energy requirements in support and in opposition
Vision is of group changes that leave the group fundamentally sound and the same. ←→	Vision is of saving the group by changing it into something fundamentally different.
The work of managers: Vision employs, protects, or perpetuates the status quo or current grouping protocols. ←→	Manifests as leadership: This vision involves a crisis-induced divorce from status quo process/protocol in order to survive.
Planning tool vision provides the normal authority of the group for direction-givers who employ low to moderate levels of rhetorical force to instigate and modulate the incremental change required in any effective group over time. ←→	Transformative vision, made salient by crisis, provides unusual and unusually strong rhetorical resources for direction-givers who make demands of the group that carry substantial rhetorical force in attempts to use the energy and member engagement stoked by crisis.

the group, and (4) the levels of *engagement* attained by grouping members, to their group, and to their vision. How group members understand and engage a vision is affected by the salience that vision has for them. (5) Level of salience is a fifth aspect of intensity. The *salience* of a vision is its perceived importance to those who embrace or oppose it. It tends to co-vary with each of the other dynamics.

Low to moderate intensities in the five dynamics can manifest anywhere on the vision continuum except, probably, at the crisis end (where folks simply must poop or get off the pot). Indeed, moderate levels of intensity are functional and desirable for most groups over the long haul. They are sufficiently productive and probably sustainable. Highest levels of intensity can create an orientation or process more subject to "burnout-level" efforts appropriate only when crisis justifies such extremes. Lowest levels of intensity, of course, may not be desirable either, though they can be a fact of life when planning tool attempts to create vision do not match exigencies perceived by group members (e.g., "today, you're gonna build a vision—yea, rah!").

Group-transformative crisis or opportunity is the most extreme end of vision intensity. That is where the most salient vision is found: the vision made salient by crisis. We need the whole continuum to cover the range of meanings found in the two clusters of conceptions: from vision as a basic planning tool (PT vision) to group transformation vision (GT vision).

At one end of the continuum, vision involves basic purposes and outcomes required by most any group. At this end of the continuum, vision is conceived of as an elaborated planning tool. Here, vision-based exigencies do not command any greater attention, concern, or intensity of effort than any other exigency for grouping. The rhetorical resources in play and the engagement of group members are relatively low when vision is a planning tool.

At the other end of the continuum, vision manifests in extreme forms because exigencies perceived for grouping are wrought by crisis. They are intense. Rhetorical responses to crisis may need to be intense as well: if the direction-giver wants to employ the copious attention and energy members bring to engagement with crisis. Because exigencies and rhetorical resources are tied to group survival, they may be used to justify action that would likely be rejected during normal times. This side of the vision continuum features a powerful rhetorical chemistry that can keep members going in extremely difficult times as they transform themselves and their group.

Planning tool vision or *PT vision* is based in a framework that requires perpetuating most of the group's status quo. That is what keeps the energy and intensity levels required relatively low in comparison to the other end of the continuum. Every group must change over time but, with proper procedures and a managerial mind-set, it can do so carefully and incrementally. Keeping the group healthy as it faces ever-changing circumstances using somewhat flexible processes to create ever-adjusted efforts and outcomes is a requirement in any successful, long-lived group. PT vision may be part of the processes used to accomplish that.

PT vision does not seek to dismantle or to fundamentally alter the basic nature of the group. It simply seeks to make the current group stronger given shifting circumstances. PT vision is carefully constituted. It provides sufficient rhetorical resources for direction-givers to address normal grouping needs. Direction-givers can use PT vision to carefully modulate reasonable efforts of group members. PT vision is used to try to manage change. Difficulties that arise, even certain crises, are dealt with by attempting to keep the group from being knocked out of kilter and fundamentally changed. A successful *PT vision allows a group to remain fundamentally sound, strong, and the same.*

Something to Consider: When Does a Group Become a Different Group?

Sometimes a group adjusts itself but remains fundamentally the same status quo. It is debatable where the point is that a group's status quo is so fundamentally altered that a new group results. We do not draw too clear a distinction because there is no particular threshold. We conceive of the possibilities within a group as a progression from one sense of grouping circumstances that morphs slowly or slaps instantly into another. Comparing the extremes of the continuum, enough difference is evident to conclude that different types of vision are involved. In the middle of the continuum, distinctions are less clear. Can you point to a time in your life when you think you became a fundamentally changed or different person? Have you ever experienced membership in a group that fundamentally transformed into a different group: as you were there? What do such differences tell you about what happened *between* the before and the after?

Group transformative or *GT vision* is for fundamental change in order to survive. Such change is not something people in their right minds should seek when all is well. Transformation is tough to contemplate and to accomplish, so it is almost always crisis induced (see Chapter 3).

Transformation requires leaving much of the status quo behind and creating new order from remnants of the old. Consequently, GT vision involves extreme intensities. Direction-givers may try to circumvent or drastically change group protocols. GT vision helps them do that (justifying and authorizing their efforts as responses to crisis).

Direction-givers may try to stimulate and direct high levels of energy and intensity that members bring to their engagement in the group. GT vision helps them do that. Crisis helps create energy needed to pay the high costs involved. Transformative vision is the sacrifice and (someday) shape of a group as it fundamentally alters itself to try to survive.

PT and GT vision are both found on the same continuum. In fact, grouping people will disagree about the nature and needs of their group and will propose and then compromise on aspects of action that approximate both types of vision. People disagree on whether their group faces a crisis, whether a change undertaken by their group is transformative, whether the effort involved is excessive, whether the opposition is loyal or treasonous, and whether management is still possible or more radical action is required. Be on the lookout for signs of such arguments. They appear much more often than do the crisis circumstances that justify transformative vision.

❖ WHAT IS THE RELATIONSHIP BETWEEN A VISION AND A DIRECTION-GIVER?

Do you remember the lyric about a woman who hears a young boy singing what sounds to her like the story of her life? "Telling my whole life with his words, killing me softly, with his song" (Fox & Gimbel, 1971). As the song continues, the woman falls under the sway of the strange singer because his words identify him so closely with her own experiences, concerns, and needs: "He sang as if he knew me in all my dark despair."

What a potent force, for someone to empathize with your experience story so well that he or she can tell the story of your life, emotion, or trauma in a way that feels authentic to you: strumming your pain with their fingers, singing your life in their words. In Chapter 2, we discuss creating a direction-conducive communication climate (see Table 2.3). This requires narrative imagination, which is the ability someone else has to "read your story" with his or her words in a way that is so powerful and spot-on that you would accept his or her words to represent you.

Sometimes people resonate with each other (Schwartz, 1973) as we share stories of our identification (see Chapters 6 and 9): showing our common values, experiences, concerns, ideas. When someone sings our life with his or her words, we are comforted: as though there is a union of souls. When someone shares a story that resonates with you (perhaps in a leadership vision), it can feel that the story was evoked or drawn right out of you (Burtis, 1989). Such evocation appears to be involved in some of the stories group members share, particularly in some group-transformative visions.

What is the relationship between a direction-giver and a vision? There are two closely related issues to address. First, where does a vision "come from"? Second, how does a vision "play out" in a group? A vision can come from a direction-giver, it can be co-created during group interaction, or it can manifest as an evocation during interaction. Probably there will be some combination of origins (see Table 10.4).

Its origins affect how vision plays out in the group. As a direction-giver, you can try to (1) *sell* your own vision to a group (e.g., a top-down effort to implement a vision). Or, the group may be (2) *seeking something* and find solace in a PT or a GT vision that addresses its need. In some cases, a vision may be (3) "*sucked right out of* grouping members," in a manner consistent with the resonance and evocation in the "killing me softly" lyric.

Table 10.4	Various Conceptions of the Origins of a Vision
Origin of Vision	*Vision Manifests as*
A dream	A vague but attractive sense of what should be different in the future.
A brilliant, inspired thought	A stroke of genius by a genius about what we ought to fear or what we ought to do or what is going to come to pass ("Eureka!").
A person with legitimate power has a big idea	A manager explains her or his vision to others and then they (better) follow (e.g., "Here is what I want us to do." Or Q: "What is your vision for our company?" A: "My vision is XYX." R: "Okay, you're hired").
An implemented co-construction	A process implemented by a guide or manager that gets (some part of) the group to "develop a vision" for us that is to be followed by us all.
An ongoing co-constructed discovery	Grouping people create both the desire for a vision and the nature of their vision as they interact: a natural, useful, though undirected and unintended by-product of interaction over time.
An evocation out of those who follow and co-create the vision	Someone articulates parts of a vision that makes us feel like they share our own experience and ideas, and so we start to chime in with resonating thoughts of our own, which excite them. We understand and are excited by and can articulate parts of the vision that we haven't even heard yet.

Direction-giving changes according to how a vision is created and plays out (see Table 10.5). Only the people's pulse reader or exemplar comes anywhere close to putting the group's ideas at the center of a vision. Leader-centric notions of vision have that blind spot.[3] If vision is evoked, people start to simultaneously speak parts of it as they experience it. People help to shape what gets said next: explaining it to themselves and to others as they do. They act as primary symbolizing agents as they co-construct their vision (see Chapter 6).

Table 10.5　　Various Conceptions of a Visionary as the Source of Vision

Visionary as long-range planner	Good manager; has ability to marshal resources so that they perpetuate status quo protocols and allow carefully modulated change.
Visionary as futurist or as sage	The general ability to see and describe future conditions that are essential to our group. A wise person or oracle who reads aspects of the future from some signs of the times and preferences of the people.
Visionary as giant in their field	A person of specialized importance or position who saw where a topic or particular industry might go and took that risky road to success.
Visionary as dreamer	Having notions about a utopic future: "I have a dream"; "You may say I'm a dreamer, but I'm not the only one."
Visionary as prophet	A voice in the wilderness warning the group to repent to avoid a coming doom (but without the position to legitimize/force an advocated change).
Visionary as rabble-rouser or hate monger	A demagogue is unethical and dangerous because he or she knows how to incite base passions of a crowd who can then (mob) rule.
Visionary as the peoples' pulse reader or exemplar	Able to capture and express the peoples' aspirations, feelings, and opinions in an articulate way: probably appearing to personify them and their hopes and dreams.

[3]The etymology of *demagogue* and of *democracy* shows their common root, both put power in the hands of the people (a demos is a self-governing group; Gastil, 1992). There is potentially great strength and danger in doing so. There is also a philosophical prejudice, whichever side of these issues you align yourself with, that ties notions of vision and leadership to a single great person versus locating leadership and vision in the group.

When group members are involved in a vision co-creation (which we believe, when possible, is the preferred form), it allows ideas to be tested and to spread as they gain traction and then authority from group consensus. Group members sort out what is meaningful to them and how new frames compare to current frames in the story they share of the group's experience (see Chapters 8 and 9). As a direction-giver, no matter how you are involved in the creation of a vision, you and others play it out and determine if it helps the group to thrive.

Something to Consider:
Does "Vision" Do Anything for You?

Although we consider the vision metaphor to be a useful heuristic, it is often overextended to apply in cases where its connotations of significance and transformation overwhelm the grouping exigencies perceived by those involved. Perhaps that is why not everyone is enthralled with the vision construct. "A number of respected leaders eschew 'vision.' " Robert J. Eaton, CEO of Chrysler Corporation states: 'Internally, we don't use the word vision.' . . . 'I believe in quantifiable, short-term results—things we can all relate to—as opposed to some esoteric thing no one can quantify.' When Louis V. Gerstner took over as CEO of IBM, he was asked about his recipe for an IBM comeback. His response was: 'The last thing IBM needs right now is a vision' . . . William Gates, CEO of Microsoft Corp., takes a dim view of vision, as evidenced by his quote: 'Being a visionary is trivial'" (Muczyk & Adler, 2002, pp. 6–7). What do you think?

❖ ARE YOU PREPARED TO GIVE DIRECTION DURING A CRISIS?

Exigencies need to be perceived by people if they are going to try to group together to do a joint task (see Chapter 1). The most extreme exigencies are crisis exigencies, with the most extreme of these being crises perceived as threatening the survival of the group.

❖ CRISIS IS DIFFERENT THAN THE TYPICAL PITFALLS AND PROBLEMS YOU FACE IN EVERY GROUP

To make sense of crisis, we need to differentiate among the sorts of struggles groups face. Every group faces a combination of pitfalls and problems, but only sometimes does a group face circumstances that may threaten its existence.

A *pitfall* is anything that might lead to a diminution of grouping outcomes, depending on how the team, organization, or community responds to the pitfall. If the group responds well, they may actually become stronger as a consequence of their struggle with the pitfall.

A *problem* is a specific task or issue that a group needs to address. Every problem is fraught with potential pitfalls. Neither pitfall nor problem is a turning point: not yet.

A pitfall or problem does not "turn into" a crisis when it reaches a particular threshold. So, determining the quality and extent of a difficulty is done through group interaction. Each individual may develop his or her own framings for whether the group faces a crisis or some less extreme form of problem or pitfall. It is a natural response to both the inquiry and influence imperatives (see Chapter 6) to try to get others to accept your own framing for these aspects of the group situation. (For a thorough discussion of potential pitfalls, see Burtis & Turman, 2006.)

Some problems and pitfalls can fester sufficiently over time to turn into a crisis. A *crisis* is something that threatens the life of the group (Burtis, 1995; Burtis & Hessenflo, 1997). Crisis is a turning point after which the group is significantly different: either substantially changed or ended (see Chapter 3). After crisis, a group may be gone entirely, it may have transformed itself, or it may still be in existence but irrevocably crippled and unable to function properly going forward.

Something to Think About and Discuss With Others

"Crises are most often framed as devastating events evoking a sense of severe urgency, serious threat and devastating loss. For organizations, crisis represents a fundamental threat to the . . . stability of the system, a questioning of core assumptions and beliefs, and risk to high priority goals, including organizational image, legitimacy . . . and ultimately survival" (Seeger & Ulmer, 2002, p. 126).[4]

As is the case with the term *vision*, the concept of *crisis* is attached to various phenomena that we sort by putting them on a continuum.

---

[4]Also see Benoit (1995); Coombs (1999); Hearit (1995); Perrow (1984); Seeger, Sellnow, and Ulmer (1998); and Turner (1976).

At one end of the continuum are problems or crises that can be addressed through careful management (do not yet threaten the life of the group). The other end is anchored by crises that threaten the life of the group and require its transformation.

On the management end of the continuum, "crises" or "problems" do not threaten the life of the system (yet) but could evolve in that direction if they are allowed to become *chronic* as they fester along insufficiently addressed. Examples include the decades-long decline in health of the "big three" in the U.S. auto industry and slow changes in financial markets and processes that result in them becoming inappropriately regulated over several decades of change.

This "management" end of the continuum also includes *acute* problems that skew group activity and must be addressed before the group returns to normal. Examples include the Exxon *Valdez* oil spill, Tylenol cyanide poisonings, the Monica Lewinsky affair, and the Bhopal chemical plant explosion. These can be framed as "fires" that must be "put out" so the group can move on. If handled properly and quickly enough, problems and crises at this end of the continuum should not evolve to the point that they require group transformation.

Where a crisis falls on the continuum is determined by the amount of change a group must undertake to deal with it. At the leadership end of the continuum are crises that require group transformation to escape. These crises are an imminent threat to system survival.

When system transformation is necessary, the group probably does not have the protocols already in place that allow a manager to respond sufficiently to address group needs. In fact, this is the definitional criterion for crisis for some experts who say a crisis exists when "a system is required or expected to handle a situation for which existing resources, procedures, policies, structures, or mechanisms are inadequate" (Hunt et al., 1999, p. 425). Preparation, where possible, is always in order, but it is not always possible.

Proper preparation should be possible for problems and crises on the management side of the continuum but will not be possible for all crises. You cannot create a protocol in advance for dealing with some crises because, until they unfold, you lack the necessary conception of their nature and potential. In those cases, understanding how GT vision works may be necessary.

The direction-giver who reads and responds well to the group's situation is the person who frames and shapes the story the group uses to guide its experience in response to the crisis. Crisis, in addition to whatever other bad things it brings to a group, also increases the likelihood of communication problems. Because crises "are chaotic, the opportunity for rumors and misperceptions to flourish is great. Add to that the plethora of outlets for information, and the potential for serious miscommunication increases exponentially" (Reynolds, 2006, p. 251).

❖ RHETORICAL RESOURCES (AND YOUR RESPONSES SHOULD) VARY ACROSS THE CIRCUMSTANCES OF CRISIS

Energy for transforming a group comes from perception of crisis exigencies. That energy may be based in feelings such as fear, misery, hurt, guilt, and anger (Sandman, 2006), which are not emotions most of us would choose to dwell upon were it not for the crisis that helps focus our attention. Consequently, framing crisis exigencies to harness that energy is difficult and sensitive direction-giving work.

Conditions must be painted as sufficiently dire to warrant uncomfortable and risky shifts in behavior that nobody can be certain will be effective. These shifts are made more difficult because they move the group away from well-established, productive norms and protocols. And despite traumatic uncertainties, the situation must be painted as hopeful if we will just act according to a vision that is unfolding as we go. To accomplish these tasks is to walk a tightrope juggling eggs. That is tough work requiring all your skill. Though you may be fearful of them, you will need to employ the rhetorical resources made available to you by the crisis.

The aspect of crisis that most interests us is how the group responds. During a "crisis condition the linkage between follower behavior and its positive consequences is severed" (Hunt et al., 1999, p. 425). Consequently, people who once knew how to behave become uncertain about how to proceed. For crisis to affect group direction, it must be perceived as exigencies for change by those who are in a position to suggest how their group should behave.

The rhetorical responses direction-givers use to frame appropriate group efforts must tell a new story about the group's experience unfolding during crisis. For example, as the world faces a dangerous recession in 2008 and 2009, key direction-givers seek drastic changes in business practices and huge governmental stimulus programs and bailouts. Many go well beyond what is possible before the crisis.

Direction-givers must articulate a vision for weathering the crisis (in management cases) or for transforming the group in response to the crisis (in leadership cases). They must link a vision to newly appropriate behaviors for those who are grouping. For example, Postmaster General John Porter met with Congress in 2009 to discuss the impending insolvency of the U.S. Postal Service. His strategy was to close some distribution centers, offer early retirement to nearly 150,000 employees, and eliminate mail delivery on Saturday.

The effective direction-giver must frame the situation so that others share their perception (1) that there is a crisis and (2) about the nature of the crisis. Only if you get others to corroborate your account of the group's current experience as constituting crisis can you marshal and employ the rhetorical resources of crisis. So, the communication challenge you face as a direction-giver is to tap the resources of crisis without doing additional damage to your goups as you do so.

There can be benefits found among the resources of crisis. Researchers say that "crises often have important positive consequences. . . . For example, . . . acceleration of needed change, resolution of latent problems, exploration of new strategies, and discovery of new competitive opportunities. Stakeholder relations may also be strengthened and positive publicity garnered" (Seeger & Ulmer, 2002, p. 129). Crisis can be an "opportunity to provide information that is otherwise difficult to get to strategic publics . . . [and crises] have a way of giving voice to many people" (R. L. Heath, 2006, p. 246). So, look for the resources, but be careful how you frame what you are attempting.

You need to keep in mind that any "crisis response is a narrative. It begins with pre-crisis . . . narratives, and continues, if all goes well, to happily ever after" (R. L. Heath, 2006, pp. 247–248). During a crisis, both "expert and lay voices will participate in the evolution of the narrative which either helps or hurts the organization's reputation/image and its relationships with its . . . publics" (R. L. Heath, 2006, p. 246). The need for integrating your framings into the story of your group's experience should always give focus to your direction-giving. Especially in times of crisis, your framings must fit well with ongoing narratives that people trust as credibly representing the group's experience.

Letting a group die or become crippled sometimes results from benign neglect in the face of crisis. Paths that lead to such poor ends appear desirable as choices are made about what the group should do: appearing easier or safer than paths to group transformation. Rhetorical resources are available but inconsequential if people do not use them to frame the crisis and to shape their group's activities in response.

❖ YOU CAN PREPARE FOR CRISES THAT RESEMBLE FIRES NEEDING TO BE PUT OUT

You should help prepare your group in advance for crises that can be anticipated (see Table 10.6). Scholars and public relations practitioners have developed these "best practices" (Venette, 2006; Seeger, 2006) for you to consider if you anticipate handling such communications. Doing so is part of stewardship (see Chapter 3).

Constructing crisis management plans should be part of every long-term group's processes. Seeger and Ulmer (2002) say this involves developing "processes whereby organizations create and exchange meanings among stakeholders regarding the risk of crisis, cause, blame, responsibility, precautionary norms, and crisis-induced changes in the organization and its relationship to stakeholders" (p. 128). These are informed by public policy reviews of past crises and case studies of effective crisis management.

The best practices for crisis communications might also be helpful when a group needs to transform itself, but those practices will not be sufficient. A transformative vision is also necessary. Though it is probably not possible to prepare a GT vision in advance of a crisis that threatens the life of your group, you can prepare yourself to understand such circumstances.

❖ YOU SHOULD UNDERSTAND DIRECTION-GIVING COMMUNICATIONS DURING TRANSFORMATIVE CRISIS

You cannot stray far from the master narrative of your group even as you seek its transformation (see Chapter 8). That master narrative provides rhetorical resources to you. It is almost always easier and a more effective approach to build vision out of it than it is to burn your group's master narrative down and try to start all over again. Keep in mind that, as they begin their journey to transformation, people are still more closely aligned to what they have been as a group than they are to what they will someday become.

It is the narrative aspects of vision that transport people from where they are to a clearer sense of where it is they want the group to go to escape the crisis. An effective vision story must integrate into already approved accounts of the personal and group experience of the people

Table 10.6	Best Practices for Crisis Communications

- Identify the most likely types of potential problems that could arise. Develop initial responses and resources with those potential problems in mind.

- Identify key stakeholders, including anyone concerned with or affected by the group. Involve them in meaningful dialog, and listen to their concerns, attempting to understand their perspectives. This should be done during preparation for a potential crisis, and it should be part of the resulting crisis management plan.

- Cultivate partnerships with various publics prior to and during crisis situations. They are stakeholders and should be integrated as legitimate partners in group considerations, whether or not they are "part" of group personnel. Frame them during your interactions as people who are contributors, having legitimate concerns and offering potential resources.

- Engage communication in all aspects of determining, testing, and explaining what will become the group's processes and policies. Communication should not just be "involved" in creating process and policy; it should be the centerpiece of crisis management. Crisis management is not something to just "turn on"; it is something to co-construct.

- Communications with group publics, especially during times of crisis, need to be honest and characterized by candor and openness (even sharing worst-case scenarios).

- Encourage risk sharing that constructs mutual responsibility for managing risk and crisis.

- When possible, craft messages of self-efficacy for your publics, providing specifics that restore some sense of control (i.e., what people can do to respond positively to the situation).

- Collaborate and coordinate with credible sources. Integrate them into your normal interaction networks, making them resources whenever and wherever possible before the onset of crisis.

- Meet the needs of the media. Remain accessible to them. Treat them as partners and as a resource: the primary conduit between the group and its many publics.

- Communicate with compassion, concern, and empathy: the basis for your credibility.

- Accept uncertainty and ambiguity: acknowledge them as a fact of life and avoid the desire to provide an answer or to behave with certainty where none, in reality, is available.

it transports even as it changes what they hope to become. Of course, the vision story must aid transformation. But such a story is not compelling if it does not allow those who hear it to integrate the new vision with their own sense of reality, which is tied to familiar framings.

It is difficult to get traction if a vision story requires folks to completely reject the frames and stories they are using successfully up to this point in time. For instance, many members of Congress are concerned about reducing the number of delivery days for the U.S. Postal Service. They think constituents expect 6-day delivery (though they might happily accept a massive layoff of postal workers—so long as their service is uninterrupted). However, if vision fails to reframe, it is not really a vision. Again, you get a tightrope to walk and a set of eggs to juggle.

❖ DO NOT MISUSE CRISIS: FROM MISTAKES TO FAUX CRISIS, FALSE PRETENSES, AND MANIPULATIONS

Crisis can be addressed (in)effectively, and crisis resources can be (mis)used rhetorically. Crisis circumstances, if they go unnoticed or unframed, can destroy a group. So, *it is a risk to not act when faced by crisis.* However, someone may attempt to create a sense of crisis exigencies when circumstances do not justify doing so. That person may be mistaken or may want access to resources crisis provides (or perhaps to use crisis as a diversion, shifting the group's attention from some other issue, pitfall, problem, or crisis). So, *it is a risk to act as though faced by crisis.*

The difference is probably more a matter of perception than of reality. The reality of a crisis is determined by its effects. In the short term, effects may manifest mostly in a group's response to what it perceives as a crisis. Over time, more objective assessments of crisis can be made after history provides sufficient distance to better understand what was really going on.

Something to Think About and Discuss With Others

Direction-givers "operate in uncertain, sometimes chaotic environments that are partly of their own creation." Though direction-givers "do not control events, they do influence how events are seen and understood . . . ; their most important tools are symbolic. . . . Language cloaks, sedates, even seduces people into believing that many of the so-called facts of our world are objectively rather than socially created. No other reason can explain why the same market fluctuations are seen as problems for some and opportunities for others. No other reason can explain why new visions and programs become future realities in some companies and remain as pipe dreams in others" (Fairhurst & Sarr, 1996, p. xi).

Who gets to decide what is faux and what is factual? "In any specific crisis, some people may be insufficiently concerned while others are appropriately concerned; some may even be excessively concerned. The same people may be excessively concerned about some aspects of the crisis, and appropriately or insufficiently concerned about other aspects" (Sandman, 2006, p. 258). What matters is how exigencies, perceived by grouping members, are framed in direction-giving attempts and used to help shape the group's experience. Is there an authentic effort to link calls for group action to helping the group thrive? If so, the group and its direction-givers are meeting the best criterion we know of for addressing crisis well.

When a group responds rhetorically to a crisis and none exists, it means it is either making a mistake or heeding unethical direction-giving that fabricates fear of faux crisis into changes in the group. Regardless, because of the extremes in resources and responses a crisis framing inspires, getting a group to respond to crisis is a distortion of grouping exigencies and energies. Doing so should be entertained only when necessary. A faux crisis shifts resources to favor an agenda other than helping a group to thrive.

Fortunately, the high levels of energy a vision involves provide a check against rhetorical misuse of crisis. This is especially true of transformative vision. Such high costs are a slow, steady, stultifying check against contrived crisis. Over time, people get worn out from paying the high costs of following a vision. When a real crisis ends or it becomes evident that a crisis is contrived, people stop following: fast! If a crisis is contrived (and even if it is not), those who hate the vision it spawns will seek to undo the group's acts in response. Their loyal opposition is the best available check on abuse.

❖ IN CONCLUSION

This book is about a "superpower" most people can actually develop and control: getting groups of folks to work well together. Most of us have to work hard to develop our direction-giving skills. We also have to make the choice (every day and over time) to use our efforts to help the group thrive (instead of serving just ourselves).

If you choose to help your group to thrive, your reputation will increase as you exercise your skills. That will make the life you lead more public and more the subject of concern for others. You can anticipate their scrutiny and criticism. Those can be a heavy burden. Our hope is that the fruits of your efforts create enough joy in you to help you pay those costs. Good luck. Don't blow it. It is very important.

Our Thing

When something needs doing, some thing one person can **do**,

Then that's all we need: not also, in addition, furthermore a president too.

When whatever we need can be done by we few,

Will you **follow** along please, to my old soft shoe?

When our something is messed up: oh, say just a bit,

We hope that some expert can **guide** us through it.

When our thing is all going as we want, A-OK,

We expect that our **manager** will keep us thata way.

But when our thing falls apart and our future we fear,

The cry emanates: 'We need a **lead**er here!' (Burtis, 1989)

Something to Think About: Juggling Eggs on Tight Ropes

Ethical leaders are people dancing over ever-changing terrain to often changing music while trying to balance community and individualism, freedom-justice-equality-order and compassion, competency with cold bureaucracy, ambition with tyranny, and conscience with dogmatism or inaction. (Shapiro, 1987)

References

Anderson, L. R., & Tolson, J. (1989). Group members' self-monitoring as a possible neutralizer of leadership. *Small Group Behavior, 20,* 24–36.

Armstrong, D. M. (1992). *Managing by storying around: A new method of leadership.* New York: Doubleday.

Baker, D., & Greenberg, C. (2007). *What happy women know.* New York: Rondale.

Bandura, A. (1997). *Self-efficacy: The exercise of control.* New York: W. H. Freeman.

Barge, K. J., & Schlueter, D. W. (2004). Memorable messages and newcomer socialization. *Western Journal of Communication, 68*(3), 233–256.

Bar-On, R. (1997). *Bar-On Emotional Quotient Inventory: Technical manual.* New York: Multi-Health Systems.

Bar-On, R., Brown, J. M., Kirkcaldy, B. D., & Thome, E. P. (2000). Emotional expression and implications for occupational stress: An application of the Emotional Quotient Inventory (EQ-I). *Personality and Individual Differences, 28,* 1107–1118.

Barrett, H. (1991). *Rhetoric and civility: Human development, narcissism, and the good audience.* Albany: State University of New York Press.

Bass, B. M. (1990). From transactional to transformational leadership: Learning to share the vision. *Organizational Dynamics, 18*(3), 19–32.

Bass, B. M., & Bass, R. (2008). *The Bass handbook of leadership theory, research, and managerial applications* (4th ed.). New York: Simon & Schuster.

Bass, B. M., & Stogdill, R. M. (1990). *Handbook of leadership: Theory, research, and managerial applications.* New York: Free Press.

Beatty, M. J., Heisel, A. D., Hall, A. E., Levine, T. R., & La France, T. L. (2002). What can we learn from the study of twins about genetic and environmental influences on interpersonal affiliation, aggressiveness, and social anxiety? A meta-analytic study. *Communication Monographs, 69*(1), 1–18.

Bell, J., & Harrison, B. T. (Eds.). (1995). *Vision and values in managing education: Successful leadership principles and practice.* London: David Fulton.

Benne, K. D., & Sheats, P. (1948). Functional roles of group members. *Journal of Social Issues, 4,* 41–49.

Benoit, W. L. (1995). *Accounts, excuses and apologies.* Albany: State University of New York Press.

Benoit, W. L., & Smythe, M. J. (2003). Rhetorical theory as message reception: A cognitive response approach to rhetorical theory and criticism. *Communication Studies, 54*, 96–114.

Benoit, W. L., & Strathman, A. J. (2004). Elaboration likelihood model. In J. S. Seiter & R. H. Gass (Eds.), *Perspectives on persuasion, social influence, and compliance gaining* (p. 102). Boston: Pearson.

Bitzer, L. (1968). The rhetorical situation. *Philosophy and Rhetoric, 1*, 1–14.

Blake, R., & Mouton, J. (1964). *The managerial grid.* Houston, TX: Gulf Publishing.

Boal, K. B., & Bryson, J. M. (1988). Charismatic leadership: A phenomenological and structural approach. In J. G. Hunt, B. R. Baligia, H. P. Dachler, & C. A. Schriesheim (Eds.), *Emerging leadership vistas* (pp. 11–28). Lexington, MA: Lexington Books.

Bodnar, J. (1992). *Remaking America: Public memory, commemoration, and patriotism in the twentieth century.* Princeton, NJ: Princeton University Press.

Bogler, R., & Nir, A. E. (2001). Organizational vision: The other side of the coin. *Journal of Leadership Studies, 8*(2), 135–144.

Bormann, E. G. (1975). *Discussion and group methods.* New York: Harper & Row.

Bormann, E. G. (1980). *Communication theory.* New York: Holt, Rinehart, & Winston.

Bormann, E. G. (1983). The symbolic convergence theory of communication and the creation, raising, and sustaining of public consciousness. In J. I. Sisco (Ed.), *The Jensen Lectures: Contemporary communication studies* (pp. 71–90). Tampa: University of South Florida.

Bormann, E. G. (1996). *Small group communication: Theory & practice.* Edina, MN: Burgess Publishing.

Bormann, E. G., & Bormann, N. C. (1996). *Effective small group communication* (6th ed.). Edina, MN: Burgess International Group.

Bormann, E. G., Cragan, J. F., & Shields, D. C. (2001). Three decades of developing, grounding, and using symbolic convergence theory (SCT). In W. B. Gudykunst (Ed.), *Communication yearbook* (Vol. 25, pp. 271–313). Thousand Oaks, CA: Sage.

Brock, T. C., Strange, J. J., & Green, M. C. (2002). Power beyond reckoning: An introduction to *narrative impact.* In M. C. Green, J. J. Strange, & T. C. Brock (Eds.), *Narrative impact: Social and cognitive foundations* (pp. 1–15). Mahwah, NJ: Lawrence Erlbaum.

Brown, M. H. (1990). Defining stories in organizations: Characteristics and functions. In J. A. Anderson (Ed.), *Communication yearbook* (Vol. 13, pp. 162–190). Newbury Park, CA: Sage.

Bruner, J. (2002). *Making stories: Law, literature, life.* New York: Farrar, Straus, & Giroux.

Burgoon, J. K. (1978). A communication model of personal space violations: Explication and an initial test. *Human Communication Research, 4*, 129–142.

Burgoon, M. (1995). Language expectancy theory: Elaboration, explication, and extension. In C. R. Berger & M. Burgoon (Eds.), *Communication and social influence processes* (pp. 29–52). East Lansing: Michigan State University Press.

Burgoon, M., & Miller, G. R. (1985). An expectancy interpretation of language and persuasion. In H. Giles & R. N. St. Clair (Eds.), *Recent advances in language communication and social psychology* (pp. 199–229). London: Lawrence Erlbaum.

Burgoon, M., & Siegel, J. T. (2004). Language expectancy theory: Insight to application. In J. S. Seiter & R. H. Gass (Eds.), *Perspectives on persuasion, social influence, and compliance gaining* (pp. 149–162). Boston: Pearson.

Burke, K. (1965). *Permanence and change.* Indianapolis, IN: Bobbs-Merrill.

Burke, K. (1969). *A rhetoric of motives.* Berkeley: University of California Press.

Burke, K. (1989). *On symbols and society* (J. R. Gusfield, Ed.). Chicago: University of Chicago Press.

Burns, J. M. (1978). *Leadership.* New York: Harper & Row.

Burtis, J. O. (1988). *Receiver as source: Richness of fantasy.* East Lansing, MI: National Center for Research on Teacher Learning. (ERIC Document Reproduction Service No. ED 290 193)

Burtis, J. O. (1989). Receiver as source: Stimulus-evoked making of meaning. In C. Roberts & K. Watson (Eds.), *Intrapersonal communication processes: Original essays* (pp. 528–546). Scottsdale, AZ: Gorsuch Scarisbrick.

Burtis, J. O. (1991). Group. In J. Austin (Ed.), *New directions, 3* (p. 4). Moorhead, MN: Concordia Leadership Center.

Burtis, J. O. (1995). Grouping and leading as citizen action. *Journal of Leadership Studies, 2,* 51–64.

Burtis, J. O. (1996). Perceptions of leadership-conducive exigencies. In A. Woodward (Ed.), *Leadership in a changing world* (pp. 16–25). Burlington, VT: Association of Leadership Educators Proceedings.

Burtis, J. O. (1997, July). *Analysis of situation and crisis resources.* Paper presented at the annual meeting of the Association of Leadership Educators, Columbus, OH.

Burtis, J. O. (1999, November). *From Purgatory to Vision (the Promised Land): A representative anecdote that describes leadership-attaining activities in the leadership-conducive group.* Poster and paper presented at the annual convention of the National Communication Association, Chicago.

Burtis, J. O. (2004a, November). *Organizational origins and vision: Four bases of exigencies and rhetorical resources for organizational leadership—the leadership-conducive system theory.* Paper presented at the annual meeting of the National Communication Association, Chicago.

Burtis, J. O. (2004b, November). *Purgatory puddle germination and attractive leadership vision: Political exigencies, rhetorical resources, and leadership-conducive systems.* Paper presented at the annual meeting of the National Communication Association, Chicago.

Burtis, J. O., & Hessenflo, S. (1997). Situation as recurring form and the nature of crisis. In R. Orr (Ed.), *Leaders in leadership education proceedings* (pp. 165–174). Columbus, OH: Association of Leadership Educators.

Burtis, J. O., & Pond-Burtis, L. K. (2001). Communication and experiential education. *Journal of Arts and Sciences in Career and Experiential Education, 1,* 4–13.

Burtis, J. O., & Turman, P. T. (2006). *Group communication pitfalls: Overcoming barriers to an effective group experience.* Thousand Oaks, CA: Sage.

Calder, B. J. (1977). An attribution theory of leadership. In B. Staw & G. Salancik (Eds.), *New directions in organizational behavior* (pp. 179–209). Chicago: St. Clair Press.

Charland, M. (1987). Constitutive rhetoric: The case of the *peuple Quebecois. Quarterly Journal of Speech, 73,* 133–150.

Cialdini, R. B. (2001). *Influence: Science and practice.* Needham Heights, MA: Allyn & Bacon.

Clampitt, P. G. (2005). *Communicating for managerial effectiveness* (3rd ed.). Thousand Oaks, CA: Sage.

Clark, L. (2005). Contesting definitional authority in the collective. *Quarterly Journal of Speech, 91,* 1–36.

Cohen, A. M., & Smith, R. D. (1976). *The critical incident in growth groups: Theory and technique.* La Jolla, CA: University Associates, Inc.

Conger, J. A. (1999). Charismatic and transformational leadership in organizations: An insider's perspective on the developing streams of research. *Leadership Quarterly, 10,* 145–180.

Coombs, W. T. (1999). *Ongoing crisis communication.* Thousand Oaks, CA: Sage.

Cronshaw, S. F., & Ellis, R. J. (1991). A process investigation of self-monitoring and leader emergence. *Small Group Research, 22,* 403–420.

Dainton, M., & Zelley, E. D. (2005). *Applying communication theory for professional life.* Thousand Oaks, CA: Sage.

Delgado, F. P. (1995). Chicano movement rhetoric: An ideographic interpretation. *Communication Quarterly, 43,* 446–455.

DeSouza, G., & Klein, H. J. (1995). Emergent leadership in the group goal-setting process. *Small Group Research, 26,* 475–496.

Douglas, A., Burtis, J. O., & Pond-Burtis, L. K. (2001). Myth and leadership vision: Rhetorical manifestations of cultural force. *Journal of Leadership Studies, 7,* 55–70.

Ellis, R. J., Adamson, R. S., Deszca, G., & Cawsey, T. F. (1988). Self-monitoring and leadership emergence. *Small Group Behavior, 19,* 312–324.

Ellis, R. J., & Cronshaw, S. F. (1992). Self-monitoring and leader emergence: A test of moderator effects. *Small Group Research, 23,* 113–129.

Engen, D. E. (2002). The communicative imagination and its cultivation. *Communication Quarterly, 50,* 41–57.

Entman, R. M. (1993). Framing: Toward clarification of a fractured paradigm. *Journal of Communication, 43,* 51–58.

Fairhurst, G. T., & Sarr, R. A. (1996). *The art of framing.* San Francisco: Jossey-Bass.

Fiedler, F. E. (1967). *Theory of leadership effectiveness.* New York: McGraw-Hill.

Fineman, S. (Ed.). (2000). *Emotion in organizations* (2nd ed.). London: Sage.

Fisher, B. A. (1980). *Small group decision-making*. New York: McGraw-Hill.

Fisher, W. R. (1978). Toward a logic of good reasons. *Quarterly Journal of Speech, 64*, 376–384.

Fisher, W. R. (1984). Narration as a human communication paradigm: The case of public moral argument. *Communication Monographs, 51*, 1–22.

Fisher, W. R. (1985a). The narrative paradigm: An elaboration. *Communication Monographs, 52*, 347–367.

Fisher, W. R. (1985b). The narrative paradigm: In the beginning. *Journal of Communication, 35*, 74–89.

Fisher, W. R. (1987). *Human communication as narration: Toward a philosophy of reason, value, and action.* Columbia: University of South Carolina Press.

Fisher, W. R. (1999). Narration as a human communication paradigm: The case of public moral argument. In J. L. Lucaites, C. M. Condit, & S. Caudill (Eds.), *Contemporary rhetorical theory* (pp. 265–287). New York: Guilford.

Flanagan, J. C. (1954). The critical incident technique. *Psychological Bulletin, 51*, 327–357.

Fox, C., & Gimbel, N. (1971). Killing me softly with his song [recorded by R. Flack]. Retrieved April 21, 2008, from http://users.cis.net/sammy/rflack.htm

French, J. R., & Raven, B. (1959). The bases of social power. In D. Cartwright (Ed.), *Studies in social power* (pp. 150–167). Ann Arbor: University of Michigan Press.

French, J. R. P., & Raven, B. (1968). The bases of social power. In D. Cartwright & A. Zander (Eds.), *Group dynamics: Research and theory* (pp. 607–623). New York: Harper & Row.

Frye, J., Kisselburgh, L. G., & Butts, D. (2007). Embracing spiritual followership. *Communication Studies, 58*, 243–260.

Gass, R. H., & Seiter, J. S. (1999). *Persuasion, social influence, and compliance gaining.* Needham Heights, MA: Allyn & Bacon.

Gastil, J. (1992). A definition of small group democracy. *Small Group Research, 23*, 278–301.

Gastil, J. (1993). Identifying obstacles to small group democracy. *Small Group Research, 24*, 5–27.

Geier, J. (1967). A trait approach to the study of leadership in small group. *Journal of Communication, 17*, 316–323.

Genovese, M. A. (1994). Thomas Jefferson and the vision of democratic leadership. *Journal of Leadership Studies, 1*, 22–25.

Gerrig, R. J. (1993). *Experiencing narrative worlds: On the psychological activities of reading.* New Haven, CT: Yale University Press.

Gitlin, T. (1980). *The whole world is watching: Mass media in the making and unmaking of the new left.* Berkeley: University of California Press.

Goffman, E. (1971). *Relations in public: Microstudies of the public order.* New York: Harper & Row.

Goffman, E. (1974). *Frame analysis: An essay on the organization of experience.* New York: Harper & Row.

Goldhaber, G. M. (1986). *Organizational communication* (4th ed.). Dubuque, IA: William C. Brown.

Goleman, D. (1995). *Emotional intelligence.* New York: Bantam.

Goleman, D. (1998a, November–December). What makes a leader? *Harvard Business Review,* pp. 94–102.

Goleman, D. (1998b). *Working with emotional intelligence.* New York: Bantam.

Goleman, D. (2000, March–April). Leadership that gets results. *Harvard Business Review,* pp. 79–90.

Gouran, D. S. (2003). Reflections on the type of question as a determinant of the form of interaction in decision-making and problem-solving discussions. *Communication Quarterly, 51,* 111–125.

Graen, G., & Cashman, J. F. (1975). A role making model of leadership in formal organizations: A developmental approach. In J. Hunt & L. Larson (Eds.), *Leadership frontiers* (pp. 187–212). Kent, OH: Kent State University Press.

Graen, G., & Uhl-Bien, M. (1995). Development of leader-member exchange theory of leadership over 25 years: Applying a multilevel perspective. *Leadership Quarterly, 6,* 219–247.

Green, M. C., & Brock, T. C. (2000). The role of transportation in the persuasiveness of public narratives. *Journal of Personality and Social Psychology, 79,* 701–721.

Green, M. C., & Brock, T. C. (2002). In the mind's eye: Transportation—imagery model of narrative persuasion. In M. C. Green, J. J. Strange, & T. C. Brock (Eds.), *Narrative impact: Social and cognitive foundations* (pp. 315–341). Mahwah, NJ: Lawrence Erlbaum.

Green, M. C., & Brock, T. C. (2005). Persuasiveness of narratives. In T. C. Brock & M. C. Green (Eds.), *Persuasion: Psychological insights and perspectives* (2nd ed., pp. 117–142). Thousand Oaks, CA: Sage.

Gregg, R. B. (1984). *Symbolic inducement and knowing.* Columbia: University of South Carolina Press.

Hahner, L. (2008). Practical patriotism: Camp Fire Girls, Girl Scouts, and Americanization. *Communication and Critical and Cultural Studies, 5,* 113–134.

Haiman, F. (1949). An experimental study of the effects of ethos in public speaking. *Speech Monographs, 16,* 190–202.

Hall, S., Critcher, C., Jefferson, T., Clarke, J., & Roberts, B. (1978). *Policing the crisis: Mugging, the state, and law and order.* New York: Holmes & Meier.

Hart, R. M. (1995). *Vision as emerging leadership phenomenon.* Unpublished master's thesis, Kansas State University.

Hart, R. P., & Burks, D. (1984). Rhetorical sensitivity and social interaction. *Speech Monographs, 39,* 75–91.

Harter, L. M., & Bochner, A. P. (2009). Healing through stories: A special issue on narrative medicine. *Journal of Applied Communication Research, 37,* 113–117.

Hasian, M., Jr., & Carlson, A. C. (2000). Revisionism and collective memory: The struggle for meaning in the Amistad affair. *Communication Monographs, 67,* 42–62.

Hauser, G. A. (1999). *Vernacular voices: The rhetoric of publics and public spheres.* Columbia: University of South Carolina Press.

Hearit, K. M. (1995). From 'We didn't do it' to 'It's not our fault': The use of apologia in public relations crises. In W. N. Elwood (Ed.), *Public relations inquiry as rhetorical criticism* (pp. 117–134). Westport, CT: Praeger.

Heath, C., & Heath, D. (2007). *Made to stick: Why some ideas survive and others die.* New York: Random House.

Heath, R. L. (2006). Best practices in crisis communication: Evolution of practice through research. *Journal of Applied Communication Research, 34,* 245–248.

Hemphill, J. K. (1949a). The leader and his group. *Journal of Educational Research, 28,* 225–229.

Hemphill, J. K. (1949b). *Situational factors in leadership.* Columbus: Ohio State University, Bureau of Educational Research.

Hersey, P., & Blanchard, K. H. (1969). Life cycle theory of leadership. *Training and Development Journal, 23,* 26–34.

Hersey, P., & Blanchard, K. H. (1982). *Management and organizational behavior* (4th ed.). Englewood Cliffs, NJ: Prentice Hall.

Hess, A. (2007). "You don't play, you volunteer": Narrative public memory construction in "Medal of Honor: Rising Sun." *Critical Studies in Media Communication, 24,* 339–356.

Hirokawa, R. Y. (1990). The role of communication in group decision-making efficacy. *Small Group Research, 21,* 190–204.

Hochschild, A. R. (1983). *The managed heart: Commercialization of human feeling.* Berkeley: University of California Press.

Holmes, G. (1993). *Essential school leadership: Developing vision and purpose in management.* London: Kogan Page.

House, R. J. (1971). A path-goal theory of leadership effectiveness. *Administrative Science Quarterly, 16,* 321–338.

Howard, D. J. (1997). Familiar phrases as peripheral persuasion cues. *Journal of Experimental Social Psychology, 33,* 231–243.

Howell, J. P., Dorfman, P. W., & Kerr, S. (1986). Moderator variables in leadership research. *Academy of Management Review, 11,* 88–102.

Hunt, J. G., Boal, K. B., & Dodge, G. E. (1999). The effects of visionary and crisis-responsive charisma on followers: An experimental examination of two kinds of charismatic leadership. *Leadership Quarterly, 10,* 423–448.

Jermier, J. M. (1993). Introduction—Charismatic leadership: Neo-Weberian perspective. *Leadership Quarterly, 4,* 217–233.

Keller, T. (1999). Images of the familiar: Individual differences and implicit leadership theories. *The Leadership Quarterly, 10,* 589–607.

Keller, T. (2003). Parental images as a guide to leadership sensemaking: An attachment perspective on implicit leadership theories. *The Leadership Quarterly, 14,* 141–160.

Kelley, H. H. (1967). Attribution theory in social psychology. *Nebraska Symposium on Motivation, 15,* 192–238.

Kelley, H. H. (1973). The processes of causal attribution. *American Psychologist, 28,* 107–128.

Ketrow, S. M. (1991). Communication role specializations and perceptions of leadership. *Small Group Research, 22,* 492–514.

Keyton, J. (2005). *Communication and organizational culture.* Thousand Oaks, CA: Sage.

Koesten, J., Miller, K. I., & Hummert, M. L. (2002). Family communication, self-efficacy, and White female adolescents' risk behavior. *Journal of Family Communication, 2,* 7–27.

Korzybski, A. (1933). *Science and sanity: An introduction to non-Aristotelian systems and general semantics.* Laxeville, CT: International Non-Aristotelian Library Pub.

Kouzes, J. M., & Posner, J. M. (1993). *Credibility: How leaders gain and lose it, why people demand it.* San Francisco: Jossey-Bass.

Kouzes, J. M., & Posner, B. Z. (1995). *The challenge of leadership.* San Francisco: Jossey-Bass.

Krayer, K. J. (1988). Exploring group maturity in the classroom: Differences in behavior, affective, and performance outcomes between mature and immature groups. *Small Group Behavior, 19,* 259–272.

Kruse, N. W. (1981). The scope of apologetic discourse: Establishing generic parameters. *Southern Speech Communication Journal, 46,* 278–291.

Lakoff, R. T. (2001). Nine ways of looking at apologies: The necessity for interdisciplinary theory and method in discourse analysis. In D. Schiffrin, D. Tannen, & H. E. Hamilton (Eds.), *The handbook of discourse analysis* (pp. 199–214). Malden, MA: Blackwell.

Latane, B., Williams, K., & Harkins, S. (1979). Many hands make light the work: The causes and consequences of social loafing. *Journal of Personal & Social Psychology, 37,* 822–832.

Lee, T. W., Locke, E. A., & Latham, G. P. (1989). Goal setting and job performance. In L. A. Pervin (Ed.), *Goal concepts in personality and social psychology* (pp. 291–326). Hillsdale, NJ: Laurence Erlbaum.

Lewin, K., & Lippitt, R. (1938). An experimental approach to the study of autocracy and democracy: A preliminary note. *Sociometry, 1,* 292–300.

Lewin, K., Lippitt, R., & White, R. K. (1939). Patterns of aggressive behavior in experimentally created 'social climates.' *Journal of Social Psychology, 10,* 271–279.

Likert, R. (1961). *New patterns of management.* New York: McGraw-Hill.

Likert, R. (1967). *The human organization.* New York: McGraw-Hill.

Locke, E. A., & Latham, G. P. (1990). *A theory of goal setting and task performance.* Englewood Cliffs, NJ: Prentice Hall.

Lucaites, J. L., & Condit, C. M. (1990). Reconstructing equality: Culturetypal and counter-cultural rhetorics in the martyred Black vision. *Communication Monographs, 57,* 5–21.

Luthans, F., Luthans, K. W., Hodgetts, R. M., & Luthans, B. C. (2001). Positive approach to leadership (PAL) implications for today's organizations. *Journal of Leadership Studies, 8*(2), 3–20.

McCombs, M. E., & Shaw, D. L. (1972). The agenda-setting function of mass media. *Public Opinion Quarterly, 36,* 176–187.

McGee, M. C. (1975). In search of 'the people': A rhetorical alternative. *Quarterly Journal of Speech, 61,* 235–249.

McGee, M. C. (1980). The 'ideograph': A link between rhetoric and ideology. *Quarterly Journal of Speech, 66,* 1–17.

McGregor, D. (1960). *The human side of enterprise.* New York: McGraw-Hill.

Meindl, J. R., Ehrlich, S. B., & Dukerich, J. M. (1985). The romance of leadership. *Administrative Science Quarterly, 30,* 78–102.

Miller, C. R. (1984). Genre as social action. *Quarterly Journal of Speech, 70,* 151–167.

Morgan, J. M., & Krone, K. J. (2001). Bending the rules of "professional" display: Emotional improvisation in caregiver performances. *Journal of Applied Communication Research, 29,* 317–340.

Morus, C. M. (2007a). The SANU Memorandum: Intellectual authority and the constitution of an exclusive Serbian 'people.' *Communication and Critical/Cultural Studies, 4,* 142–165.

Morus, C. M. (2007b). Slobo the redeemer: The rhetoric of Slobodan Milosevic and the construction of the Serbian 'people.' *Southern States Communication Association, 72,* 1–20.

Muczyk, J. P., & Adler, T. (2002). An attempt at a consentience regarding formal leadership. *Journal of Leadership and Organizational Studies, 9,* 2–17.

Mumford, M. D., & Strange, J. M. (2004). Vision and mental models: The case of charismatic and ideological leadership. In B. J. Avolio & F. J. Yammarino (Eds.), *Charismatic and transformational leadership: The road ahead* (pp. 109–142). New York: Elsevier.

Nye, J. L., & Forsyth, D. R. (1991). The effects of prototype-based biases on leadership appraisals: A test of leadership categorization theory. *Small Group Research, 22,* 360–379.

Oatley, K. (2002). Emotions and the story worlds of fiction. In M. C. Green, J. J. Strange, & T. C. Brock (Eds.), *Narrative impact: Social and cognitive foundations* (pp. 39–69). Mahwah, NJ: Lawrence Erlbaum.

Offerman, L. R., Kennedy, J. K., & Wirtz, P. W. (1994). Implicit leadership theories: Content, structure, and generalizability. *The Leadership Quarterly, 5,* 43–58.

Olson, C. (1987). *A case study analysis of credentialing in small groups.* Unpublished doctoral dissertation, University of Minnesota.

Osborn, M. (1986). Rhetorical depiction. In H. W. Simons & A. A. Aghazarian (Eds.), *Form, genre, and the study of political discourse* (pp. 79–107). Columbia: University of South Carolina Press.

Park, H. S., & Guan, X. (2009). Cross-cultural comparison of verbal and non-verbal strategies of apologizing. *Journal of International and Intercultural Communication, 2,* 66–87.

Pavitt, C., & Sackgroff, P. (1990). Implicit theories of leadership and judgments of leadership among group members. *Small Group Research, 21,* 374–392.

Perreault, G. (1997). Ethical followers: A link to ethical leadership. *Journal of Leadership Studies, 4,* 78–89.

Perrow, C. (1984). *Normal accidents.* New York: Basic Books.

Petty, R. E., & Cacioppo, J. T. (1986a). *Communication and persuasion: Central and peripheral routes to attitude change.* New York: Springer-Verlag.

Petty, R. E., & Cacioppo, J. T. (1986b). The elaboration likelihood model of persuasion. In L. Berkowitz (Ed.), *Advances in experimental social psychology* (Vol. 19, pp. 123–205). San Diego: Academic Press.

Petty, R. E., Cacioppo, J. T., Strathman, A. J., & Priester, J. R. (2005). To think or not to think. In T. C. Brock & M. C. Green (Eds.), *Persuasion: Psychological insights and perspectives* (2nd ed., pp. 81–116). Thousand Oaks, CA: Sage.

Phillips, K. R. (2004). *Framing public memory.* Tuscaloosa: University of Alabama Press.

Polichak, J. W., & Gerrig, R. J. (2002). Get up and win! Participatory responses to narratives. In M. C. Green, J. J. Strange, & T. C. Brock (Eds.), *Narrative impact: Social and cognitive foundations* (pp. 71–95). Mahwah, NJ: Lawrence Erlbaum.

Pond, L. K., & Burtis, J. O. (1998). Group discussion exercises, Part I: Direction givers, direction giving, and becoming a direction giver. In *Leading learning organizations proceedings* (pp. 121–139). Charleston, SC: Association of Leadership Educators.

Porto, M. P. (2007). Frame diversity and citizen competence: Towards a critical approach to news quality. *Critical Studies in Media Communication, 24,* 303–321.

Powers, W. G., & Bodie, G. D. (2003). Listening fidelity: Seeking congruence between cognitions of the listener and the sender. *International Journal of Listening, 17,* 19–31.

Powers, W. G., & Love, D. (1989). Basic communication fidelity: An extension. *Communication Research Reports, 6,* 79–83.

Powers, W. G., & Lowry, D. N. (1984). Basic communication fidelity: A fundamental approach. In R. L. Bostrom (Ed.), *Communication competence* (pp. 57–71). Beverly Hills, CA: Sage.

Powers, W. G., & Witt, P. L. (2008). Expanding the theoretical framework of communication fidelity. *Communication Quarterly, 56,* 247–267.

Quigley, J. V. (1993). *Vision: How leaders develop it, share it, and sustain it.* New York: McGraw-Hill.

Reynolds, B. (2006). Response to best practices. *Journal of Applied Communication Research, 34,* 249–252.

Ricoeur, P. (1980). Narrative time. *Critical Inquiry, 7,* 169–190.

Roy, A., & Rowland, R. C. (2003). The rhetoric of Hindu nationalism: A narrative of mythic redefinition. *Western Journal of Communication, 67,* 225–248.

Ryan, H. R. (Ed.). (1988). *Oratorical encounters: Selected studies and sources of twentieth-century political accusations and apologies.* New York: Greenwood.

Ryfe, D. M. (2006). Narrative and deliberation in small group forums. *Journal of Applied Communication Research, 34,* 72–93.

Salovey, P., & Mayer, J. D. (1990). Emotional intelligence. *Imagination, Cognition and Personality, 9,* 185–211.

Sandman, P. M. (2006). Crisis communication best practices: Some quibbles and additions. *Journal of Applied Communication Research, 34,* 257–262.

Scheibel, D., Gibson, K., & Anderson, C. (2002). Practicing 'sorority rush': Mockery and the dramatistic rehearsing of organizational conversations. *Communication Studies, 53*, 219–233.

Schiappa, E. (2003). *Defining reality: Definitions and politics of meaning*. Carbondale: Southern Illinois University.

Schwartz, T. (1973). *The responsive chord*. New York: Anchor Press/Doubleday.

Seeger, M. W. (2006). Best practices in crisis communication: An expert panel process. *Journal of Applied Communication Research, 34*, 232–244.

Seeger, M. W., Sellnow, T. L., & Ulmer, R. R. (1998). Communication, organization and crisis. In M. E. Roloff (Ed.), *Communication yearbook* (Vol. 21, pp. 231–275). Thousand Oaks, CA: Sage.

Seeger, M. W., & Ulmer, R. R. (2002). A post-crisis discourse of renewal: The cases of Malden Mills and Cole Hardwoods. *Journal of Applied Communication Research, 30*, 126–142.

Seligman, M. E. P. (2002). Positive psychology, positive prevention, and positive therapy. In C. R. Snyder & S. J. Lopez (Eds.), *Handbook of positive psychology* (pp. 3–9) New York: Oxford University Press.

Shannon, C. E., & Weaver, W. (1949). *The mathematical theory of communication*. Urbana: University of Illinois Press.

Shapiro, G. (1987). How its done: Ideas for ongoing programs. In M. B. Clark (Ed.), *The cultivation of leadership roles, methods and responsibilities* (pp. 75–83 & 199–203). Greensboro, NC: Center for Creative Leadership.

Shaw, M. E. (1981). *Group dynamics: The psychology of small group behavior* (3rd ed.). New York: McGraw-Hill.

Sheldon, C. (1896). *In his steps*. Retrieved June 10, 2008, from http://en.wikipedia .org/wiki/What_would_jesus_do

Simons, H. W. (2001). *Persuasion in society*. Thousand Oaks, CA: Sage.

Snyder, C. R., & Lopez, S. J. (2006). *Positive psychology: The scientific and practical explorations of human strengths*. Thousand Oaks, CA: Sage.

Snyder, M. (1974). Self-monitoring of expressive behavior. *Journal of Personality and Social Psychology, 30*, 526–537.

Stephenson, M. T., Benoit, W. L., & Tschida, D. A. (2001). Testing the mediating role of cognitive responses in the elaboration likelihood model. *Communication Studies, 52*, 324–337.

Stogdill, R. M. (1948). Personal factors associated with leadership: A survey of the literature. *Journal of Psychology, 25*, 35–71.

Stohl, C. (1986). The role of memorable messages in the process of organizational socialization. *Communication Quarterly, 34*, 231–249.

Strange, J. M., & Mumford, M. D. (2002). The origins of vision: Charismatic versus ideological leadership. *The Leadership Quarterly, 13*, 374–373.

Taylor, F. (1911). *The principles of scientific management*. New York: Harper Bros.

Turman, P. (2005). Coaches' use of anticipatory and counterfactual regret messages during competition. *Journal of Applied Communication Research, 33*(2), 116–138.

Turner, B. (1976). The organizational and interorganizational development of disasters. *Administrative Science Quarterly, 21*, 378–397.

Venette, S. J. (2006). Special section introduction: Best practices in risk and crisis communication. *Journal of Applied Communication Research, 34,* 229–231.

Vroom, V. H., & Yetton, P. W. (1973). *Leadership and decision making.* Pittsburgh: University of Pittsburgh Press.

Waisanen, D. J. (2009). A citizen's guides to democracy inaction: Jon Stewart and Stephen Colbert's comic rhetorical criticism. *Southern Communication Journal, 74,* 119–140.

Waldron, V. R. (1994). Once more, with feeling: Reconsidering the role of emotion in work. In S. A. Deetz (Ed.), *Communication yearbook* (Vol. 17, pp. 388–416). Thousand Oaks, CA: Sage.

Walicki, A. (1995). *Marxism and the leap to the kingdom of freedom: The rise and fall of the Communist utopia.* Stanford, CA: Stanford University Press.

Ware, B. L., & Linkugel, W. A. (1973). They spoke in defense of themselves: On the generic criticism of apologia. *Quarterly Journal of Speech, 59,* 273–283.

Weick, K. E. (1995). *Sensemaking in organizations.* Thousand Oaks, CA: Sage.

West, R., & Turner, L. H. (2004). *Introducing communication theory: Analysis and application* (2nd ed.). Boston: McGraw-Hill.

White, H. (1980). The value of narrativity in the representation of reality. *Critical Inquiry, 7,* 5–23.

White, R. K., & Lippitt, R. (1960). *Autocracy and democracy.* New York: Harper & Row.

Yukl, G. (1994). *Leadership in organizations* (3rd ed.). Englewood Cliffs, NJ: Prentice Hall.

Yukl, G. J. (1998). *Leadership in organizations.* Englewood Cliffs, NJ: Prentice Hall.

Zaleznik, A. (1977). Managers and leaders: Are they different? *Harvard Business Review, 55,* 67–78.

Zorn, T. E. (1993). Motivation to communicate: A critical review with suggested alternatives. In S. A. Deetz (Ed.), *Communication yearbook* (Vol. 16, pp. 515–549). Newbury Park, CA: Sage.

Index

About the Authors

John O. Burtis is Professor of Communication Studies at the University of Northern Iowa. He has served as the director of the Concordia Leadership Center and of the West Central Minnesota Leadership Program and the head of the Department of Communication Studies at the University of Northern Iowa. He was the Director of Forensics at Kansas State University and at Concordia College while students in those intercollegiate speech and debate programs won many awards, including more than 20 national championships in individual and team competitions. He has taught undergraduate and graduate courses in leadership, persuasion, group communication, public speaking, argumentation, communication theory, and management. He has been a consultant, trainer, and speaker on related subjects in both the private and public sectors. He holds a doctorate in speech-communication from the University of Minnesota and both master's and bachelor's degrees in speech from Kansas State University.

Paul D. Turman is Associate Vice President for Academic Affairs and Director of Academic Assessment for the South Dakota Board of Regents. Prior to his work with the Regents, Paul was an Associate Professor at the University of Northern Iowa, where he taught undergraduate and graduate courses in group and interpersonal communication, technology and human communication, research methods, and public speaking. His extensive research program includes publications examining interpersonal and group communication variables, such as assessments of the roles played by coaches of athletic teams as facilitators of effective interaction. The coauthor of three textbooks on these subjects, he holds a doctorate in interpersonal communication from the University of Nebraska–Lincoln and both master's and bachelor's degrees in communication from South Dakota State University.

Supporting researchers for more than 40 years

Research methods have always been at the core of SAGE's publishing program. Founder Sara Miller McCune published SAGE's first methods book, *Public Policy Evaluation*, in 1970. Soon after, she launched the *Quantitative Applications in the Social Sciences* series—affectionately known as the "little green books."

Always at the forefront of developing and supporting new approaches in methods, SAGE published early groundbreaking texts and journals in the fields of qualitative methods and evaluation.

Today, more than 40 years and two million little green books later, SAGE continues to push the boundaries with a growing list of more than 1,200 research methods books, journals, and reference works across the social, behavioral, and health sciences. Its imprints—Pine Forge Press, home of innovative textbooks in sociology, and Corwin, publisher of PreK–12 resources for teachers and administrators—broaden SAGE's range of offerings in methods. SAGE further extended its impact in 2008 when it acquired CQ Press and its best-selling and highly respected political science research methods list.

From qualitative, quantitative, and mixed methods to evaluation, SAGE is the essential resource for academics and practitioners looking for the latest methods by leading scholars.

For more information, visit **www.sagepub.com**.